The Motorhome Touring Handbook

Practical Advice From Buying Your First Motorhome to a Year-Long Tour of Europe

Julie and Jason Buckley

An OurTour Publication - OurTour.co.uk

Contents

Part Two: Your First Time Abroad in a Motorhome   87

Awaiting the Tour de France

Introduction

Thanks for buying our book about motorhome touring. We've put it together in response to the questions we've had over the years asking about the practical aspects of buying a motorhome and using it to explore the UK and continental Europe. Our aim is to give useful information, hints and tips gained from first-hand experience of long-term touring. If you're in need of inspiration, it'll hopefully give you some of that too. Motorhomes have offered us a unique way to holiday, tour and even live in full time, and we'd love you to experience this for yourself!

Awning out on a sunny seaside pitch in Croatia. Heaven!

We're motorhome enthusiasts, rather than experts, and don't know everything there is to know about motorhome touring, so we've referred throughout this book to sources of additional information. Where these are websites, we've given the address in italics, like this: *ourtour.co.uk*.

Please don't be put off by the volume of information in this book, by the way. When we started out, we knew very little of what's in here, picking it up as we went along, and we're still in one piece! By reading this book, you'll hopefully avoid some of the errors we made though, and quickly get the most from your motorhome.

The book is separated into three parts, each building on the previous one:

- **Part One** looks at choosing a motorhome and taking your first trips.
- **Part Two** takes the journey abroad for the first time.
- **Part Three** focuses on the big one: full-timing on a year-long, or even multi-year, tour of Europe.

Before we dive into Part One, here's some background information on our motorhome story, so you've some idea who we are, and why we enjoy life in a motorhome.

1

Our Motorhome Story

We're Julie and Jason Buckley, in our mid-forties, and we're based in Nottingham in the UK when we're not travelling. Motorhomes have given us experiences we never dreamed we'd have. They've granted us a sense of unrivalled freedom. Their windscreens display epic vistas, through which we pass as though living a shared dream. It's no exaggeration, to our minds at least, that stepping through the door of a motorhome shaves decades from our lives. Motorhomes lift us into a world where a simple life is once again, as in our youth, wondrous.

Us two with our long-time travelling pooch Charlie

Over years of touring, making as best use of words, videos and photos as we can, we've rendered these sensations into a blog: *ourtour.co.uk*. This book aims to collate the practical information we've peppered throughout the blog, which has grown into something of an unwieldy beast. Our hope is this information will inspire you to expand your own world of adventure, whether that means taking your first motorhome holiday, heading abroad for the first time, or making the leap into a year or more of touring our diverse European continent.

Before the blog came to life, we owned Harvey. Harvey was our first campervan, who we chugged around in during holidays from work. Harvey was about five and a half meters long, twenty years old, based on a Talbot Express petrol panel van with a high top, kitchen and a tiny bathroom. He stoically handled the abuses of a couple of laughing 30-somethings, both clueless about how to handle his delicate innards.

The British seaside seemed to really bring out our inner nitwits. Parked alongside a butter-coloured sandy beach on Scotland's west coast, we sat outside one evening to watch the sunset with a cheeky glass of rosé wine. In the dark hours of the night, we woke to an alarming bang, finding the wind had whipped up and ripped off our awning. The following morning, shame-faced, we threw the weighty thing in a fisherman's skip and narrowly avoided abandoning the rest of the trip in a huff. Another time, on a frozen cliff-top farm near Skegness, the heating failed ushering in a layer of duvet-frost in the morning. It turned out we'd killed the leisure battery needed to power it, by discharging it over winter.

These were but a gentle warm-up for things to come. Twice we forgot to drain Harvey's water system in the winter, allowing cold nights to freeze his water heater solid, and twice we had to repair it as pipes ruptured and poured with water in the spring. His water pump seized solid one winter, and his engine decided no, it wasn't taking another step, while on the way to fetch some holiday fish and chips.

Despite these minor calamities, enough of Harvey survived to carry us across the English Channel on forays into France. Each time nervous that our ancient engine would spitefully destroy itself, we'd gridlock a country driving the wrong way around a roundabout, annoy locals by being entirely ignorant of 'la priorité à droite' (France's arcane 'give way to the right' rule), or die of embarrassment trying to utter long-forgotten foreign phrases in the bakers.

Each time we survived the worst our imaginations could conjure our confidence grew that tiny bit. While pottering around France's stone-built shuttered towns and villages, we'd notice clusters of motorhomes huddled together close to the town. While we were usually parked in a remote campsite somewhere, they were a stone's throw from the town centre. We were jealous, but also afraid to join them. This was our introduction to 'aires' (motorhome parking areas), the French system of welcoming campers into towns, many of them great places, all devoid of 'no overnight' signs and height barriers.

Once we'd broken our aires duck, edging ourselves in among 20 or so French motorhomes by a lake in the Jura region, there was no looking back. Although we still use campsites, the low cost and high convenience of aires is just too good to be true. Harvey had everything we needed on board for at least a few days at a time 'off-grid', and we revelled in our independence.

A little later we came across the France Passion scheme. This stroke of genius sells you a book listing out participating vineyards, restaurants, farm shops, and other businesses, which welcome motorhomes to stay for free for a night or two. In return you agree not to overstay your welcome, and not to wreck the place. If you like, you can take a meal, or buy a bottle of their wine, goat's cheese, olive oil, snails, fruit juice or whatever they produce. In business-speak,

Introduction

it's a win-win. A similar scheme has since launched in the UK called Brit Stops, which mostly lists out pubs which welcome us 'vanners' under roughly the same terms.

While in the car park of a forest-bound France Passion auberge (farm restaurant) in the Vosges Mountains, having eaten one of the most wonderful meals we've ever tasted, we pulled out a map and hatched a plan to stretch our two-week holiday route into Germany. As we drove over the Rhine, almost missing the border sign, we realised just how simple it was to travel from country to country. Another step up in confidence. On the way home, having been treated to a cow-worshipping festival in the Black Forest, with copious drinking and strapping blokes literally whipping out candle flames, we nipped into Belgium for a few Trappist Monk beers, because we could!

Back at home and work, time passed, and our wanderlust increased. Cutting a years-long story short, we eventually opted for a simpler life than the one we already had. Online auctions saw lots of our excess stuff sold, and what didn't sell was given away. Our mortgage company must have winced at the pace we attacked the balance, denying them a decade or so in interest payments by ploughing everything we had into it. A map of Europe appeared on the wall of our lounge, and our imaginations started to fire as stickers appeared one by one, pointing at places we might visit.

One day, a particularly bad day for reasons we don't fully recall, something inside snapped. The mortgage was gone. Our savings weren't as much as we'd have liked, but we needed an escape from our work, badly. Sitting in the garden we talked, one of those life-turning talks, and made the decision: we'd quit, and we'd travel. As romantic as it might sound, guilt and fear were our prominent emotions at this point, the joy came later.

A year on the road, we decided, meant Harvey wouldn't cut the mustard. His bed had to be slotted together each night by winding the front seats down, folding out seat supports, shifting cushions and making up the bedding. All of this produced a flat-ish, double-ish bed, which had to be disassembled in reverse each morning. Once the bed assembly process was complete, which one of us (mentioning no names) tended to hide from by walking the dog, there wasn't much room to move around, so no choice but for both of us to hit the sack. No, we needed a vehicle which wouldn't result in divorce after a month!

It's an odd sight, seeing your beloved vehicle being driven off by a stranger. Harvey went that way one afternoon, bought by a prison warden from London, and our search for a long-term motorhome started in earnest. Vicarious trawls of dealers while we were paying the mortgage down had located the kind of thing we wanted, only now we had about half the money to spend. We reverted to the private market and after a while ended up buying a slightly yellowing

1991 A Class Hymer B544 with a full service history but many, many miles on the clock (well, kilometres, as he was left hand drive).

Motorhomes and campervans tend to attract a name. Ours became Dave, named after the previous owner's nickname for his cat. Nope, we can't recall why! As the months of notice at work ticked by, we fettled him, fitting a solar panel, getting the gas system tested, servicing his engine and rubbing surface rust from his LPG tank. With great emotional effort, the house emptied further of our beloved possessions, and Dave gradually filled up. The map bristled with a forest of arrows. Our stomachs twisted and turned with anticipation, fear, excitement and a general fog of confusion. *Ourtour.co.uk* came into being, in a pretty half-hearted fashion at first, as we tentatively started to tell our story.

One day a 'To Let' sign appeared, attached to our front gate, and shortly after the agent called to say he had someone interested. Our friends all arrived one evening and, in an empty, echoing house, we had a small riot, fuelled by the remnants of our drinks cabinet. A few days later, our brains had finally rehydrated and, under a grey sky in October, we locked the house and gave the keys to the letting agent. Sat in Dave, we drove off towards Milton Keynes, staying in a field behind a village pub, and eating our last traditional English meal for a year. Despite the months of planning, and all the tearful goodbyes, this point was a shock, a surreal sensation of departure.

Dave, first in line at Dover at the start of our year-long tour

A year later we came home, hugged family and friends, treated Dave to a service and MOT, turned around and left for continental Europe again. Another year later, the funds finally ran out, and we reluctantly rolled Dave back home to Nottingham. Those two years were an incredible experience, and something which indelibly altered the both of us.

Introduction

On our return, folks back home would ask us "what was it like?", "what were your favourite places?" They're good questions, but we couldn't answer them. Not succinctly anyway, and we quickly learned few folks wanted the long and boring version, everyone's living their own story after all.

What could we say? We'd visited 23 countries, slept in 494 different places and driven 29,773 miles (and spent over £28,000). As well as 21 countries in Europe, we'd driven to the edge of the Sahara Desert twice, once in Morocco and once in Tunisia. In the latter we'd knelt at Ju's grandfather's war grave, making a pilgrimage on behalf of family. We'd crossed France so many times it now felt like home. Northern Spain surprised us with its high mountains and deserted coves. Croatia delighted the snorkelling senses. Greece had us horizontally laid back. Ukraine scared the monkeys out of us but rewarded us too. Switzerland's MacDonald's prices had us wishing we'd made a sarnie.

Dave the motorhome had enabled us to move at our own pace. He gifted us choices we'd never have had with another means of travel. The route we took meandered about the map, only ever firming up on the day we drove. Some days we arrived at our planned place, didn't like it much, and simply drove to another spot. Other times we loved the place enough to stay a week. Well, almost a week. There were just too many places to see, feel, smell, taste and live in, to keep us still that long.

Dave at a cracking overnight spot in Tropea in Calabria, Italy

Our house back in Nottingham didn't become our home again. The tenants wanted to stay, and the house now suited them much better than us. We emptied the loft of the things we stored there and now no longer needed, and as we were both unemployed, the only way for us to rent a house was to pay six month's rent in advance. Fortunately, we'd stored up a 'get back into life at home' fund and had resisted the very strong temptation to spend our last penny to keep travelling.

Within a few weeks of our wheels touching down at Dover, we were living in bricks and mortar, and had joined the commuter traffic heading to office jobs once again. We'd wondered for two years how hard this point might be, of 'coming back' and 'getting back in'. We almost convinced ourselves we were now unemployable, with a two-year gap on our CVs. Luckily for us, finding work turned out to be fairly easy. At least the logistics were.

Going from footloose to nine-to-fivers proved a mental challenge. The both of us faced up to it but couldn't stomach the idea of settling long-term back into the rat race. Thankfully, we already knew this wasn't going to happen, and started preparing for it almost as soon as we arrived back. Over a glass of wine and a large blank sheet of paper on the living room floor, we started to plan. Our aim was simple: to get free again, and this time for good. On the face of it this was going to take another nine years, to arrange our finances to enable this new life. Dave wasn't going to get the use he needed, so one day we stood and cried as he was driven off to live with a new family.

Luck came our way. An IT contracting business we set up did well and generated a chunk of income which we invested into an old butcher's shop in an adjacent town. Behind the shop was a three-bedroom house, and behind that a small outbuilding which used to be an abattoir and was now full of walk-in chiller units and meat cookers. We moved in to save on rent and months of work and many brick-dust-filled sandwiches later, we'd removed all trace of butchery and had a shop we could let, rooms in the house we could also rent out, and a large en-suite bedroom we could live in while in the UK.

Another intense attack on our remaining belongings shrank them to the point we could store them all at home. For Jay, selling his tools, each of which reminded him of the job he bought it for, was perhaps the hardest. Ju agonised over selling some of our wedding presents, many of which we'd hardly used, but all were treasured.

Only two years after coming home, we'd found a way to create enough income to say a second goodbye to the office, admittedly having revised our overall goal figure down rather a lot! A dash down south after work one evening bought us another motorhome, another Hymer B544, a newer version of Dave which we named Zagan. Perhaps a little more exotic than 'Dave', this name came from the town we visited in Poland where the real version of the film 'The

Great Escape' took place at the nearby Stalag Luft III prisoner of war camp. Zagan was, for us, our own (second!) Great Escape.

Four years after his predecessor tentatively headed for Dover, Zagan followed. The idea that we'd done it, that we'd managed to free ourselves forever, seemed more than a little incredulous, and yet, here we were. Over the course of the next 18 months Zagan proved himself to be as tough and capable as Dave, carrying us across the Pyrenees, under and over the Alps, across the Baltics, up through the Arctic and back again to the edge of the Sahara. This time we visited 20 countries and increased the number of places we've slept in a motorhome to around 900.

Zagan at Eggum, Lofoten Istands, Arctic Norway

This updated version was released in 2020, over eight years after originally setting off on that fateful first year-long tour and we've given up counting countries and places. Our lives now flow between nomadic wandering in our motorhome for six or so months of the year, while the rest of the time we're happy to put down roots at our home in the English Midlands. This feels the best of both worlds to us: the adventure of being on the road coupled with the sense of belonging from a fixed community. There remains a truth though: every time we step into our motorhome, we feel the memories rush upwards, and the promise of new horizons lifting our souls.

The Joy of Life in a Motorhome

Our years spent travelling in our campervan and motorhomes were punctuated with episodes of adventure, fun, serenity, drunken-foolery and companionship, with the occasional splash of fear, loneliness and anti-climax. The overall, abiding sensation though is one of joy. The following sections try and capture some of the reasons we find motorhome life so easy to enjoy.

Simple Living

We suspect you've noticed, that life can get complicated at times. Heavy traffic commutes, deadlines, grim news stories coming at you from every angle, bad bosses, relentless politics, you name it. While a motorhome can't solve all of life's problems, it can help to reduce them to more realistic proportions. During time spent away in a van, the issues you need to solve are simplified to ones you can control: where to sleep, where to get fuel, where to get fresh water, what to eat, what to visit and so on. Working with these simple, solve-able problems can be a delightful breath of fresh air to a tired soul.

The simple but comfortable living area in our Hymer B544 motorhome

Low Cost of Living

Motorhomes aren't cheap, but they can be a very cost-effective way to travel, especially for long-term touring. Once we'd bought the van, around £40 a day for two people and a dog proved a realistic long-term touring budget for us. This covered all our travelling costs, including insurance, fuel, van depreciation, food, overnight fees, entry fees, meals out, replacing clothes and gadgets, ferries and the odd foray up a cable car or some such. We've met people who spend more, and many who spend much less.

Self-Contained Luxury

Travelling in a motorhome is unlike any other form of transport. Each evening you get to stay in your own bed, under your own duvet with your favourite pillow. Open the fridge, and there's your favourite tipple nicely cooled, ready to be sipped as you read a book or sit outside watching the sun drop down over the sea. Your clothes stay happily inside the wardrobe, no need to drag them around in a rucksack or suitcase, no need to pack or unpack. And when it comes to ablutions, your shower, sink and loo are en-suite, always there, with hot and cold running water, always clean.

Incredible Flexibility
There is no 'fixed itinerary' in a motorhome. With Europe's enormous array of campsites, dedicated motorhome parking locations, car parks and simply flat parcels of land, there's little need to book ahead. You can choose your route and parking places at will, at least outside the school holidays and summer peak season. One morning you could wake up in the Italian Alps, perhaps feel a little chilly and be on the French Riviera that evening. The flexibility granted by a motorhome is second to none.

Proximity to Nature
When you're in a motorhome and it rains, you know about it! A thousand drums beat out the rhythm, either annoyingly drowning out the TV, or reminding you that you're comfortably dry and warm, depending on your mood. Near the ocean, opening a door in the morning lets in the salty waft of the sea. On a windy night, you can lie awake as your home gets rocked by each passing blast of air, or you can let it rock you to sleep like a baby. The calming influence of nature isn't far away when you're out and about in your van.

The World Through Your Windscreen
Driving yourself across a landscape, rather than flying thousands of feet above it, you get a sense of living in a three-dimensional dream. In control of your own destiny, the fields, forests, villages, beaches, lakes and rivers ease into sight, filling your windscreen and lifting your spirit. Further afield, mountains rise, glaciers glint and waterfalls thunder. The scene ahead draws you in.

A Norwegian vista through our motorhome's window, magical

Part One: Your First Motorhome

Right, let's get started! If you've never owned a motorhome before, this part of the book is for you. Its aim is to get you up to speed quickly on some of the terminology which bounces around the world of motorhomes and campervans, and to help you choose a suitable home on wheels from the mind-boggling range available.

There's not going to be enough space in any book to cover every aspect of every type, make and model motorhome. We don't have the technical skills either to explain how all types of equipment work (or why they annoyingly don't work). Fortunately, there are lots of supportive internet resources out there which will do just that with thousands of hugely knowledgeable and friendly folks providing their time for free. *Motorhomefacts.com* and *motorhomefun.co.uk* are two of the biggest UK forums. If you have a Facebook account, try searching there too, as there are often groups full of dedicated individuals who know everything worth knowing about specific makes of van. We're members of the Hymer Owners Group and Classic Hymers groups on Facebook, for example.

If you prefer your information in print, the Practical Motorhome and Motorhome Monthly Magazine (often called MMM) publications are widely available at UK newsagents and supermarkets. They have very informative websites too: *www.practicalmotorhome.com* and *outandaboutlive.co.uk*.

Campervans, Motorcaravans, Motorhomes and RVs

First up, what's the difference between a campervan, a motorcaravan, a motorhome and an RV? They're ambiguous, debatable terms, to be honest. The term 'RV' isn't used much in Europe. It stands for Recreational Vehicle and when it is used on this side of the pond, it generally refers to large 'Rock Star' style American motorhomes. There are a few RVs knocking about in the UK and Europe, but they're relatively rare as they're not very well suited to the smaller roads and campsite pitches here.

The term 'motorcaravan' is one which is hardly ever used in day-to-day conversation either. However, the British DVLA like to use it as a catch-all term for motorhomes and campervans when classifying vehicles on the V5C (log book). Unless you're converting a commercial van into a campervan, you don't need to worry about any of that stuff.

That leaves us with the terms: 'campervan' and 'motorhome'. Hmmmm, let's see. Some would say campervans are the colourful classic, old style VW campers. However, with the rise in popularity of smaller vans of various makes, the term 'campervan' is more likely to be used for any van suitable for holidays or a short tour of a few weeks, typically lacking a shower and built-in toilet.

'Motorhomes' have more space and facilities so they can be easily used to live in for years at a time, including washing and toilet facilities. That's roughly it but, as they are all based on commercial vans, there's a big overlap between the two names, and in the end it's only a debate of semantics. While we're at it with the definitions, here are a few more terms which crop-up in the motorhome world to classify the huge range of vehicles available:

A Class Motorhomes: often on a Fiat or Mercedes-Benz base, these types of motorhome don't retain the standard van cab area. Instead the motorhome conversion company (Hymer, Pilote, Niesmann & Bischoff, Dethleffs and so on) build a motorhome-specific cab which fits over the standard van dashboard and is the full width of the motorhome.

Zagan, our A Class Hymer B544 motorhome

Panel Van Conversions (B Class in the USA): these are the easiest to drive, as they retain the entirety of the original van, cutting holes in the sides and roof for windows etc. Those fitted with high roofs enable you to walk around inside, which is essential for comfort on longer trips. They do tend to be much smaller than A and C Class motorhomes, but many cleverly cram in lots of features so they can still easily be used for long-term touring.

Our first motorhome Harvey the RV - a high top panel van conversion

C Class Motorhomes: along with A Class vans, these are sometimes referred to as 'coachbuilts'. C Class motorhomes keep the original cab area which the rest of the living area is attached to. As they use the original cab, features which require a wider-than-standard cab cannot be used, such as the cab area drop-down bed often found in A Class vans. Many have a bed or storage cupboards over the cab giving them the distinctive 'quiff' look, those that don't are called 'low profile'. The cab area on a C Class tends to be a little less well insulated than an A Class, and in general C Class motorhomes cost less than A Class to buy.

Our friends' C Class motorhome in Morocco

Campervans and Day Vans: these are intended for shorter periods of use. They are small and agile, so easier to drive than any other type of motorhome, but they tend not to have a separate bathroom, and the bed has to be made every night. Some have a pop-up roof so you can stand up inside, or sleep in the space it creates.

A VW Campervan at a festival in the UK

13

Expedition Vehicles: rarely seen in the UK, they can look like something from Hollywood: a gigantic MAN truck or Unimog which only the military or emergency services would use. They can also be something less overpowering, like a pick-up truck with a 'demountable' living space attached to the rear, or even a four-wheel drive with a tent mounted on the roof. Unless you're planning on mounting an expedition across the desert or driving to China you won't need one of these, but they're fascinating, amazing vehicles nevertheless.

A MAN Truck expedition vehicle at an aire in France

Fifth Wheelers: these are closer to being caravans than motorhomes, as they need a tow vehicle to move them around. They can be highly luxurious, with slide-outs to add additional space, but are not common in the UK or mainland Europe.

A UK-made Fifth Wheeler at a campsite in Oslo, Norway

RVs (Winnebagos): these are the 'Rock Star' vehicles mentioned earlier on. Winnebago is a specific make of RV but is sometimes used as a generic term. They have a reputation for being very comfortable; sides that slide out to create wide rooms with huge comfy chairs and sofas, a washing machine, large garages (some of which will squeeze a car inside) and a king-sized bed. They also have a reputation for poor fuel consumption.

A Winnebago (nicknamed 'The Beast') camping in Croatia

As a rule, almost everyone touring in the UK and continental Europe by motorhome uses either an A or C Class motorhome, with quite a few Panel Van Conversions also being used. Some people shift between different types over time as their needs change, or they better understand their needs. Throughout this book we'll be using the terms motorhome, campervan and van interchangeably, as from here onwards they will all refer to our homes on wheels.

Tips for Choosing a Motorhome

Over the years, we've been asked a fair few times for advice on choosing a motorhome and have generally resisted the urge to help. Why? Partly because we've only ever bought three of them, so maybe we're not well enough qualified to answer. But the main reason is this: choosing a motorhome is like choosing a home; it's a very personal thing. What works for one individual, couple or family just won't work for another.

Which type of van to choose depends on your own circumstances: your budget, the features you need, what you can legally drive, how many beds (berths) and belted seats you need, the storage space and so on. As well as the big things like price, age, layout, make and condition, smaller things also drive our choices of motorhome: the interior colour scheme, whether there is a built-in oven, whether the toilet and shower are in separate compartments and so on. Finally, there's that unknown factor which no-one can predict: the heart! When you walk into the motorhome which is the one for you, your heart may well overrule your head, and the 'must have features' you thought were essential disappear.

Considerations Before Starting to Look

We strongly suspect that if you've read this far, you've already spent time drooling over *autotrader.co.uk* or *motorhomedepot.com*, reading reports in Motorhome Monthly Magazine, or have visited your local motorhome dealer for a sniff around. Even if you have, assuming you haven't already bought the van, the following sections cover off the things it's helpful to be aware of before making a purchase, and ideally even before you start looking at vehicles.

With the above in mind, here are some thoughts from our time on the road, of how our own vehicles have worked out for us, and from experience built up from chatting with fellow travellers in all shapes and sizes of van.

How You Will Use Your Motorhome?

Although it's impossible to predict the future, by answering a few questions you can probably get an idea how you will use your motorhome. Have a think about the following, which should all have a big impact on the van you buy:

- **Who will travel in it?** This will affect the number of belted seats and berths (beds) you need, as well as the space for all your belongings, room to sit around the table and so on. Try to be honest with yourselves. We've met a few people who've regretted buying a larger vehicle than they wanted to drive, in order to accommodate teenage children who, it turned out, never want to travel in it. If you have young children who need car seats you'll need to ensure there are enough 'three point' seat belts as some seats only have lap belts in older vehicles.
- **Are you comfortable driving a larger vehicle and can you legally do so**? Wider and longer vans can be stressful to drive and park, outweighing the benefit of additional living space. We've met owners of large motorhomes who manage this by carrying electric bikes or a moped, enabling them to explore a larger area without moving the van so often. We've also met people who bought a large van, found it no fun to drive and park, and ended up selling it at a loss and buying a smaller one.
- **How much do you have to spend?** It's not just the purchase cost of the motorhome. You'll need to budget for road tax, insurance, servicing and MOT costs, repairs, depreciation, maybe storage and so on.
- **Do you plan short trips, or extensive touring?** For longer tours the van's storage and layout become more critical. A fixed bed becomes a must for many people, removing the need to store bedding and

assemble/disassemble the bed every day. But there's no hard-and-fast rule: we met a Canadian family of four happily travelling for months in a small VW campervan.

- **Do you plan to mostly stay on campsites**? This will reduce your reliance on the van's built-in facilities such as the shower and toilet, making them less critical in your buying decision.
- **Will you travel in winter?** Some vans are better than others at keeping you warm and safe in cold weather. Look into the *Winterisation* section on page 23 for more thoughts on this.
- **Are you planning on heading into the wilds**? If you really want to get away from it all and go searching for moose up dirt tracks in Norway or sleeping alone under a star-spangled Saharan sky, you need to consider a specialist four-wheel drive (4x4) vehicle. Otherwise, a two-wheel drive motorhome will do just fine.

OK, let's look into some of these areas in more detail.

Check Your Driving Licence

This is a really important point: don't assume that you can drive every motorhome available. To work out whether you can legally drive your preferred van, you need to know three things:

- Which **category entitlements** do you have on your driving licence? To find these, look on the back of your licence. If there are dates next to the respective letter, then you have that entitlement. While you're looking at it, check the entitlement isn't about to expire. If more than one person will drive the motorhome, all drivers need the correct entitlement. Also bear in mind that if a driver is under 18 or over 70, or has certain medical conditions, additional restrictions may apply (*www.gov.uk/driving-medical-conditions*).
- What is the **maximum legal weight** of the motorhome? This is known by various names which all mean the same thing: the Maximum Authorised Mass (MAM), Maximum Technically Permissible Laden Mass (MTPLM) and Gross Vehicle Weight (GVW). We'll use the term 'MAM' in his book. The MAM is the maximum legal weight of the van, plus everything inside it, including fuel, water, clothes, bikes, food and drink, spare wheel, tools, pets, the driver and passengers, everything (*www.gov.uk/vehicle-weights-explained*). The MAM figure is printed on a plaque or label attached to the van and will normally be between around 3000Kg and 5000Kg for most motorhomes. The sticker will also show the van's gross train weight (GTW), which is the maximum combined van plus trailer weight, this will be higher than the MAM. It's easy to confuse this with the MAM, be careful folks.

- Is the motorhome's **MAM enough for you**? Just because a motorhome has a 3500Kg MAM, that doesn't necessarily mean you'll be able to legally carry all your stuff. See the section on *Payload* on page 19.

The rest of this section summarises the driving licences rules. As there are a few exceptions, we suggest also running through the questions on this website to be sure you can drive the van you want: *www.gov.uk/vehicles-can-drive*. If you have a full UK car driving licence (category B entitlement), you can drive any motorhome with a MAM up to 3500Kg. You can carry up to 8 passengers (most motorhomes don't have that many belted seats), and tow a 750Kg trailer.

If you want to drive a motorhome which has a MAM more than 3500Kg but less than 7500Kg, you need category entitlement C1 (see *www.gov.uk/driving-motorhome*). This also allows you to tow a 750Kg trailer. For vans with a MAM over 7500Kg you need entitlement C, which again lets you tow a 750Kg trailer.

For trailers over 750Kg, you need category E entitlement: shown as BE, C1E or CE on your licence. For reference, a Smart Fortwo car plus trailer weigh roughly 1000Kg combined, so you would need E entitlement. A trailer and moped might come in at 350Kg to 500Kg, so no need for need category E. If you're planning on towing, it's best to get the trailer weighed to ensure you stay legal.

Motorhome adverts often fail to state the MAM for the vehicle. Ask the seller before travelling, to save you a wasted trip. Bear in mind that individual motorhomes may have been 'uprated' after leaving the factory (given a higher MAM) or 'downrated' (given a lower MAM), so you can't rely on just knowing the make and model.

Thoughts on the 3500Kg Cut Off

For whatever reason, 3500Kg is generally the maximum MAM before officialdom across the UK and Europe starts to make things just that little bit more complicated for drivers. Even if your licence allows you to drive a heavier van, it's worth at least considering the following before deciding on a motorhome over 3500Kg MAM.

Speed Limits
Speed limits are lower in many European countries for vehicles over 3500Kg, including Austria, Belgium, France, Germany, The Netherlands and Spain (*www.caravanclub.co.uk/overseas-holidays/planning-your-route/european-speed-limits*). In practice most motorhome trips are relatively leisurely things, so the loss of speed hopefully won't be a big issue. In the UK, the speed is weirdly based on a van's 'unladen weight' (not including passengers, cupboard contents, bikes and the like) not the MAM. Unladen vans less than 3050Kg (not the usual 3500kg) can travel more quickly than heavier vans. How these speed limits are policed without you being pulled over and asked to take everything out of your motorhome, we don't know!

Some roads and bridges are also legally off-limits to vehicles over 3500Kg, but friends who drive a heavier van report this is relatively easy to work around by using alternative routes.

Tolls
In some countries, notably Austria, Czech Republic, Norway and Slovenia, vehicles over 3500Kg which want to use the toll roads must source a tag or electronic box. This records your mileage to enable you to pay for using the road, rather than simply buying an unlimited mileage 'vignette' (a physical sticker to go in your windscreen, or an electronic record), see *www.tolls.eu* for more details. With planning and patience, you can sometimes avoid the toll roads and therefore avoid the need for the tag or box, should you want to.

Breakdown Cover
Some breakdown policies exclude vehicles over 3500Kg (as well as restricting the maximum age, length, width and height of vehicles they cover). Other policies will cover vehicles over 3500Kg but with restrictions, so be sure to read the small print.

Payload
OK, here's the rub. Motorhomes are heavy things, even before you load it up with all your stuff. This means you need to be careful to buy a motorhome which can legally carry all your party, and all your essential travel belongings. In other words, you need to be careful not to exceed the MAM; it's surprisingly easy to go over your van's legal weight. Whichever type of motorhome you intend to drive, you need to carefully consider your payload. For example:

- If the motorhome weighs 3000Kg completely empty, and has a MAM of 3500Kg, then you've 500Kg of payload to play with.
- If you and your partner weigh 150Kg (about 12 stone each), then you're down to 350Kg.
- Each litre of water weighs 1Kg so a 100-litre tank weighs another 100Kg when full (or if 50% of the water is in the fresh tank and the rest in the waste tanks) so your available payload is now 250Kg.
- With gas weighing 20Kg, and 70 litres of diesel (at about 0.9Kg per litre) is 63Kg, you've now got 167Kg left.
- That's 167Kg for everything else: food, bedding, toilet cassette contents (oh yes), bikes, clothes, gadgets, books, beer, pets, tools, maps, spare wheel, cooking equipment, wetsuits, outside chairs and table, everything.

There are assumptions in the points above (some people travel with empty water tanks, for example), but the point is that it's very, very easy to use up your payload. It's a source of constant surprise and frustration among motorhome owners how low the payload can be. In our current motorhome, we have far more storage space available than we can use, as otherwise we'd go over the weight limit.

What happens if you go over your weight limit? You're breaking the law, so you'll face a fine if you're pulled over and weighed. This doesn't happen often (it's never happened to us), but folks on forums periodically report spot checks. If you're in an accident and your insurer gets wind of your van being overweight and deems this a contributing factor, you could find your claim is disputed. The biggest consideration for us personally is safety: we need to be able to stop our vans safely and quickly, even if we're descending a miles-long mountain pass, and don't want to risk tyre blowouts. See *Weighbridges and Uprating* on page 47 for information on how to check your van's weight.

How Much do You Really Need to Spend?

You can easily spend £60,000 or more on a new motorhome, and you should get something frankly stunning as a result. But do you need to? Obviously, what you do with your money is entirely your choice, but you really don't need to spend loads of money to get a great motorhome, unless you really want to.

In 2019, a Camping and Caravanning Club survey reported the average cost of a new motorhome to be just over £53,000. Most second-hand vans were reported to cost between £20,000 and £39,999, with the 'sweet spot' being around £31,000. The same survey stated: "six times as many respondents paid less than £10,000 than paid over £100,000". Autotrader is a great place to get an idea for how much different types, age, make and model of motorhome cost (*www.autotrader.co.uk*).

Prices will be higher from dealers, or agents working on behalf of the seller, probably by a few thousand pounds. Whether any additional warranty you get from a dealer is worth the additional cost is debateable. We bought our first panel van from a dealer, with a three-year RAC warranty. The peace of mind was worth it to start with, but as our confidence grew, we found it much cheaper to buy second hand with no warranty, and get repairs done on the road. None of our motorhomes have cost more than £17,000 to buy, although our repair bills have probably been a little higher as a result.

Insurance Costs

Get an idea of how much it will cost to insure your motorhome and prepare yourself to have cover when you buy up your van. Everyone's circumstances will be different, and costs could range from a few hundred pounds a year to over a thousand, especially if you plan to 'full time' (live) in your motorhome.

There are dozens of motorhome insurance companies. We've listed some of the most well-known ones in *Appendix B* starting on page 230. It pays to shop around for the best deal and when doing so, also consider:

- Buying comprehensive insurance, as third-party won't cover the costs to repair your vehicle in the event of an accident, so you could lose your entire motorhome's value.
- If your policy includes breakdown cover, check there are no restrictions on the age, size or weight of the vehicle.
- If you have an A Class motorhome with a large windscreen, check to see if there is a limit on windscreen replacement cover.

Cost of Road Tax

The cost of your yearly road tax (Vehicle Excise Duty or VED) can run into several hundred, or even thousands of, pounds. The tax due will depend on a range of factors, including the weight of the vehicle, when it was registered and, potentially, the price when new and the CO_2 emissions. Ask the seller or check on *www.gov.uk* to find out the cost so you can budget accordingly.

New Versus Used

We've never bought a brand-new motorhome, partly because they've been well outside our budget and partly to avoid the depreciation in value. Buying a new motorhome has the obvious advantages of a warranty, of being pristine and having a three-year period before an MOT is needed. Once a van is over three years old, if you plan to tour Europe you'll have to come back to the UK at least once a year to renew the MOT, it can't be done anywhere abroad.

New motorhomes have VAT included in the price. In theory this shouldn't affect the resale value but it seems to, and they lose a large percentage of their value as soon as you take ownership. With new motorhomes costing upwards of £60,000, a 20% depreciation in the first year equates to an enormous £12,000 drop, although hopefully it would be much less than that. If you plan to keep the van for years, of course, this is largely irrelevant until the point you come to sell. If you never sell, it's completely irrelevant.

Our approach has been to buy used vehicles with a full service history (FSH) from private sellers. We accepted the risk we would have no warranty, and could incur higher repair costs, but balanced off against the potentially high depreciation of a new vehicle. The trade-off has worked well for us.

Where Will You Store the Motorhome?

If you are planning to store your motorhome at home, you'll need to get the tape measure out and check it will fit on your driveway. While doing this, also consider which way any gates you have open and if there is anything overhanging which may encroach on the motorhome's roof. Our first van nearly took out the guttering on our front porch when we first drove it onto the drive without looking up! We had to widen our drive to fit our second van and swap the normal gates for bi-folding ones.

Also check there are no restrictive covenants on your property title deeds or lease which forbid storing a motorhome, commercial van or caravan on your driveway. If you can't store your motorhome at home, there are specialised storage sites around the UK where you can rent a space. We pay around £1 a day to keep ours at a nearby farm which is CaSSOA-accredited (*cassoa.co.uk*), which is recognised by our insurance company as a secure site.

Right-Hand Drive (RHD) and Left-Hand Drive (LHD)

"Do I need a LHD motorhome to tour Europe?" This question pops up from time to time on our blog. Our answer's always the same: "no, but it helps if you plan to spend a long time outside the UK". The same goes for driving a LHD motorhome in the UK: we do it often, but if we planned to only tour the UK we'd get a RHD one.

We've met many people who tour Europe in right-hand drive (RHD) motorhomes. Friends we made in Northern Spain on our first tour had a right-hand drive van. They toured several countries working together at junctions and when overtaking and had no issues. If you don't have a partner to 'spot' for you, a RHD vehicle is a little more difficult to drive abroad. To overtake on two-way roads, it helps if the driver is in the middle of the road, so they can see any oncoming vehicles. In a LHD van you'll be in the right place to get the best view. Same for turning right at a wide junction. In a LHD van you get a far better view both ways than if you're in the right-hand seat and are up against the kerb.

If you're thinking "but I'm a steady driver and hardly overtake anyone", consider roadworks, accidents or large vehicles parked in the road forcing you out into oncoming traffic, whether you want to overtake or not. Very slow agricultural vehicles do the same when you've a string of impatient cars and lorries behind you.

If you plan to sell a LHD vehicle in the UK, it may be a little more difficult than a RHD. Take this into account when deciding how much you want to pay in the first place. We've only sold one LHD van, and it didn't seem to be important to buyers compared with the engine mileage and the van's interior condition.

Front Wheel Drive Versus Rear Wheel Drive

There are various pros and cons of going for front versus rear wheel drive motorhomes. One of the biggest discussion points is traction: the ability to get the motorhome off wet grass, up a gravel or snow-bound slope and so on. This becomes more of an issue if you have a lot of weight behind the rear axle of your motorhome, such as a scooter in the garage or on a rack. By no means do you need a rear wheel drive vehicle to avoid getting stuck but depending on how you plan to use your van it's worth considering it when making your choice.

There are also cost implications: front wheel drive vehicles are cheaper to buy than equivalent rear wheel drive, but some engine repairs can be more expensive on front wheel drive.

We've only used front wheel drive motorhomes and haven't suffered with traction issues. Our tours have taken us over a fair few mountain ranges and into lots of types of terrain, including river beds and sand-filled tracks. That said, we are careful about where we park, and don't often park on wet grass or drive for long periods in snow or ice.

Towing Capability
We've seen all sorts being towed behind motorhomes. Cars on A frames, cars on trailers, motorbikes on length-ways and sideways-on trailers, boats on trailers, box trailers with quad bikes or Harley Davidsons inside, you name it.

Like most motorhomes touring the UK and Europe, we opted not to tow anything, so can't comment first hand on towing capabilities. If you plan to tow, do your research to ensure your licence(s) allow it, your motorhome can legally tow the trailer and load (check the van's Gross Train Weight), whether the trailer needs to be braked and so on. Also, think carefully about access to aires, free camping spaces, car parks and motorhome campsites. Some of these are geared up to large motorhomes with trailers, but most are not. .

Being able to manoeuvre and park with a trailer in tight spots can be awkward and may restrict where you can stay. If you plan to take a moped or motorbike, a side-loading trailer will shorten your overall rig length. We've seen a few swivel wheel side-loading motorbike trailers on our travels. These have two ball hitches instead of one and can be reversed without risk of jack-knifing. They would be worth looking into, although again we've never used one.

Winterisation
If you plan to travel in your van in winter, especially if you plan to ski or snowboard, here are a few tips for looking for a suitable motorhome:

- Motorhomes are small spaces, which are easy to heat using built-in heating. This is normally powered by gas, but electric and diesel heaters (like those from Eberspächer) are also available.
- Lots of heat is lost through the cab windscreen and side windows. This can be reduced by fitting insulated windscreen thermal covers, often known as Silver Screens, while stationary. If the van doesn't come with them, you can buy them to fit (*www.silverscreens.co.uk* or *taylormade-covers.co.uk*). We recommend external covers, rather than ones which go inside the van,

as they keep ice off the windows, reduce condensation and avoid super-cold air (or super-hot air in summer) on the inside of the windscreen.

- The fresh and grey water tanks need to be very well insulated to stop them freezing. They'll need to be in a heated space inside the van and not slung underneath, or have immersion or stick-on heaters to stop them freezing.

- The grey water tank tap, used to empty the water, needs to be insulated to prevent it freezing, unless you plan to leave it open with a bucket beneath (which itself will freeze). Ideally the tap will be in a heated space.

- The toilet cassette space should ideally be heated to prevent the contents freezing and stopping you being able to empty it.

- Our current Hymer has a 'double floor' based on the AL-KO chassis (*www.alko-tech.com*). This chassis is lighter and lower than the standard Fiat commercial van chassis, and allows the water and waste tanks to be located between the floors where they are better insulated. This also means the floor stays warmer, so we don't end up with cold feet. Finally, it gives us full-width under-van storage, which can be used for skis.

Our fresh water tank, stored and insulated in between two floors

- If the van has curtains, thermal/blackout linings can be fitted if they're not already in place. Also, if the bed can be curtained off from the main living space this can make it easier to maintain a cosier sleeping area.

Even in the coldest conditions you can stay warm in your motorhome

Refine Your Criteria While Searching

OK, let's get looking at motorhomes. If you're after a brand-new motorhome, there are various shows around the UK (*www.outandaboutlive.co.uk/shows*) which will let you get up close with plenty of vans and chat with friendly and knowledgeable folks. For new and second-hand vans, motorhome dealers are great places to look around lots of different vehicles, normally without any pressure. While you're looking, here are a few more things to think about when choosing the right type of van, the base vehicle, and the layout for you.

Types of Van

For the majority of us, the choice of vehicle will be between an A Class, C Class (or coachbuilt) and a Panel Van. Finding your local dealer and going to look at a few makes and model of each type of vehicle really helps you get a feel for what works for you. These are the kinds of things we've considered when making the decision on the type of vehicle:

A Class

- The cab area has been built specifically to function as a motorhome. This means the cab is better insulated than a C Class (useful in winter). The cabs are also wide enough for a drop-down bed, which is effectively a fixed bed, avoiding the need to assemble it every night.
- They tend to be fairly long (although both of ours have been under six metres), this allows more space inside for fixed tables, fixed beds, storage, seating areas and so on, but larger vans can be intimidating to drive.

- Generally speaking, A Class vans are more expensive than C Class ones of a similar specification.
- Huge windscreens offer a magnificent view but can be expensive (possibly £2000 to £3000 including fitting) and difficult to source in the event they break. In reality we've only heard of a handful of times when someone's needed to replace their screen. Most insurance policies cover replacement windscreens with a relatively low excess, but some impose a maximum pay-out limit, so check.
- May have only one cab door (like our first Hymer B544) or none at all (like our current B544). This hasn't been an issue for us, although we do keep a fire extinguisher by the bed in case of a fire near the habitation door.

C Class

- C Class vans tend to be less expensive than A Class, while offering a similar level of living space and facilities.
- May have a bed mounted in a 'bubble' area above the cab, which like the A Class drop-down bed is fixed, and avoids the need to make up a bed each evening and put it away again in the morning.
- As they retain the standard cab, servicing and maintenance can be simpler. Changing a headlight on our A Class motorhome takes us at least an hour of fiddling with fingertips.
- A minority of owners report issues with water ingress where the cab bodywork meets the habitation area bodywork.
- The cab doors might need some additional security installing (this can apply to A Class and panel vans too).

Panel Van or Campervan

- Less conspicuous, making free camping easier.
- May be low enough to get under height barriers on car parks.
- Better fuel consumption than heavier A and C Class vans.
- Not as wide as A and C Class motorhomes, so easier to drive on narrow roads, and to park in standard-sized car spaces.
- Can still have a fixed bed, although this reduces the already-limited living space in the rest of the van.
- At the smaller end of the spectrum, campervans often won't have a toilet/shower, limiting where you can park.

Base Vehicle and Engine

Dave, our first motorhome, turned out to have a non-turbo diesel engine. We didn't find this out until a year after we'd bought him, by which point he'd hauled us up and over various mountain ranges. Clearly neither of us are experts on engines or base vehicles!

Our view is when it comes to the base vehicle and engine specification, it's more about what you do with it, and less about what you've got, as long as it's reliable. When it comes to reliability, our approach has been:

- To look for vehicles with a record of a full service history.
- To check when the cam belt change (if the engine needs one) is due. These can cost a few hundred pounds to get done every three or four years, and if left too long can wreck the engine if the belt snaps.
- To get a lower mileage vehicle (less than 70,000 miles, as an arbitrary figure) when the budget allowed.
- To ignore potentially expensive preconceptions, like Fiat being less reliable than Mercedes-Benz. Surveys suggest these biases may not have basis in reality.
- To see the vehicle in person, has it been well looked after?

If you're not comfortable taking this approach, various companies offer inspection services. Some of these are habitation checks only (looking at the van's living space and facilities) and don't look at the underlying chassis or engine, so make sure you ask what is covered.

Our latest 3.5 tonne van has a 2.8 litre JTD Turbo Diesel engine, which works well for us. In terms of speed we normally travel at 50 to 60mph, although the van comfortably handles 70mph on motorways. We don't tow anything. The van easily handles high mountain passes in the Alps without overheating, although at no great speed. The engine isn't very clean though, and over time we'll slowly find our access to low emission zones being tightened (see page 119). Also, our older engine means we don't have to use AdBlue, a liquid additive needed by some of the newest diesel engines.

We've only ever had manual gearbox motorhomes, never automatics. Chatting with folks who have an automatic they've raved about them, saying they'd never go back to manual. Same goes for cruise control. We're both comfortable driving with a manual gearbox, with no cruise control, perhaps because we've never tried the alternatives. Having huffed and puffed and arm-pumped our old Autosleeper Harmony panel van around the UK, we'd suggest power-assisted steering (PAS) is a must for anything other than the smallest campervan.

When it comes to fuel type, our campervan was petrol and our two motorhomes were diesel. Diesel is (generally) cheaper then unleaded petrol outside the UK (*www.fuel-prices-europe.info*), but otherwise we've no preference either way.

All our campers and motorhomes have been relatively light, with only two axles, and four wheels. You'll come across 'tag axle' motorhomes, which have two axles mounted one behind the other at the rear of the van, and others with rear wheel drive and twin rear wheels. Both these configurations have six wheels. The latter seems to be preferred by experts on forums, as they're expected to have fewer issues getting grip on the drive wheels, have a better turning circle and attract lower toll road fees in some countries.

Our first motorhome had air-assisted suspension: basically two heavy duty rubber bags which could be inflated to take some of the load from the rear leaf springs. They made little difference to the vehicle handling but did reduce the squeaks and knocking noises from the aged springs!

Length, Width, Height and Ground Clearance
Keeping the physical length of the van down to 6m or less has been helpful for us, although in reality most motorhomes we see while touring are now longer than 7m. With a longer van, consider the points below.

Depending on where you plan to go, some ferry companies increase their prices for longer vans, although not by a huge amount. If you get a chance to head to Norway, with its endless stream of fjords and ferries, prices increase dramatically above 6m, and for every additional metre.

Six metres is about the limit for fitting in a standard car parking space (overhanging the back over a low kerb if you're not blocking a path). While this isn't a show-stopper for getting a longer van, it does help if you plan to free camp, and is useful in busier car parks at supermarkets and tourist attractions.

Have a look at the height of the van above the ground too. Our current motorhome had low ground clearance at the front, which meant the front bumper caught on levelling ramps and high kerbs until we had heavy-duty springs installed. Motorhomes with a long overhang at the back also suffer from grounding when the road gradient changes, when driving on and off the ramp at ferries or if they have to be loaded onto a breakdown vehicle. You can consider fitting 'skid wheels' which hit the ground before your rear chassis, helping protect it from damage.

We've found that even with a 6m long motorhome, our A Class vans have been a challenge to drive on some roads due to their width. At around 2.2m wide, they're about 40cm to 50cm wider than an average car of around 1.7m to 1.8m. There are plenty of places in the UK and Europe where we really notice that additional width; at entrances to campsites, in tunnels, on mountain roads, at 'pinch points' in medieval towns and villages, you name it. That said, we've only ever hit wing mirrors a couple of times, so while the additional width can cause tight shoulders, it's not a huge issue for us.

The height of the vehicle has never been much of a consideration for us. Our motorhomes have been around 3m high, which means almost every car park with a height barrier is off-limits. We fit under most bridges, although we've almost been caught out a time or two (like the time we had to reverse through traffic in Italy to avoid a low railway bridge)! Getting on the roof requires a ladder (or being parked alongside a high wall), so we'd need to carry or fit one if we planned to spend a long time in snow-bound conditions so we could clear the roof, or if we had a canoe stored up there.

The Layout
When picking a layout – rear lounge, two sofas, rear bed, one sofa and a dinette, two single beds – think about how you'll live in it. If there are two of you, can one of you lie in bed while the other watches TV from the sofa or cooks in the kitchen? Can you both use the table at the same time? Can one of you work in the kitchen while the other gets in and out of the van, or walks into or out of the bathroom?

We suggest visiting a few motorhome dealers and physically trying out as many layouts as you can. Sit in the chairs. Use the table. Take your shoes off and lie in the bed, pointing your toes to make sure you're really comfortable. Pretend to have a shower and see if your elbows get whacked. Think about how you'll prepare and cook a meal. We found it helpful to take photos and video our favourite layouts on our phones, making notes of which were which and what they cost. That way we could look at them later without any pressure felt being at the dealer.

Just be aware that every motorhome will be a compromise in some way; because unless you self-build it to your specification you'll struggle to find one which is 100% perfect. That doesn't matter though, as your gut feel (also known as 'falling in love') for a van is always going to beat any analysis by your brain. Here are some lessons we've learned from living in our motorhomes.

The Bed
Sleep is important! Unless you're an insomniac, you're going to need it, and if you can't get it because your bed's not comfortable then you won't much enjoy life. Getting a comfortable bed is critical!

The bed in Harvey, our old panel van, had to be made up each night using the driving seats (which folded right back), and a series of cushion and chair moves. Eventually this rendered an almost-but-not-quite-flat bed across the width of the van. Sadly, at 5ft 10" we were about two inches too tall to sleep comfortably in it, so we had to make up two single beds with one of us sleeping with our legs under the steering wheel. This was fine for a few nights, but awkward and uncomfortable over time. Whoever was assembling the beds got trapped fingers, a twisted back, and a black humour. The bedding had to be kept under the seats, which took up a lot of the storage space and once the beds were made there wasn't room for anyone to be sat down anywhere but the loo.

When we came to buy our first motorhome, we tried over-cab (Luton) beds on C Class vans but found the headroom to be a little too low for us. We also tried fixed beds, but they didn't work well for us personally, as they either made the vans too long, or restricted the living space.

The van we chose, a Hymer B544, had a good compromise solution for us. It had a drop-down bed, common in A Class motorhomes. The bed could be assembled quickly by closing the cab curtains, using quick release catches to drop the cab chairs forward (optional), unclipping a seatbelt safety clip, and pulling the bed down. It came down to about chest height, giving us enough headroom to be comfortable, and was wide enough to let us sleep with toes pointed (something we didn't realise we did until we tried to sleep in our panel van).

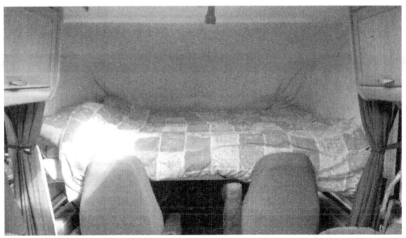

The cab drop-down bed on our Hymer A Class motorhome

We could leave the bedding on the bed when it wasn't in use, so only had to move a few pillows, which we spread out across the bed to help stop it bouncing about while driving, and it was made. The time to get the bed ready was less than a couple of minutes, and even though the van was only 5.5m long, with the bed down you could still access the sofa and dinette. When one of us was ill for a few days, this arrangement really helped us both stay comfortable.

Our second van is also a B544, although newer, and has the same bed set up. We've spent over four years sleeping in this type of bed and while we can both stretch out and get a good night's sleep across the width of the van, they aren't perfect:

- It can get very warm up there when it's hot. One of us takes to a sofa-based bed when this happens, so we both get a good night's sleep.
- One of us has to be 'on the inside'. We take it in turns, as it means:
  - sleeping up against the windscreen, which is cold in winter or in the mountains, and hot in summer when the sun hits it,
  - having a little less headroom,
  - and having to climb over the other one to get out of bed.
- It takes a bit of back power to push the bed back up with all our bedding on it (although it lifts up easily without bedding).

These issues, coupled with the agility needed to get into the bed (we don't take the ladder and use the edge of the sofa to climb up), it would be hard to recommend to anyone who wants or needs to just roll into or out of bed.

Berths and Privacy
Over time we've come across a few folks driving much larger motorhomes than they're comfortable with. Some openly admit they were upsold at the dealers, and the motorhome's become something of a fearsome pain to get from one place to another. Some tell us they made sure they had additional beds so that their grown-up children could visit them, but they never had, or had only visited for a few days when they could have easily stated in a nearby cabin or hotel.

What we're trying to say is this: think very carefully about how many beds and belted seats you really, truly need, and get this down to as few as possible. This will likely make the van easier to park, easier to manoeuvre, more fuel efficient and something you're more likely to cherish rather than fear. Remember, if your children need car seats, you'll need full belts, and not just lap belts.

While we have no children, we've met many couples and single parents travelling for long periods with children. They reported few issues in day-to-day living in the van. One couple had deliberately specified a van where their front bed could be separated from the rear area of the van where the children slept, using a door. This offered night-time privacy to both parents and kids. Another had altered a single rear bed into two short beds, to accommodate their two young girls for a 24-month tour.

Cooking Facilities
Cooking in a motorhome's tiny kitchen offers a chance to perfect your small-space living skills! How you cook in the van compared to being at home can be very different. Here are a few points to consider when making a decision based on cooking facilities:

- As standard, you'll usually get two or three gas burners on a hob. We also carry a single electric hob for use when on electric hook-up and have seen some newer motorhomes with a built-in electric hob.
- Many motorhomes, particularly those built outside the UK, don't have a fitted oven. Have a think if you really need one, as finding a van with an oven might reduce the options available to you. If you love to cook and don't think a three-ring hob will be enough for you, maybe have a trip to one of the motorhome shows. There are many gadgets and other cooking devices out there. We're oven-less, so we use a Remoska and a Double Skillet. See *Cooking* on page 75.
- If you plan to wild camp/free camp and use aires a lot of the time, is it worth the weight and space of carrying a microwave? Yes, you could power one using an inverter (see *Inverters* on page 71), but you'll need a big device, and batteries to match.
- Is there enough worktop space to allow you to prepare food and cook for everyone on board? Does the kitchen sink have a worktop cover, so you can work over it while preparing, and remove when you need to wash up?
- Charcoal BBQs aren't always allowed on campsites due to the fire risk, so gas BBQs become useful, especially if you're cooking something like fish that will stink up your motorhome. Gas BBQs are either powered with a small gas bottle or canister or attached to an external gas BBQ point.

Fridge and Freezer

These are the main fridge-freezer things to think about when looking at a motorhome, other than 'does it work?'

- Is the fridge and freezer big enough? On first sight, they might look tiny (especially the under-counter ones) but bear in mind you can frequently re-stock fresh food at supermarkets while driving between sites, or even better from local markets. We switch from fresh milk to UHT while on the road, as it's easier to keep a store of it.
- Can you access the freezer without opening the fridge too? This isn't a big issue unless the weather's very warm and you want to avoid losing the cold air from your fridge.
- Does the fridge automatically change between heat sources (see *The Fridge* on page 76)? If not, you'll need remember to switch between the heat sources (which becomes a habit but if you forget can ruin a full fridge and freezer's worth of food).

The Table

The table in our first campervan was stored in the wardrobe. It fitted onto a wide, pipe-like single leg, which was stored above the sliding side door. In all, it took about a minute to get it out and set it up. During our years in the campervan, we were quite happy with this set up, although when the wardrobe was packed, it could be awkward to extract the table.

When it came to choosing a second van, we knew a fixed table was essential. On shorter trips we could easily put up with installing and removing the table each time we needed it. But we knew something which was only a mild irritation needed fixing for our long-term layout.

When we got Dave, our first Hymer B544, he had a fixed table in a dinette arrangement. The table could also be used to make up a second double bed, but we only ever did that when it was too hot for both of us to sleep in the drop-down bed. Most of the time the table stayed solidly in place, ready for us to use whenever the hand brake went on. It was easily large enough for us both to eat at and, at a push, we could seat six people around it.

In Zagan, our current motorhome, we have two sofas and a table which 'swings' out from above one of the sofas, on a single dog-leg shaped mount. While not as stable or large as Dave's table, we find the ability to store the table out of the way gives the van a great open feel.

Shower and Toilet

We've met plenty of people who have never used the shower and toilet in their motorhome. When we bought our current motorhome, its 14-year-old bathroom had a piece of carpet in the shower tray as it was never used, and the toilet cassette was free of scratches, effectively unused. If you plan to use your motorhome only on campsites, always using the site's shower and toilet facilities, then you don't need to worry too much about your on-board facilities.

Once we'd gotten over the idea of using the toilet while the other one of us was in the van (turning up the radio helps!), we found having access to our own toilet meant we could stay anywhere. This opened up the possibility of free camping and use of the European aires in addition to campsites. This in turn dramatically reduced our overnight costs, freeing up money for eating out, diesel, and entrance fees and so on.

If you plan to use your bathroom fully, have a look for these features:

- Can you comfortably fit in the shower and lift your arms and legs in a way which lets you properly get washed and towel yourself down?
- If the shower and loo share the same floor space, are you OK with the floor being wet after each shower (not usually an issue as you can quickly dry the floor if you need to)?

- Is there room to keep the loo roll, clothes and your towel dry during a shower?
- Is the shower room heated?
- Is there only one plug hole in the shower? If there is, it can be a bit of a job emptying the shower tray with the 'uphill foot sweep to the plug hole' technique if you're on a slope.
- If you're into sea swimming, water sports or have a pooch who likes to get muddy, can the shower be used outside?

Don't expect too much from the shower, by the way. Back home, you can easily get through 50 or 60 litres of water taking a single shower. Given the fact most vans aren't likely to have more than 100 litres of fresh water available, motorhome makers don't bother installing a power-pump to blast you with water! You'd use all your supply in just a couple of showers, which means hunting out water continually. Instead you can expect a pretty weak flow of water, but it should be enough to wash shampoo from your hair.

Storage and Garage
Motorhomes typically have a wardrobe, under-seat storage, kitchen cupboards and high-level cupboards above the seats or bed. Some have under-bed storage and/or a garage area. Others have under-van storage, especially if they have a double floor, and some have storage space on the roof or back, either using racks or a roof-mounted locker.

Remembering the payload limitations, storage isn't usually a huge problem, on vans under 3.5 tonnes at least, unless you need to carry specialist equipment like skis, snowboards, surfboards, an inflatable boat with outboard motor (yes, we've seen this) or a moped. That said, have a think about where you'll keep some of the larger items you're likely to be carrying. Being able to easily get at outdoor equipment such as a camping table and chairs and BBQ, makes you more likely to use them. Being able to access internal lockers from outside can be useful too: we store our levelling ramps under one of the benches for example.

Some vans have special 'wet lockers', which are sealed units designed for, well, wet stuff, although some have a 230V socket installed so stuffing wet stuff in there might not be sensible while hooked-up.

If you are thinking of taking bikes with you, have a think about where you'll store them. If they are on a bike rack on the back is it easy to reach to get the bikes on and off (you can get racks which drop down to a lower level for easier access)? If it's in a garage will they fit easily? If they're heavy, like electric bikes, will you overload your rear axle?

Watching TV

With such a wealth of culture around you, why on Earth would you want to watch TV? So the argument goes. We've a foot in both pro and anti-TV camps, having travelled for two years with no TV, and having travelled for over two years with a satellite TV system. When we're parked somewhere quiet or rainy, just need some down time, or want to watch the Olympics 100m final, we like having the option to use the TV.

As well as receiving live TV in your motorhome, you also have the option to watch DVD box sets (we pick them up from charity shops) or downloaded programs on your laptop, tablet or even your phone. There are various methods of doing this, some of dubious legality, but having DVD or downloaded media is the best guarantee you'll be able to watch something. The options for watching live TV below aren't 100% infallible, and can lead to frustration if you have a strong expectation to be able to watch what you want, when you want:

- Using a roof, floor or tripod-mounted satellite dish, decoder and TV (some vans have a satellite dish mounted on a pole on the back). We have a FreeView decoder built into our TV, so cannot watch Sky channels, for example.
- Using a roof-mounted digital antenna and a TV which can receive digital terrestrial signals.
- Watching internet TV via 3G, 4G or 5G uses the mobile phone networks, so depending on where you are parked, you can't always guarantee a connection which is fast and consistent enough for a good experience. Mobile data is usually metered too, you pay per GB (gigabyte). Streaming TV can get through between 0.5GB and 3GB of data per hour, depending on the quality of the video. You may also need to pay for a VPN (a virtual private network, a method of hiding your location around the World, see page 129) if you are outside the UK, as some channels may be blocked for viewing outside the country. If your TV isn't internet-enabled, it's not an issue. You can buy an adapter like Amazon's Fire TV Stick or the Now TV Stick, which plugs into your TV's HDMI port, converting it to an internet TV.

When you're choosing a motorhome, if you're certain you'll want to watch satellite TV then have a think about these things:

- The satellite dish, TV and (if you don't use a built-in Freeview version) separate decoder will all impact your payload. You'll also need space on the roof to mount the dish.
- Automatic systems seek out the correct satellite for you. Our system is manual, which means we have to spend a few minutes finding the satellite each time we use it. Using a signal strength meter and a smartphone app which indicates the direction of the satellite, this has proved to be easy.

- If you'll want to watch TV away from mains hook-up, make sure your system works with 12V or specify a suitable inverter. Also, if you won't be on campsites bear in mind it's more difficult to have a floor-mounted dish alongside your van when on aires or free-camping.
- If you plan to travel continental Europe, UK channels get harder to receive. The further you are away from the UK, the bigger dish you'll need. Research satellite footprints and dish sizes to make sure your system will work where you need it to.
- Remember you can't reliably use a satellite system in high winds, while driving, in heavy rain or when there's a tree, hill, building or some such in the way.

Leisure Batteries
Except for the mains sockets, all the electrical power in your motorhome's habitation space will come from one or more leisure batteries. These aren't used by the motorhome's engine; that has a separate battery just for the job of starting the engine, running the vehicle's lights and so on. The leisure battery provides a 12V DC power supply for the lights inside the van, runs the fridge while driving, powers the water pump, runs the heating fan, and charges your gadgets and so on. See *12V DC System* on page 65 for more information.

During buying, check the battery voltages using the built-in meter/control panel in the van. As a very rough rule of thumb, if the batteries in the van read less than 12V, they may be old or damaged, so budget for new ones.

Awnings
A wind out awning is great for providing shade not only for you to sit under but for the side of the van when it's hot. Ours also gets used for cooking under in light rain (drop one leg lower so the rain runs off) and hanging a washing line from.

Awnings aren't light; a 2.5m long awning can take around 20Kg out of your payload, but we believe they are worth it. Always wind in your awning if there's a chance of gusting or strong wind. Heavy duty tie-down straps help prevent the thing flying off the ground, but the fabric can still tear, and it's no fun trying to sleep in heavy wind with your awning flapping like mad outside.

You can get sides for some awnings, which can be mesh-screens to reduce strong sunlight, or a tent-like material (safari rooms) to offer full protection from wind and rain and effectively double the size of your living space. Our second van came with both types of side, but we didn't use either. We've also seen inflatable awnings and ones that can be left standing when you go out in your motorhomes, known as 'drive away' awnings. If there will be a few of you in your van, it might be worth looking into these space creators.

Things You Can Change After Buying

If you hate the brightly patterned upholstery in a motorhome that ticks all your other boxes, it doesn't have to stop you from buying it. In this section we look at areas which, although important, can potentially be changed after you've bought the vehicle. We also look at things you might want to add to your motorhome. Of course, there'll be a cost consideration to making any changes, so it's worth having a read through before committing to buy.

Safety

The van should have at least one smoke/fire/carbon monoxide (CO) alarm, a small, but very important thing. It needs to be loud enough to wake you up in the event of a fire or fault on your heating system. If your motorhome has a garage, consider popping a separate alarm in there too.

In the event of a fire, a fire extinguisher or two could be the difference between a blackened cupboard and a molten mess of motorhome. We have one extinguisher in the kitchen and another by the bed. Both are the powder type. We also have a fire blanket in the kitchen in case we set our 'coq-au-vin' alight.

Ideally the van will have had a recent habitation check, with a certificate to prove that the gas system is safe. If the van doesn't come with this, you can get one done (we searched the Gas Safe Register for local plumbers who dealt with LPG and caravans and rang a few for quotes) but be aware if it reveals the water heater's had it, it will be very expensive to replace.

Bike Rack

Most motorhomes can take a rear-mounted cycle rack, which itself can typically hold up to four bikes (*www.fiammastore.com*). Some vans have the fittings for these built-in, so as long as you get a compatible rack you can easily fit it without drilling holes in your van. If you plan to carry bikes and the van has no rack, have a look at how easy it will be to buy and fit one.

Security Features

If the van has an alarm, tracker and/or immobiliser, check it works and ask your insurance company whether they offer a discount for that particular make and model. We've always used secondary locks (in addition to the standard ones fitted by the manufacturer) on the habitation door and cab doors. Secondary locks on exterior lockers are only really helpful if you've expensive or irreplaceable stuff in there: otherwise they're just awkward.

While parked at home you might also want to think about additional 'static' security, like a wheel clamp, steering wheel lock and the like. We've never used any of these, and very rarely see them in use by anyone touring. That's not to say they don't have value, especially if your van is parked somewhere highly visible.

Lighting

Lighting can be a big draw on your leisure battery, especially during long winter evenings. Check whether the van has LED lighting, as this uses far, far less power. If it doesn't, you can retrofit it, but budget for the price of the replacement lights.

Solar Panels

Solar panels are useful in any motorhome which isn't frequently hooked up to the mains electricity network (see *Solar Panels* on page 67). If you plan to free camp, use the aires network in Europe, or want to avoid the cost of using mains hook-up on sites, having at least one solar panel really helps increase your flexibility. Solar panels also help maintain your batteries when the van isn't in use, as long as it's not parked under a roof, tree or blanketed under snow.

If you're thinking of having a panel fitted after buying the van, or an additional panel fitted, check there's physically enough roof space to take it.

Upholstery

This seems to be the first thing we all spot when walking through the habitation door of a potential buy. Unless it's worn out, or a livid colour, the upholstery shouldn't (in theory!) be an enormous factor when deciding on a motorhome. That said, if it does burn your eyeballs in a technicolour blaze, you can either cover it with throws and car seat covers or get it reupholstered. There are specialist companies that do this, but it can cost around £1000 or more, depending on how much needs doing and the fabric you choose.

Anti-Fly Measures

Depending on where you are and when, you might find yourself sharing your van with a variety of flying critters, mosquitoes and midges being the worse. If it happens to be warm and sunny at the same time, then you'll likely be wanting some fresh air in the van, requiring the door, windows and/or skylights to be open, inviting the bugs in too.

We fitted a net fly curtain on the habitation door of our first motorhome, which worked to a degree but kept getting caught in the door. Our current motorhome has a mesh screen attached to the door which swings into place with the main door open. That approach works much better. In extreme mozzy-infected zones like Finland, we fit a mosquito net above our bed.

Blackout Capability

Even if you aren't heading to the Arctic in summer, where you'd have the midnight sun to contend with, being parked under a bright streetlight at night can be a challenge to sleep. Check the skylights can be blacked-out and how well any blinds or curtains keep light out. If needs be, you can sew blackout material onto the back of curtains.

Final Checks and the Buying Process

Once you've found the right vehicle for you, there are a few final checks you may want to carry out before signing on the dotted line. Once you've completed these, the process for buying the motorhome is summarised below.

DVLA and MOT Checks

You can pay to have online checks done to ensure the motorhome you are buying isn't stolen, doesn't have existing finance on it etc. There are also a couple of quick online checks you can do yourself for free, to make sure what you are being told by the seller stacks up.

With just the registration number, you can check the past results of the vehicle's MOT tests including details of any failures, advisories, mileage and so on at *www.gov.uk/check-mot-history*.

You can also do a search to find out when the tax and MOT are due, as well as the first registration date and fuel type, once again with just the registration at *vehicleenquiry.service.gov.uk*. If you have the 11-digit code from the V5 log book you can also use this site to find out how much the road tax will be.

Test Driving

It makes a lot of sense to test drive your chosen van before agreeing to buy it, especially if you've not driven that type of vehicle before. Is the driving position comfortable, are you happy with visibility, are you able to get the van through gaps and around corners without all your hair falling out? The test drive will also, in theory at least, give you confidence a second-hand van's engine and chassis actually function!

That said, we didn't test drive either of our private-bought motorhomes. We started the engine to check for plumes of smoke and to listen to it, but otherwise we relied on the service history and the seller's honesty that the van engine was functioning. Our trust was repaid and, being relatively small vans, we got used to the vehicle size over time.

Are the Main Habitation Area Utilities Working?

When we bought our vans we mainly relied on the honesty of the sellers, as we were too excited to think of what we should be checking and asking. We have been lucky, but the high cost of a new fridge (maybe £500 unfitted) or heater (over £1000 unfitted for combi heaters) makes it hard for us to suggest you do the same. For any future purchases we'll be going through the following checks.

It makes sense to ask the seller what 'quirks' the van has, and have a checklist which, if you're serious about buying the van, you can ask the seller to demonstrate these items before agreeing a price. If possible, send your list to the seller in advance, so they can prepare the van. The list could include things like:

- Hot water flowing from the taps and shower (this might take 10 or 20 minutes for the water to heat up).
- Hot air coming from the heater (this might take a few minutes to heat up).
- The freezer keeping ice frozen (this will take overnight if the van isn't being used and will only demonstrate electric or gas as a heating source, not both).
- The toilet flush working.
- Each of the gas hobs lighting.

Damp Check

Water can make it into a motorhome over time, through leaking windows, seams or cable connections through the vehicle's external skin or from a leaking water pipe or tank inside the van. A van which has been stood for a while in the cold will start to smell musty, but it shouldn't smell strongly of damp. The floor and walls should feel solid, and not bouncy or soft. There should be no signs of damp getting in around skylights and windows: stains, mould or black marks. Take a damp meter and if you're concerned walk away.

Age, Suitability and Condition of Tyres

Tyres are critical to keeping you safe and on the road. If you need to replace five tyres with new motorhome-specific ones, you'll need to budget around £400 to £600. Think about these things when looking at the tyres:

- Do they have (at the very least) the legal tread limit? If you plan to travel outside the UK in winter, more stringent tread limits can apply.
- Are they over five years old (they should have a date on the sidewall)? If they are, they'll need closer professional inspection to be sure they're safe.
- Do they have any cracks in the sidewalls? If they do, expect to replace them.
- Do they have the M+S or Winter Tyre marking on the sidewall (see page 163 for more details)?
- Are they specialist motorhome tyres (not essential, but nice to have)?
- What state is the spare tyre in, if there is one?
- If you don't have a spare wheel, is there an 'emergency inflation' kit supplied?

If your van has a spare wheel, does it have a suitable jack and tyre brace, and would you be happy using them at the roadside on a heavy vehicle with large lorries blowing it about as they pass? If not, will you have breakdown cover, so you can call them out to replace your wheel for you? We have a spare wheel, brace and jack, but would most likely call our breakdown company unless we were somewhere we felt safe to change it, like at an aire or on a campsite.

If you're close to your payload weight limit, spare wheels aren't light. You could consider leaving it at home, and carrying just a spare tyre, tyre repair kit and air pump, then use your breakdown cover to get you to a suitable garage for the tyre to be fitted.

Getting a Walkthrough of the Facilities

If you've found your perfect van and everything is looking good, before you hand over your cash, get the owner to run though how the facilities work. Consider asking if you can video them on your phone, so you can watch it again later when you're not as excited/rushed. They may not know all of these but asking now might save you from hunting around or having to experiment later on. Sending them the list beforehand would be helpful for the seller so they can prepare.

- How to turn the air heating on, adjust the temperature and turn it off.
- How to turn the water heating on and off, along with any temperature adjustment.
- If the gas system is refillable, or has an auto cut-over valve, talk through how they work.
- How to turn the fridge onto gas, 12V and mains hook-up.
- Where the fresh water refill point is and where the mains hook-up point is on the outside of the van, and how to use any locks.
- How to empty the grey water tank.
- How to access the grey and fresh water tanks from inside the van (if this is possible), and how to drain down the fresh water system.
- Where the water pump is located.
- Where the 12V and mains sockets are all located.
- Where the 230V mains consumer unit is inside the van.
- If the van has an inverter, where it is and how you turn it on and off.
- Where the van's leisure batteries are stored.
- Where you top up the engine fuel tank, and with which type of fuel, and how to use any locking fuel cap.
- If the van has a satellite dish/terrestrial antenna and/or TV, get a demonstration of how they work.
- How to open the bonnet.
- How to open and lock the lockers, habitation door and cab doors.
- Where the fuses are for the habitation area, and the underlying vehicle.
- How to make the bed up, if needed.

Going Through the Buying Process

Once you're finally ready to buy, the process for transferring ownership is fairly straightforward:

1. You can get a background check done to ensure the vehicle has no outstanding HPI (loan payments), hasn't been stolen and so on (for example: *www.mycarcheck.com*).
2. Check the registration number, engine and chassis numbers on the V5C are the same as those physically on the vehicle.
3. If you haven't already, check the sticker or plaque on the van to ensure the MAM weight limit is what you expect it to be.
4. Before making payment, contact your bank to agree the best option for moving the money. There may be a value limit on some types of payment, so check well in advance. You're supposed to avoid paying with cash by the way, as you can't prove you paid it as easily as more 'auditable' methods like a bank transfer.
5. We tend to take our passports with us, just to give the buyer confidence we are who we say we are.
6. If you leave a deposit, make sure you get a receipt for it stating how much deposit you paid, the vehicle registration and how much is outstanding. When you make the final payment, get another receipt stating you've paid the full amount.
7. After you've completed your details on the V5C, the current owner should give you the section with your details and send the rest to the DVLA to change ownership to you.
8. You'll need to tax the vehicle and arrange insurance before driving it away. It makes sense to contact your insurers well in advance to get an idea of cost. You can buy the tax online, using the part of the V5C the seller gives you, at *www.gov.uk/vehicle-tax*.
9. The owner should give you the MOT certificate, if it is old enough to need one.
10. Remember to ask for all paperwork relating to the van's service history and any warranty.

Take your time driving away! Unless you've driven a similar vehicle, it will feel odd, and possibly very large. Get the mirrors lined up before you drive off, work out where the indicators and lights are, and make sure you're comfortable before hitting the road.

Other Options for Sourcing a Motorhome

Most of us will source a motorhome from a dealer or private seller within the UK and buy it. This isn't the only option though. You could choose to rent a motorhome instead, import one from abroad or even buy a base vehicle and convert it into a motorhome yourself. The following sections take a brief look at these options (none of which we've done personally).

Rent Versus Buy

Some advice regularly given to first time motorhome buyers is to rent a van first. The reasoning is simple: it's hard to know what you like (and what you really don't like) until you've tried living in it. This is sage advice, but we'd attach a serious caveat to it: it might be much, much cheaper to buy an older van, and sell it on if you don't like it, than it is to rent one.

A month's hire of a 'standard' 4-berth motorhome in the UK in May can set you back £2000 (*www.justgo.uk.com*). This includes basic insurance; to add full collision damage waiver, add another £500. To add insurance for selected European countries, add another £200. And for a 'travel pack' of child seats, linen, GPS, an additional driver and picnic table and chairs, add another £300. The full package comes in at £3000.

Compare that with buying a £15,000 motorhome second hand from a private seller, with £500 for a year's comprehensive insurance, £250 for tax and a generous £750 for MOT and repairs. If the van depreciated at a rate of 10%, it would take a year to go down in value by £1500. Adding it all up, this gives you a full year of motorhome fun for around £3,000 instead of a month. We met one Australian couple who'd spent £15,000 hiring a van to tour Europe for a year. This didn't make much financial sense to us, although it certainly simplified issues with insurance and registration.

Of course, if you plan to buy a brand new £60,000 motorhome, the sums can change significantly. This vehicle could depreciate by £12,000 in its first year on the road, so the case for renting for a while to test the layout and so on makes more sense.

Importing a Motorhome

Another alternative to buying a motorhome in the UK is to find one abroad and import it. The main reasons to do this are to get a better price, or to get a specification which isn't available in the UK (perhaps a LHD version). If this option interests you, think about these implications during your research:

- Get a free Import Pack from the DVLA for information on what you need to do to register the van in the UK (*forms.dft.gov.uk/order-dvla-forms*).
- Websites such as *mobile.de* will give you some ideas of prices in Germany.
- The price of a van outside the UK will vary with the exchange rate from Sterling. If the pound is weak, the price will obviously increase. You can look at using a forward contract to mitigate the risk of the rate worsening (check if your bank offers this).
- Vans intended for a non-UK market may have a different specification for the same make and model. For example, they may not have an oven, or may have a larger fuel tank.

- If you're buying a brand-new van, you'll probably have to pay VAT in the country you buy the van, then inform HMRC of the import within 14 days of arriving in the UK (*www.gov.uk/nova-log-in*). HMRC will bill you for the UK VAT which you'll need to pay before you can reclaim the VAT from the dealer abroad, so for a while you'll have paid the VAT twice.
- Make sure the dealer provides you with a certificate of conformity, which you'll need to complete UK paperwork.
- Consider how you'll insure the vehicle once you've picked it up and before you can register it in the UK. If buying in Germany, dealers can provide you with export plates which include third-party insurance. People who've imported a van have reported getting comprehensive insurance prior to arriving in the UK is difficult.
- Remember you'll need to budget for alterations to make the van legal in the UK, as specified by the UK Vehicle Certification Agency (VCA). The headlights, fog light and speedometer may all need changing, and you'll need an MOT station to provide proof that the VCA requirements are met.
- Once you have a suitable invoice from the MOT station, you can apply for type approval from the VCA, who'll send you the UK log book (the V5C). You can now have UK number plates made.

We've chatted with people who've imported motorhomes and made significant savings on their new vehicles. They advised the import process to be reasonably simple, especially with help from dealers in Germany.

Self-Building a Motorhome

As an alternative to buying a motorhome, some talented and industrious souls do a self-build. This enables you to fully customise the van to your needs. We've never done this, or even contemplated it, so can only direct you to some people who have:

- The Self Build Motor Caravanner's Club (*sbmcc.co.uk*)
- DIY Motorhome (*www.diymotorhome.co.uk*)
- Campervan Conversion (*campervanconversion.co.uk*)
- Vandog Traveller (*vandogtraveller.com*)

Even if you don't plan to self-build, these sources are useful to get an idea of how motorhomes are put together, how the electrical system works, how the heater works and so on.

Your First Trips Out in the UK

Right, you have your motorhome! Woo hoo! You've driven it home and are (fairly) comfortable with it. Time to pack your essentials, weigh the van and get ready for your first 'shakedown trips'.

Packing Your Motorhome

We've been guilty of going too mad over-worrying about having exactly the right stuff with us on our trips and trying to pack everything! There are shops everywhere of course, as folks have to dress and eat wherever you're going. Most of the time you can get anything you've missed. Also, it's only when you've been going a day, week, month or even a year before you start to realise you've not used half the 'essential' stuff clogging up the lockers or garage.

That said, whatever you do, don't forget your potato masher if you're going to Italy. It took us months to find one. The forgotten and broken corkscrews, on the other hand, were replaced just like that. Working out what to take's a challenge, so we've put together some information below to give you a hand and some thoughts about how best to place it all in your van's various storage cupboards and lockers.

What to Take

One rainy day in our motorhome, we wrote out everything we had in there as we took a year-long tour of Europe. This has now become our packing checklist and you can find a copy in *Appendix A* starting on page 219. To help you work out your own packing list, we've summarised below the sorts of things to think about:

- **Legal Stuff** and **Documentation** – unless you plan to travel outside the UK, you don't need to carry anything in this regard. However, the UK police may ask to see your driving licence, insurance certificate and MOT certificate, and if you don't have them with you, then you only have seven days to produce them at a police station (*www.gov.uk/stopped-by-police-while-driving-your-rights*).
- **Daily Servicing** – things you'll need to fill with water, top up with gas or swap bottles, hook-up to mains electricity and keep the loo smelling fresh.
- **Navigation and Finding Places to Sleep** – databases, books, satnav (GPS) and maps for finding your way around.
- **Outdoor Stuff** – table, chair, BBQs and other fun stuff.
- **Tools** – bits and bobs for making minor repairs on the road, including tape, fuses, screwdrivers, spare bulbs and the like.
- **Kitchen Essentials** – bowls, plates, glasses, utensils, saucepans, everything you need for feeding your crew in the van.
- **Store Cupboard Food** – essentials for flavouring your grub, making brews, a couple of bottles of wine and the like.

- **Bathroom** – towels, toothbrushes, first aid kit, sunscreen, toiletries, shaving kit, loo rolls and so on.
- **Bedroom** – duvet, pillows, mattress topping, bed sheet and all the things you need for a warm and comfy kip.
- **Soft Furnishings** – cushions and throws for keeping your seating area looking and feeling inviting.
- **Clothing and Laundry** – clothes for all the weather you expect to experience! Plus, if you plan longer trips, a clothes line, pegs and washing liquid, etc.
- **Entertainment, Leisure and Tech** – books, board games, wetsuit, laptop, camera, blow-up kayak, drone, whatever you want to keep you entertained.
- **Pet Stuff** – bowls, food, tick and flea treatment, ID disk, lead and harness, towel... Our pampered pooch had more stuff than us!

How to Pack Your Van
There are a few golden rules we've learned over time for packing our van:

- Our main 'rule' is 'a place for everything, and everything in its place'. This means stuff gets put away when not in use (at least in theory!). You'll be amazed at how quickly your motorhome can start to feel small when the surfaces are full.
- Ensure things used all the time are easy to get to: cups for tea, cutlery, bowls and plates, your favourite shoes and coat, outdoor chairs, toothbrush, shampoo and so on. If you have to remove a glass from a cupboard before you can get your plate out, it'll slowly but surely drive you nuts.
- Also think about things you use at the same time and store them together if you can. We keep our coffee in the same cupboard as our mugs, which saves opening two cupboards.
- Try not to use the bathroom for storage. We hang our coats (suction hooks are great for this) and pop our shoes in there if we've gotten soaked, but it quickly becomes unfunny having to shift a load of stuff out of the bathroom every time we need the loo.
- Pack so stuff doesn't move around when you drive. Think about using separators like paper plates or sponges between glasses and plates, especially if you don't use plastic ones. Using rubberised non-slip matting in your cupboards will stop stuff sliding about. We pop a tea towel under our hob's glass lid after it's cooled down to stop the racks rattling, and avoid hanging anything up like keys, which scrape the walls as we drive, driving us nuts. We've hit the odd speed bump far too quickly in the past, which really tested how well we'd wedged our stuff in.
- When we visit countries where food is expensive, we sometimes buy a larger selection of foods in cheaper countries and store it under a bench.

We write down what we've got in there and cross it off as we use it, to save us hunting about with a head torch for something we ate weeks ago.

- Do you really need clothes hanging on a rail in the wardrobe? We fitted shelves, creating a lot of space. It also makes it easier for each of us to have our own designated clothes spaces.
- Using lightweight plastic boxes underneath the seats and in the garage can really help you put your hands on your stuff quickly and easily.
- Load heavier stuff lower down in the van to improve handling, and if a locker says '15Kg max', maybe don't store scuba weights and tanks in there.
- Consider spreading the weight as evenly as possible so you aren't heavier on one side. Keeping heavier stuff lower down will also save you from having to lift it.
- Having too much weight on the back (a scooter in the garage or on a rack) may reduce traction if your van is front wheel drive.

Weighbridges and Uprating

Once you have your van loaded up as much as it will ever be (full diesel tank, full fresh water, everyone on board, bikes on the rack, fridge full and so on), we recommend that you visit a weighbridge. It only costs around £10 and can usually be done without an appointment. To find a weighbridge and their opening times, either contact your local council, search the internet for 'public weighbridge' or go here: *www.gov.uk/find-weighbridge*.

Once complete, you'll know the actual weight of your vehicle, to compare with the legal maximum (the MAM, GVW or MTPLM – they all mean the same thing) and can make a call on what to do if you're overweight.

As well as the overall vehicle weight, you need to know each axle's weight, to compare with the individual limits printed on the vehicle. Otherwise your overall weight may be less than your MAM, but your vehicle could still be illegal as one axle is overloaded. To weigh the individual axles, get the weighbridge operator to weigh the van with all four wheels on the weighbridge (to get the overall weight figure to compare with the MAM). Then weigh with just the rear wheels on the weighbridge, to give the weight on the back axle. Subtract this figure from the overall weight to get the weight on the front axle. Note that heavy weights behind the rear axle, such as a moped on a rack, will unload the front axle (which may be the drive wheels), and add more weight to the rear axle than the weight of the bike and rack.

Once out and about, realistically, no-one is going to be stopping every time they've done a big food shop and weighing their vehicle. One approach to ensure you remain within the law could be to buy a van (or uprate your vehicle) well above the payload you intend to ever carry. Specialist companies like SVTech Ltd may be able to do the uprating for you, depending on the specification of your motorhome, giving up to 500Kg additional payload in some cases (*www.svtech.co.uk/our-services/uprating*). However, doing this may take you over 3500kg, see *Thoughts on the 3500Kg Cut Off* on page 18 for the implications of this.

Use a Pre-Flight Checklist

We've driven off from parking spots thousands of times, and we still manage to get the process wrong from time-to-time. Having a simple pre-flight checklist and getting into the habit of running through it every time you move off helps a lot. This is what's on our checklist:

1. **Step Up?**
   Have we pulled the habitation step in? Some vans have a warning buzzer if you start the engine with the step down, but these sometimes fail, so a visual check's helpful. The step sticks out and will probably get damaged or ripped off if we drive with it down.

2. **Fridge On 12V and Locked Down?**
   Our fridge needs us to manually switch heat sources. This check asks whether we've flipped it to 12V for driving. We also ensure both the top and bottom catches on the fridge are shut as we have had the door swing open before when braking heavily.

3. **Gas Off?**
   For safety in the event of a crash, we isolate our bottles each time we set off. This check makes sure one of us has opened the gas locker and closed off both bottles. Some motorhomes have specialist gas systems which isolate themselves in the event of an accident, so you wouldn't have to do this. While shutting off the bottles, we also check the gauges to see how much gas we have left so we can stop en-route and fill up if needed.

4. **Pooch Stowed?**
   When we travelled with a dog, this check made sure he was in a secure place in the van and couldn't get in the cab area.

5. **Awning In?**
   If we've had the awning out, is it fully wound back in and the handle put away? If the awning's sticking out more than it should, there's a reasonable chance it'll hit something while driving.

6. **Cable In?**
   If we've been hooked up to the mains, this check makes sure we don't try and drive off with the cable attached.

7. **Skylights Down, Windows Closed?**

We always make sure our skylights are closed before driving off. Some designs don't need this, but after ripping our main skylight off once by not closing it, we always make sure ours are down.

8. **Satellite or Antenna Down?**

We have a TV satellite dish, which needs to be manually wound back into its home position for driving. We have a fabric cover for our TV, which we don't put back on until the sat dish is down. This step also applies to any terrestrial TV antenna fitted to the van: have you lowered it?

9. **Steadies Up?**

If we've wound down the two steadying legs under the rear of the van, which we only do if it's very windy or we're staying put for a few days, then they need manually winding back up before we leave. We place the winder for the steadies on the dashboard when they're down, to remind us to wind them up before driving.

10. **SatNav Set?**

We use a dash-mounted satnav (GPS). This check just confirms the satnav's programmed for the right place and we're ready to go.

11. **Chocks Away!**

That doesn't mean go, it's a final check we aren't on our levelling chocks (ramps). They make quite a bang if you drive off them the wrong way...

We also do quick visual checks, both:

Inside the van:

To check the habitation door is closed and locked, the bathroom door is closed, the cupboard and drawer catches are all locked, there's nothing on the worktops, table or seats, the curtains and blinds are open, the heating is switched off and our table is locked in place.

Outside the van:

To check the bikes are securely on the rack, the rack itself isn't coming loose, the lights are clear of dirt and the external lockers, the fuel cap, electrical and water filler covers and doors are all closed and there's nothing under or around the van for us to hit.

For your first few trips, it's worth writing down these lists and running through them each time you move off. Our list is on a small laminated card we keep in the cab. The other side has the van's height, width and length and the tyre pressures, so we don't have to try and remember them.

Finding Places to Stay Overnight

There are loads of places to overnight in your motorhome. In general, UK official stopovers are usually on private campsites, in pub car parks and at a relatively small number of local council-approved overnight-friendly car parks.

Enjoying a fire at a campsite in Latvia

Websites and mobile phone apps are probably the best way to find places to stay these days. 'Aggregator' websites like *searchforsites.co.uk*, pull together campsites and other parking locations from various sources, so can speed up your search. Websites and apps often carry reviews too, so you can get an idea what other people think of the site, its facilities, location and the management team:

- *www.ukcampsite.co.uk*
- *searchforsites.co.uk*
- *park4night.com*
- *campercontact.com*

We started our campervan life on campsites, and enjoyed holidays on sites in England, Wales, Scotland, France, Germany and Belgium before starting to use other types of overnight locations.

In our first year we were members of the Camping and Caravanning Club. Along with the Caravan and Motorhome Club, these clubs offer a range of benefits including exclusive member-only sites, discounts on site fees, insurance and ferry crossings. We only stayed with them for a year as we found there are so many campsites out there, we didn't need their exclusive ones. Also, we didn't stay in enough of their campsites for the discounts to cover the membership fee. If you do intend to spend more of your time in the UK than abroad, these clubs are well worth looking into.

If you like small campsites, both clubs offer them too. The Camping and Caravanning Club call theirs 'Certificated Sites', and the Caravan and Motorhome Clubs call theirs 'Certified Locations' or CLs. Check out their websites for more information:

- The Camping and Caravanning Club -
  www.campingandcaravanningclub.co.uk
- The Caravan and Motorhome Club - *www.caravanclub.co.uk*

If you have children or dogs, be aware that some sites won't allow them. Use the above websites to check or call the site you plan to visit well in advance to be sure.

For pubs, and other places, which accept motorhomes for overnight stops in the UK, the Brit Stops scheme (*www.britstops.com*) is a great place to start. You buy the current book (there's a new one each year) and it lists pubs and other businesses that will let you sleep in their car park overnight. It says that no purchase is necessary, but it's common practice (in reality, a necessity to keep the scheme going), to nip in for a couple of drinks and/or a meal.

Some car parks are sloping, some small, some busy, some noisy. Cracking open Google Maps before you go and having a look at the place from above can be handy. Most of them offer no services, so come full of water and with an empty loo and grey water tank.

For your first few nights it is sensible to head for a campsite close to home. That way you have electrical hook-up, a service point and a nice clean shower block, so you can get used to your motorhome's facilities but aren't 100% reliant on them. For our first stays we booked a pitch in advance, to ensure they had space for us, allowed dogs and had electrical hook-up available.

Checking In to a Campsite

Different sites let you check-in at different times. Best to check with the site before setting off, so you know what to expect when you get there. On arrival, we find it best for the driver to stay with the van while the passenger goes to check in. By having the non-driver check in, the driver gets a few minutes to relax after the drive and is available in case the van needs moving. Some campsites have clear areas for you to park and wait during check-in, at others you just have to guess.

Whoever goes to reception needs to have money (sometimes you have to pay in advance), passports (needed for ID on some campsites), the motorhome registration and any club or discount cards that may be required.

Choosing a Pitch and Parking Up

Depending on the site, and how busy it is, you might be allocated a pitch, or they may tell you to pick one. If you do get to choose a pitch, obviously you'll grab one which looks good to you, maybe with a tree for shade in summer, or a nice view. Here are a few things we look for when choosing a pitch:

- Will our cable reach to the nearest electrical hook-up point?
- Will we be able to get off any wet grass or mud, and if heavy rain is forecast, is it likely to flood?
- How near or far are we from the shower block?
- Are we next to the playground?
- Are there roads nearby, and will they be noisy until late at night?
- Is there enough space to wind out our awning?
- Are we under a tree which might drop sap, pine cones and so on, or if it rains will it drip on the roof all night?
- How exposed is it if high winds are forecast?

A few hints and tips for parking up:

- Think about where the sun will come up. If it's hot, you might not want the sun hitting the windscreen first thing in the morning.
- Try not to have your habitation door facing the habitation door of the van on the next pitch. This is good etiquette, as it gives you both a little more privacy.
- If you have a manual gearbox, leave your van in gear, so it shouldn't move if the handbrake's not working fully. One time in the Spanish Pyrenees we found ourselves rolling backwards into trees when we didn't properly pull on the handbrake and had left the van in neutral.

Getting Your Van Level

Occasionally we get to sit in awe as a motorhome on a nearby pitch levels itself using hydraulic legs. These lift the entire van off the ground, each leg by a different amount to get the van perfectly level. Sadly, most motorhomes don't have these, and they cost a few thousand pounds to retrofit, so you'll probably need to use plastic ramps to get level.

Being level's fairly important in motorhome life. It means that you don't find yourself rolling out of bed at night, all your food gathering in one side of the pan when cooking, your fridge not staying cool and the shower water all gathering at the opposite corner to the plug hole. Not being level, which we've taken to calling 'being on a wonk', isn't all that much fun, although we've met folks who it really doesn't bother. To get level using ramps (chocks):

- Have a small two-way or bullseye spirit level fixed on a flat surface near the driver. It will give you an idea which wheels need to be lifted up. If needs be, you can lift just the one wheel. There are also mobile phone apps that will do the same thing, try searching the app stores for 'motorhome camper leveller'.

- If you're facing uphill, place the ramps behind the rear wheels and reverse onto them. Don't try and drive uphill onto ramps; we've smelt the sickly whiff of burnt clutch from many folks trying to do this.
- If you're facing downhill, place the ramps in front of the front wheels and drive forwards onto them.
- If you're on a side-to-side slope, place the ramps in front of or behind both side wheels and drive onto them. If one wheel needs to be higher than another one, place that wheel's ramp right against it, and the other one a little way back.
- Small plastic chocks (or a big rock) wedged under your wheel will also give you peace of mind that you won't start rolling off down the hill in the night.

We use hand signals to try and avoid the embarrassing bang when you drive off the end of the ramps. One of us goes outside and 'spots'. If the ramp has a series of 'steps', they hold up fingers to the driver to show how many steps they are up the ramp. If they're straight ramps, hold up two hands and bring them together, so the driver can see how close to the edge they are. Even with all of this, we rarely get it perfectly level.

On more extreme slopes, if the surface allows, you can dig down to help you get level, using a shovel or even your hands when on gravel. Be careful when you do this not to dig too far and find the van touching the ground or being unable to get the van's wheels out of the holes. Once when we did this on a mountain pass while waiting for the Tour de France, we were woken by a mouse that had crawled into the air ducts behind the dashboard through a damaged mesh under the engine which was almost touching the ground. No, the mouse didn't want to leave, and yes, we were up half the night.

Setting the Van Up

Parked and level(ish), the beauty of a motorhome is that the set-up process is quick. It's pretty much the reverse of the pre-flight checklist: lower the step, unlock the habitation door, hook up to mains if it's available, turn on your gas bottles, turn the fridge to gas or mains, spin round the cab chairs (if possible), pop the kettle on and you're in business.

Getting Your Bearings

Campsite receptions are usually very helpful, providing information on how to access local attractions, find the nearest pub or restaurant, how to get a bus or taxi into a nearby city, where you can walk your dog and so on. We also find our electronic friends come in handy too:

- The *maps.me* smartphone app quickly pinpoints our location and shows (usually very accurately) everything from post boxes, ATMs, paths, bus stops, pubs, galleries, petrol stations, car parks, public toilets, sports grounds, restaurants and even benches.

- *Google Maps* is online-only but has the added bonuses of satellite photography and better navigation information than *maps.me*. In many countries it will tell you which bus or train to get and where from, although it won't yet tell you how to pay for a ticket!

Leaving Your Pitch

When it comes to leaving your pitch, let reception know and pay any balance, then run through your pre-flight checklist before you set off.

Should you find yourself stuck on soft grass or sand, don't keep wheel-spinning until you're buried up to the bumpers! If you have traction mats, try popping them under the wheels and see if they give you enough grip to escape. Parked on sand by the Dune du Pilat in France, we got stuck, so after digging to the base of the tyre we used the cab floor mats for traction. It worked but did make them dirty. If this fails, find someone to tow you out, making sure they tie the rope to a solid part of your van's chassis. Don't worry, you won't be the first person that has needed a tow, and you won't be the last!

Free or Wild Camping in the UK

As well as campsites, Brit Stop locations and official aires, there are also semi-official and unofficial places to stay across the UK, sometimes referred to as 'wild camping' or 'free camping' locations. These spots are usually free of charge, or attract car-parking rates only, but the motivation for many motorhome and campervan travellers is to get a greater sense of freedom and individuality compared with more formal sites. That said, 'camping' in this sense is probably a poor choice of word, as you're almost certainly restricted to non-camping activities in these locations. Getting your chairs out, hanging washing anywhere outside or even opening windows wide might upset locals, resulting in a visit from the police or the landowner.

At least compared with much of mainland Europe, free camping is generally frowned upon across the UK, with signs indicating 'no overnight parking' or height barriers liberally spread across the country. With care and planning and some acceptance of risk (you may not get a good night's sleep!), free camping is still possible of course, although awareness of local sensitivities is needed, and a lack of access to disposal points necessitates periodic use of campsites if out wandering for longer than a few days. Some campsites will let you pay just for use of the service point without staying overnight, you just have to ask. A solar panel or two and an additional leisure battery is also very useful to reduce your reliance on mains hook-up.

Scotland is perhaps the UK country with the most relaxed attitude to motorhome off-site parking. Although the Scottish Outdoor Access Code (*www.outdooraccess-scotland.scot*) outlines how tent-based campers can legally wild camp in Scotland, these rights don't formally extend to motorhomes and campervans. However, in practice many areas of Scotland are easy-going and allow stays for a night or two (albeit sometimes with a permit, for example: *www.lochlomond-trossachs.org/things-to-do/camping/get-a-permit*).

If you do want to spend more time free camping across the UK, this subscription-only site is a good starting point for finding suitable places: *www.wildcamping.co.uk* and you'll also find quite a few listed here: *park4night.com*. We haven't done much free camping in England or Wales but have enjoyed a few weeks in Scotland on the famous North Coast 500 route. The NC500 runs through spectacular scenery and has long sections of single-track road and is reputed to be very busy in summer (*www.northcoast500.com*). We've enjoyed an autumn tour of some of this beautiful route with very few fellow travellers though.

One final point on wild camping: be aware of how much alcohol you're consuming while you're parked in a 'public place'. Even if you're parked for the night and have no intention of moving your motorhome until you're safe to drive the following day, if you're over the legal limit you might find you have an issue with the police if they come to move you. We've never had an issue with this 'Drunk in Charge' offence, or heard of anyone who has, but nevertheless we're more careful to avoid drinking when we're free camping.

Day-to-Day Motorhome Life Survival Guide

We once arrived at a *pueblo blanco* (an Andalusian white town in southern Spain) to find an enigmatic French chap in his 70s living in a tiny Citroën Berlingo van with his dog. He had no bed, no bathroom and no built-in cooker, and he intended to live like that for a few years. It goes to show you can live with very little, but we're thankful we have all the modern comforts of a motorhome. There are still practicalities to handle though, so let's pile in and have a look at them.

Driving and Navigation

We can recall sitting in the front seats of Dave, our first A Class motorhome for the first time. The windscreen seemed wider than the world! To say we were nervous as we pulled off, waving goodbye to the couple we'd bought him from, would be a huge understatement.

Neither of us had run through any pre-flight checklist as second gear was awkwardly selected from the left hand drive seat. We were stealing glances in the mirrors to check the step was up, and none of the locker doors were flapping about. We risked the odd glance behind us to see if everything was stowed inside, scaring ourselves silly at the sight of an entire room following us down the road. The rest of the time was spent trying to work out how far we were from the kerb and the cars we were passing at the roadside. It wasn't fun, but it was exhilarating!

Over time, as well as building up and using a pre-departure checklist, we've come up with a few tricks for driving, not just for the first few times but whenever we're on the road:

- **Drive past junctions.** Motorhomes are generally longer than cars, so you need to drive further past a junction you want to take before turning into it, or you'll find your rear wheels up the kerb. This quickly becomes second nature.

- **Use windscreen markers to position the van on the road.** We have two vertical 2cm high pieces of white tape stuck on the inside of the windscreen. These are placed at the bottom of the screen, and when we're on tight roads the driver can look at them, or see them in their peripheral vision, and use them to perfectly line the van up against the kerb or centre of the road. To position the tape we find a quiet bit of road and line the van up so the side is right against the road's centre line. The driver looks through the bottom of the windscreen and finds the point the white line crosses the dashboard. That's where the first bit of tape goes. We then repeat the process for the kerb side of the road. This leaves us with two pieces of tape on the windscreen which we can use to know the van is almost as far across as it will go while driving along (if it's really tight, we slow down and use the wing mirrors too). You don't need to use tape and can instead remember a couple of reference points like windscreen mounts, but the tape works well in the dark, at night or in unlit tunnels.

- **Drive only as fast as you're comfortable with.** Motorhomes aren't fast. They seem even slower when you've a car close to your rear bumper, seemingly shoving you down the road. Speed up if it's legal, and you feel safe, otherwise keep going at your comfortable pace. At spots where it's safe for a following vehicle to pass, we indicate to the side of the road to show following cars it's safe to overtake. On slow roads like in the mountains, we pull over now and again, or at larger roundabouts we go all the way around to let following cars get past us. We call this 'de-tailing' and you'll be amazed at the length of car tails that motorhomes and tractors can grow.

- **Manage the traffic behind you, gently.** A trick taught to us by an advanced motorist is to use our brake lights to control the traffic behind us. We're not talking about getting upset with someone driving too close and slamming the anchors on to shake 'em up a bit. Tempting as that might be, it's not recommended. Nope, we're talking about choosing braking points well before those we'd use in a car, getting the brakes on early but gently at roundabouts and junctions, so those big red lights at the back come on. This alerts the car driver behind us to the fact that the motorhome up front is slowing down and gives them plenty of time to react.

- **Expect the push-pull effect from large vehicles.** When a bus, lorry, motorhome or other large vehicle passes, it will first push you away, and then pull you in as it passes. The effect can be unnerving at first, but you quickly get used to it. Like with crosswinds, the best way to handle it is to try and steer gently, don't over-react or you'll find yourself bouncing back and forth as you over-correct, which isn't fun.

- **Indicate early for push bikes and pedestrians.** If you spot a push bike in front of you, indicate to overtake much earlier than you might in a car. We once had a following car, who was unable to see up the road, try to overtake us just as we were pulling out to overtake a pushbike, resulting in a near-miss for everyone.

- **Use your passenger if you have one.** If you're lucky enough to have someone sat in the seat alongside you in the cab, make the most of them! Even if you're using a satnav, they can be hard to interpret, especially at complicated or fast junctions. Assuming they can stay awake and aren't busy looking after children, get them involved looking out for signs pointing you down the correct lane or junction, and double-checking junctions and roundabouts are clear.

- **Don't trust your satnav.** Satnavs are programmed to take you on the shortest or fastest route, when often in a large vehicle like a motorhome you probably want the easiest route. If it looks like we're being directed on a 'satnav shortcut', down a tiny route which isn't much shorter than the main road, the satnav gets ignored. If your passenger's tracking your location on a map, these narrow rat-run roads are easier to spot. Also, if there's no signpost pointing down a route, consider carrying on to the next main road.

Satnav and GPS

Getting from one place to another in your motorhome can be a bit of a challenge, unless you know exactly where you're off to. Satellite Navigation (satnav GPS) systems, are brilliant. Most of the time. But big old paper maps and a passenger looking out for 'low bridge' signs still very much have their place.

Whenever we set off to a new place, we use our TomTom satnav to come up with a route to our destination. Wherever possible, we use GPS co-ordinates rather than postcodes and addresses, which aren't always accurate enough to find the place. We get the GPS co-ordinates from various websites, books and apps listed in *Appendix B*, starting on page 230.

GPS co-ordinates are written as latitude first (always north for Europe) and longitude (a positive number for places east of Greenwich, and negative for places to the west). They can be written in a few ways, the examples below, are all the same place:

- Decimal Degrees: 46.2471385, -1.4867974
- Decimal Degrees: N46.2471385°, W1.4867974°
- Degrees Minutes: 46°14.82831', -1°29.20784'
- Degrees Minutes Seconds: 46°14'49.6986", -1°29'12.4706"

We use decimal degrees (the first format listed above) as it's the simplest to type into our satnav, and the easiest to write down. You can usually change the format you use to input co-ordinates in your satnav in the settings or you can convert between various formats using website tools like the one at *www.earthpoint.us*.

You can get satnav apps on your phone too, some of which are free, like *maps.me*. We use *maps.me* a lot, mainly to see where a town is relative to the parking site, where cash points and tourist attractions are, where there are paths we can walk, run or cycle and to work out exactly where we currently are when out and about. When it comes to navigation, we've found ourselves using our TomTom rather than *maps.me*, as long as it has the maps for the country we're going to. The apps are great, and work fairly well for navigation, but we found the TomTom generally did a better job, being easier to mount and see, and tracking satellites better.

Some satnavs and apps are designed to create better routes for trucks or motorhomes. You can enter your van's dimensions and weight, and the satnav aims to avoid low bridges, weight-limited roads and the like. Perhaps because we drive relatively small motorhomes (6m long, 3m high, 3.5 tonnes), we haven't found the need to invest in one of these as they are often quite a bit more expensive than a standard satnav. They're worth investigating though, if you don't have confidence in your current system.

We don't tend to use toll roads, so use the 'avoid toll roads' feature on our GPS. Most of the time this works well, especially in France where they have good A roads running next to the toll motorways, but sometimes it makes far more sense to pay tolls. A drive across Greece's mountainous Central Macedonia took us several hours of wheel-swinging, while another couple took the arrow-straight toll roads for a whole €6, cutting the journey time in half. Heading through Naples to Mount Vesuvius, fellow travellers advised "whatever you do, don't try to avoid the toll road, the traffic's TERRIBLE!" We took their advice, stumped up a few Euros and had a pretty easy ride as a result. Having sampled them a few times, the French and Spanish roads through the natural bottleneck squeezed by the Pyrenees and the Bay of Biscay seem perpetually clogged. The A63 and AP-8 toll motorways, on the other hand, are blissfully empty and devoid of endless roundabouts. So, sometimes we use toll roads on purpose.

Once we've a route planned in the satnav, we look at the route on a paper map, so we can just check there's nothing daft going on, like:

- We've entered the GPS co-ordinates slightly wrong, resulting in us driving in the opposite direction (that's happened in various places).
- A tiny car ferry on the route, which we would never fit on (which happened to us in Poland – that was quite a detour!).
- The route including a tunnel only a bicycle can fit through (in France, we had to get a big hedge-cutting contraption to move twice – once on the way to the tunnel and once, red-faced, on the way back).

Out on the road, satnav lane assistance comes in very useful, as does watching what lorries are doing on multi-lane roads. If they're weirdly staying out of the slow lane, it could well be because that lane's about to merge or turn off.

As a final point: sometimes neither paper road maps nor satnavs will give you a sensible route, especially in mountainous areas. Several of the roads running east-west across the Vercors in south-east France are impassable even in a small motorhome (look up the 'Combe Laval' or 'Gorges de la Bourne'), even though they have 3.5m height and 3.5 tonne weight limits. Thankfully, this is rare, but if you do take to the mountains, it pays to research your route.

Reversing a Motorhome

We've pulled this out into a section of its own, as it's one of the hardest parts of motorhome driving. All too often we've seen couples, who may have been married for decades, storming about and shouting at each other after making a hash of a reversing manoeuvre.

We've ignored our own advice below, to our peril. Once this resulted in us reversing into a car in Slovenia. Another time we pierced our motorhome with a piece of metal sticking from a wall in Italy, almost taking out the fridge.

If you have no-one to spot for you, getting a reversing camera and parking sensors fitted makes a lot of sense. If you do have someone who can get out and help you reverse, they can be much better than technology, but you need to get the communication right. Here's how we've learned to reverse. Don't be embarrassed to do this stuff, even though few other people do it this way, it works and may save your marriage!

- One of us gets out and stands behind the van where they can see the driver in a wing mirror, and the driver can see them – if at any point the driver loses sight of 'spotter' (the one stood behind the van) the van is stopped until the spotter moves themselves back into view.
- We don't bother trying to shout instructions to each other or banging on the van as the engine is normally too loud to hear over. Instead, the spotter uses a series of visual arm and hand gestures, as though they're guiding a plane into its parking position:
  - **Come straight back** – hold both arms out in front of you, palms facing up. Slowly move both hands to your shoulders and back down again in a waving motion.
  - **Come back and turn** – one arm held out to the side in the direction of the turn, while the other arm waves in the same motion as above.
  - **Stop** – both hands are held up palm forwards. Can be helpful when the spotter needs to walk from one side of the van to the other for a better view in a tight spot.
  - **Go forwards** – both hands held up pointing forwards.
  - **Come back slowly** – when getting near to where you want to be, hold one arm up in the air and one down by your thighs, palms facing each other. Slowly bring your hands together to indicate how much distance there is left to go. Then use the stop signal when done.
  - **Two thumbs up** – phew, we did it again without hitting anything!
- The driver sees all of these in the side mirrors, and yes, we do occasionally get confused which way to turn the wheel! We move the van slowly though, and if the driver gets it wrong, the spotter's hands being thrown in the air gets the message across.
- The spotter's job is to look for things which might catch the driver out: overhanging branches or parts of buildings, pets or children running about, cars or other motorhomes driving past, rocks, high kerbs, soft ground, broken glass, walls and the like. Once in the Slovenian mountains we avoided running over a tiny kitten this way.
- In the dark, the spotter can carry a torch or two to help make their gestures more visible, but we generally try not to arrive after dark.

Fresh and Grey Water

We all need water to stay alive and to stay clean! Motorhomes typically have a big plastic tank on board to enable you to carry fresh water for a few day's use. Once this has flowed down the sink or shower plug-holes, it ends up in another plastic 'grey water' tank which you can later empty into a suitable drain. Finally, there's a third type of 'water' referred to in motorhome life as 'black water'. This isn't water at all, but the contents of your chemical loo.

Fresh Water

You're likely to have a fresh water tank either under a seat or under the floor, holding 70 to 100 litres when full. This water's pumped out through the taps in the kitchen and bathroom, with hot water coming from the water heater when you have it switched on. The pump itself is normally (but not always) submerged in the tank, and micro-switches in the taps turn it on and off. You'll hear it whirring away when you're using water. Remember not to run the pump if there's no water in the tank as you'll damage it.

Inside the van there'll be a control panel which shows you how much water's left in your fresh water tank. When you're getting low, there's a fill point on the outside the van, often lockable. Most folks use a hose pipe dedicated to refilling. It should ideally be food grade if you plan to drink direct from your fresh water tank. If you carry three Hozelock screw-on connector sizes: ½ inch, ¾ inch and 1 inch, and a male-to-male connector, these will suit most taps which have a thread.

The set of Hozelock tap adapters we carry

Sometimes taps are awkward to get at, have no thread, or you don't want to move your van to get the water. A water carrier comes in handy for these instances. We've met folks using standard watering cans to do this, or if you don't have space for a watering can we use a 15-litre collapsible water carrier with a funnel fabricated from an ice-cream tub lid or plastic pop bottle.

When staying on campsites, water is very easy to find. Just ask reception if you can't spot a tap. Away from campsites the some of the books and apps listed in *Finding Places to Stay Overnight* on page 50 indicate where you can find water.

When filling up we use an antibacterial wipe on the tap before attaching our hose, as we regularly see folks cleaning their chemical toilet under the fresh water tap, instead of the dedicated cassette toilet tap. We then run the water through for a few seconds and fill a clear water bottle for a visual check to see if it's cloudy before we put it in our tank.

Unlike many people, we don't drink water direct from our motorhome's taps unless it has been boiled first. This is because we don't sterilise the tank and pipes in the van or our hose pipe as often as we should. We've learned not to trust the water going into the tank (as we've travelled across lots of countries) and we don't want to have to treat the water every single time we fill up. After getting ill a couple of times from dodgy water we've switched to using bottles for drinking water, stored in a dark cupboard (which we re-use several times before recycling). We could also look at using a fitted water filter, or a filter in a jug, but haven't done yet.

One small note on washing up: none of our vans have had a draining board. Instead of carrying a portable one, we use a thick tea towel to place washed pots on while they either drip dry, or to rest for a minute while the other one of us dries them.

Grey Water
Any water (and other gunk) which goes down the sink and shower plug holes will end up in your grey water tank. This tank's usually slung under the van or under the floor, and also has a gauge on the control panel which shows how full it is. Ours rarely works, probably due to bits of fat or grease getting onto the sensor.

The grey tank can be emptied directly into a grey waste drain or into a bucket if you don't want to move your van or can't get over the drain. Each van has its own process for opening the grey waste, so it is best to ask when you buy it. It took us ages to find a flexible hose hidden in the rear bumper of our first motorhome which made it much easier to empty in awkward drains. The place where the grey water drops from the van also varies depending on the van design, so again its best to check you have this information when you buy.

Grey water and the tank itself have a habit of smelling like rotten eggs, especially in hot weather. Cooking oil, grease, bits of food, starchy water from pasta, shampoo, you name it, they end up in the tank to create a pong. Our noses have wrinkled many times over the years, and even though we try to stop this stuff going into the tank, some still ends up in there. We've met people who wipe their pots and plates with kitchen roll before washing them and scrub out their grey tanks on a regular basis, so we know we're not the only people this happens to.

If we get a smell inside the van, as a temporary measure we'll close all the plugs in the sinks and shower to try to fend it off. To eliminate the nasty niffs, we empty the grey tank, then either fill the sink with hot water and dissolve a couple of dishwasher tablets in it or pour a bottle or two of cheap cola down the sink. After a drive to our next destination, we empty the grey tank again and the cola or dishwasher water has done the trick.

For the above whiffy reason, dumping grey water anywhere other than a drain is not a good idea. Some campsites and many aires have motorhome drains, where you can park your van over them and open the grey tap. The water flows across a concrete surface and, if you're parked in the right spot, into a drain and away. Once you've emptied and closed your grey tank tap, hose down the area with fresh water to get rid of any grey water and bits of food. Sometimes you can't get over the drain though, so it's useful to have a flexible pipe which fits over your grey emptying pipe or empty into a bucket.

Black Water and the Infamous Cassette Toilet!

"How do you go to the toilet in a motorhome?" This question comes up a lot, unsurprisingly, and the answer is: "pretty much the same as in a house". Our motorhome has a small private bathroom, with a sit-on cassette loo, which looks much like a 'normal' house toilet. The main differences between a cassette and the house loo are:

- There's no water sitting in the bowl of a motorhome loo, just a 'flush' which washes the bowl a bit.
- Your wee and poop drop through a hole in the loo into a plastic box called a cassette, rather than heading off to the sewers; these cassettes are usually made by either Thetford or Dometic.
- A plastic 'blade' covers the hole and is opened to allow your wee and poop to drop into the cassette. You can open the blade either before or afterward doing your business, it's up to you. If you open it after, you may need to clean the blade more frequently.

Unless you've a strong constitution, you'll need to do something to control the smell in a motorhome loo. Most people use specialist chemicals or biological washing tablets, which is what we did for the first two years. We now use something called a SOG, see *Chemical-Free Toilet - SOG Unit* on page 164.

The cassette will fill up between one and four days, depending on the number of people using it and if you have access to other facilities. At that point, the nominated person has to remove the cassette via a small door in the side of the motorhome and carry it to a suitable disposal point (sometimes called an Elsan Point) to empty it into a sewer.

This job is without doubt the cause of the most hilarity when fellow motorhomers get together, the toilet tales usually start after a couple of drinks! We've never found the emptying job quite as bad as you might imagine, especially once we got the hang of it. That said, we've made our fair share of cock-ups with the thing too, the worst of which resulted from over-shaking the box to remove a blockage, spraying one of us head to toe with the contents of the box at a forest campsite in Finland. This is not recommended and resulted in a clothed shower followed by a naked sauna to start feeling clean again.

So you don't end up in the sauna too, here are some loo lessons we've learned:

- Avoid using fancy three-ply loo paper. It blocks the cassette and makes emptying difficult. You have to keep filling the cassette with water, shaking it to try and remove the blockage and trying to empty it again. You can buy expensive 'specialist' paper for the loo, but there is no need, just buy cheaper two-ply stuff from the supermarket, it works just as well.
- Use the loo with the blade open as we found in a previous van a hard deposit builds up on the blade if it is left closed, making it stick.
- Clean and pop some olive oil on the blade from time to time to help avoid damaging the seal on the cassette, preventing a leaky loo.
- During emptying, stay well away from the pipe on the cassette where the nasty stuff comes out. Hold the pipe as far inside the emptying point / receptacle as you can before pressing the vent button, keep your mouth closed and always be sober while emptying!
- Toilet cassettes have an automatic pressure release valve, which doesn't always work. One couple told us how after travelling to altitude they went to go to the loo. As they opened the toilet blade the cassette contents sprayed around the bathroom. Leaving the blade open slightly would help prevent this, but thankfully our SOG unit means we don't risk this issue.
- Some folks wear washing up gloves to empty. We don't, and simply scrub down well with soap and water as soon as emptying is finished. Neither of us has ever been made ill from loo emptying duties.
- During emptying, make sure the screw cap for the cassette is placed well away from any hole it could fall into.
- A full loo cassette can weigh quite a bit. Some have built-in wheels and handles like little suitcases, and some folks carry a trolley do a similar job. We just lug ours around, and if we're staying still for a while, we'll empty it when only part-full to avoid having to carry the full weight across a large aire or campsite.

Larger motorhomes, typically only American RVs, have marine-style toilets. These have a built-in holding tank rather than a cassette, which has to be emptied by driving the vehicle to a suitable waste point and using a large bore pipe to route the sewage.

Electricity

There are two kinds of electricity in the majority of European motorhomes:

- **12 Volts Direct Current (DC)** – from your leisure and starter batteries. This is used by three-way fridges (when driving only), compression fridges (all the time), habitation lights, water pump, heating fan, electric step, satnav and some TVs.
- **230 Volts Alternating Current (AC)** – usually only available when hooked up to the mains with a cable but can be created in a limited way using an inverter. This is used by mains electrical appliances like hair dryers, microwave ovens, Remoskas and Sky TV boxes.

12V DC System

Your motorhome's engine will have a starter battery (also called a 'shallow cycle' battery) which is used for starting the engine. It also runs the vehicle's lights and provides power to other engine systems and the underlying chassis. Apart from the dashboard fans, radio and possibly the auxiliary (cigarette lighter) socket, it doesn't power the habitation area of your van, instead separate leisure batteries (also called 'deep cycle') do this, for these reasons:

- The starter battery's internal construction is designed for it to be fully charged almost all of the time. It provides a large kick of several amps to start the engine and is then immediately recharged by the alternator.
- Leisure batteries are specially constructed for 'deep cycling', meaning they can be regularly depleted down to 50% of their capacity (some types even lower), without being damaged. At least that's the theory – we bought a starter battery in Spain and used it as a leisure battery when full-timing for two years without any problems. Starter batteries are cheaper and more widely available than leisure batteries.
- If you accidentally flatten your leisure batteries, your starter battery should remain charged, so you can start your engine, move your vehicle, and subsequently recharge your leisure batteries.
- Note that even on mains hook-up, your 12V appliances will run from your leisure battery. If the battery is damaged and can no longer hold charge, these appliances won't work.

Leisure batteries have a capacity measured in amp-hours (Ah), which is printed on the battery label. You can't always easily get at the batteries to see this label; ours are under bolted-down front seats. A new 100Ah battery will provide, for example, 1 amp of current for 100 hours, so a device which draws 2 amps could

⌐d for 50 hours. However, you can't regularly discharge lead-acid type ⌐ batteries (the most common type) to less than 50% of capacity without ⌐maging them, so a 100Ah battery can actually provide 2 amps for only 25 hours. Very heavy current loads will flatten your batteries more quickly than lighter ones, so a 100Ah battery cannot provide 100 amps for an hour, but closer to 38 minutes.

Our first motorhome had a single 110Ah lead-acid battery, and our current one has two 86Ah batteries, so 86Ah of 'usable' capacity from the 172Ah total. Both have worked well for us. We only flattened the 110Ah battery once and have never flattened the 86Ah batteries. We use inexpensive sealed, maintenance-free lead-acid batteries, spending around £100 on each of the 86Ah NUMAX brand batteries. It's worth noting that if you change the type of battery in your van (to gel ones for example), you may need to change a setting on your charger; check the instruction manual. Also, lead-acid batteries may need a vent pipe fitting, even if they're of a sealed construction. If the batteries or charging system malfunction, this vent pipe ensures any excess explosive gas is pushed outside.

Motorhomes have a meter or digital display showing the voltage of the starter and leisure batteries, which gives an indication how charged they are. Your batteries will over-read voltage during charging and under-read when they're being used, so it's hard to get a truly accurate figure. It takes 12 to 24 hours with no charge or load for the batteries to reach their 'resting voltage', which gives the most accurate indication of their charge state (*www.batterystuff.com*). This rarely happens in heavy day-to-day use, so treat these figures with a lot of caution: 100% full batteries read roughly 12.7V or over, 50% is around 12.2V and 11.9V or less is empty.

The voltage and water meters in our motorhome, which get a lot of use!

There are various ways to recharge your leisure batteries:

- **Running the engine.** Motorhomes with a split charge relay system (which most have) will charge the leisure batteries from the alternator when the engine's running. Our system generates about 5 to 10 amps for the batteries, so a 5-hour drive will generate between 25 and 50Ah (less if you are using the heating or air-conditioning fans in your cab area while driving). You can run your engine while stationary too, although this isn't recommended as it's annoying to be sat inside or near a big diesel engine that's idling, and it can damage newer types of diesel engine. We've only found the need to do this once in over a thousand days of touring, with lots of 'off-grid' camping.

- **Using mains hook-up.** Most motorhomes have a built-in battery charger which automatically starts working when you connect your van to the mains using a cable. On our long tours, we did lots of off-grid camping in winter, which increases the load on the batteries as they have to run the heating fan, lights and so on for much longer than in summer. We've found we need to hook-up to the mains every couple of weeks (very roughly) in the winter to keep our batteries topped-up.

- **Using solar panels.** Lots of motorhomes which don't stay on campsites all the time have a solar panel or two on the roof. These slowly charge your batteries during daylight and are useful both in day-to-day use, and if the van's parked up unused for any length of time, to prevent the batteries being drained and damaged.

- **Using a generator.** A few motorhomes have a generator built in or a portable one placed outside, although it's rare to see them as the more cost-effective diesel ones are noisy and hard to use sociably. There are quieter LPG suitcase generators available, which are worth a look if you'll be free camping a lot, especially in winter. Fuel cell power sources like those from Efoy (*www.efoy-comfort.com*) and Dynad (*www.dynad-hydromax.com*) are silent, but generate 12V power, not 230V, and look expensive to buy and run.

- **Using wind turbines**. We've hardly ever seen these in use out on the road and they seem to have a poor reputation for being noisy, awkward to mount, inefficient and causing vibration in the van.

In theory you can work out how much leisure battery capacity you need by adding up the amp-hours (Ah) needed to run your appliances each day, and taking away the input from your solar panel, driving and so on. In practice this is really hard:

- Write a list of every appliance you will use, including the habitation LED lights, the heater fan, water pump, TV, laptop, phone chargers and so on.

- Find out the current (in amps) needed for each appliance. The current drawn will depend on whether you run the device from the mains or an inverter. To find the current you first need to know the wattage of the appliance, which should be on a label attached to it. To get the number of amps, divide the wattage by either 230 (if you run the device from the mains) or 12 (if you run the device through an inverter from your leisure batteries). So, a 750W camping kettle will draw 750/230 = 3.3A if run from the mains, or 750/12 = 63A if run from your inverter. More accurately, you should multiply the inverter amps by 1.1 to account for inefficiencies, so the travel kettle would really draw closer to 63 x 1.1 = 69A. Some more examples are given below, with (very) approximate wattages and current draws. These can also be useful to avoid using more than a site's maximum current when on mains hook-up and tripping the supply, which could be as low as 4A to 10A on older sites.

Appliance	Wattage	Mains Current	12V Current
Camping Kettle	750W	3A	69A
Domestic House Kettle	2000W	9A	180A
Halogen Heater	1200W	5A	110A
12V Truma Heater Fan	16W	0.07A	1.5A
12V Water Pump	50W	0.2A	5A
12V LED Light (Each)	2W	0.01A	0.2A
Travel Iron	1000W	4A	90A
Microwave Oven	700W	3A	65A
Two Litre Remoska	400W	2A	35A
Laptop Charger	65W	0.3A	6A
Smart Phone Charger	10W	0.04A	0.9A
Colour LED TV	15W	0.06A	1.5A
Domestic Hair Dryer	2000W	9A	180A

- Guess how many hours you'll use that appliance for each day and multiply it by that device's amps to get the number of Ah each appliance needs daily. For example, running a 2000W hair dryer for 10 minutes from an inverter will use around 180 x (10/60) = 30Ah.
- Add together all the Ah figures and compare it with the capacity of your leisure batteries (remember you can only use half your overall capacity).
- Try and work out how often you'll drive and for how long and work out how many Ah that will put back into the leisure battery each day (our system generates about 5 to 10Ah per hour of driving).
- Work out how much energy you might get back from solar panels on the roof. This is going to vary with the size and type of panel(s) you have, the latitude you're at, how sunny it is, any shading on the panel(s) and the time of year.

Eventually you'll have an idea how many hours, days or weeks your leisure batteries can last before you need to connect to the mains, to recharge them. It is possible, by the way, to never need mains hook-up if your electrical use is low enough, and you generate enough electricity by driving, using a generator and/or using solar panels.

While you can of course have a crack at the above calculations, it'll likely only be a very rough guess. Our approach has been to do this instead:

- We avoid using high-wattage devices on our inverter. We only use things like our Remoska, electric kettle and fan heater when we're on mains hook-up.
- We've changed most of our lights to LEDs, as these use much less power than older types of light.
- We've a 100W roof-mounted solar panel and charge controller fitted which charges our batteries during daylight.
- We charge phones, laptops and so on while we're driving. This helps ensure we arrive at our destination with the leisure batteries full.
- We always switch off our inverter when not in use, to avoid it slowly draining our batteries.
- We keep an eye on the battery voltage on our control panel to get an understanding of how much current we're using. Over time we get to understand how we can best use the batteries to avoid flattening them.

In this way, during summer we can avoid the need for mains hook-up for months, although we do tend to hook-up periodically as and when we use campsites. In winter, especially if we're in a ski resort and our solar panels is covered in snow, we might only last a handful of days before we need mains hook up (or we could choose to carry a generator).

Solar Panels

Both of our motorhomes had a solar photovoltaic (PV) panel fitted to the roof (we installed one of these ourselves). This charges the leisure battery from direct or diffuse sunlight. The panels were around 100Wp, meaning the maximum (the p stands for 'peak') they would ever generate was 100 Watts, with the sun high in the sky on a summer's day. This translates to (very roughly), an absolute maximum of 50Ah a day under the best possible summer conditions in the UK, dropping to maybe 7Ah a day in winter.

Our panels are mounted flat on the roof, with an air gap underneath to keep them cool. Some more dedicated free campers have panels on brackets which are manually rotated to face the sun. Others have an additional flexible panel which they place outside or behind the windscreen when parked up.

A 100W solar panel, mounting brackets, waterproof roof entry point (gland), Sikaflex sealant/glue, charge regulator, cable and inline fuse kit can cost around £200 (*www.outdoorbits.com*). There are lots of videos on *youtube.com* showing how to fit the panel, and we've successfully fitted a panel in this way. If you can't or don't want to fit it yourself, budget another £200 to £300 for professional fitting.

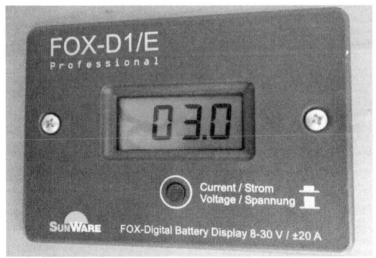

3 amps being generated by our solar panel on a sunny day

More information on sizing panels, types of panel, charge controllers and so on, can be found on this website:

www.campingandcaravanningclub.co.uk/helpandadvice/
technicalhelp/solar-power

Mains Electricity

Campsites (and some other locations) usually offer the option to connect your motorhome to 230V mains electricity, usually using a 3-pin 16A weatherproof blue connector and a 20A-rated cable (which is usually orange coloured). This is sometimes called a 'hook-up', and the power's routed around your van via a small consumer unit.

Over the long term, mains hook-up can be very expensive compared to paying for electricity at home or using gas, so we try to avoid having it unless it is included in the cost of the pitch. When we do get hook up it fully recharges our leisure batteries and we make sure we get the most from it by:

- Charging up all gadgets – electric toothbrushes, Kindle, laptop, tablet, phones and so on.

- Running our 3-way fridge on the mains (useful in places where we couldn't easily top up our gas supply: Finland and Morocco in particular).
- Using an electric fan or halogen heaters (again to save gas).
- Using a travel kettle to boil water for drinks (saving gas).
- Cooking on an electric hotplate (saving gas) or in our Remoska (to bake food as we have no oven).
- Running a fan when in hot places (for cooling).

Campsite 230V supplies usually provide about 16 amps, although we've seen it as low as 4 amps on campsites in North Africa. This means you can overload the supply by running too many mains appliances at the same time. We've managed this by running a fan heater and trying to boil the kettle at the same time. The result is an RCD device 'trips' the site supply and it goes off. To get it going again switch some of your appliances off (or it will trip again), find the RCD switch and flick it back on again. Some campsites lock their electric supply cupboards, if this is the case you'll need to ask reception to come out and reset it for you.

A plug-in tester, which came with our second motorhome, revealed mains supplies were often reverse-polarity or lacked an Earth connection, more so outside the UK. We hadn't noticed either of these before in two years of travelling, as they're only a problem with equipment not designed to handle it, and in very specific circumstances. For safety, you can fix reverse polarity connections using a cross-over lead (or if outside the UK and using a two-pin plug, turn the plug around). You can't fix the lack of Earth though, you just have to decide if you want to continue using the supply or not.

Inverters

If you want to use 230V equipment when you're not hooked up to the mains, you can fit an inverter. This converts the 12V DC from the leisure batteries to 230V AC. You can get different sizes and types of inverter, depending on the equipment you want to power.

If you plan to charge electronics like laptops and mobile phones from an inverter, consider paying more to get a pure sine one, rather than the cheaper modified sine. Pure sine inverters create a cleaner output signal and are less likely to damage chargers and batteries. We went through a few mains laptop chargers before upgrading to a 300W pure sine one, which cost about £50.

Our inverter is next to the leisure battery under the driver's seat, and it's connected directly to the batteries via short, heavy-duty cables. We've had a four-way extension lead plugged into it so we can charge multiple items at once. We initially ordered a 1kW inverter but sent it back when we saw how physically big and heavy it was. 300W works fine for our needs; charging smart phones, laptop, camera and for running 230V hair clippers. If you wanted to run a decent mains hair dryer though, you'd need a much bigger inverter, with a continual use rating around 2kW. This would draw roughly 180 amps from your batteries, so best used while the engine is running.

Check the equipment you want to run, looking for the peak wattage it needs (some kit needs more power to start up than to run afterwards). Inverters have two power ratings: peak and continual use. The peak rating is the wattage they can sustain for short periods of time. The continual use rating indicates how much power the inverter can sustain after the initial peak is over. As we personally don't use high-demand equipment like microwaves, we've not needed to worry too much about this.

Consider how quickly the inverter will deplete your leisure batteries. There are various calculators at *www.batterystuff.com* to help size your 12V system. Also, read reviews on the inverter to find out how noisy it is. Cheaper ones have more basic cooling systems, which means an irritating fan buzz. More expensive ones run silently and are worth the extra money if the inverter is in earshot.

Inverters aren't as efficient as running devices directly from your 12V system. In other words, using a 12V charger for your laptop is going to drain your batteries more slowly than having a mains laptop charger run through an inverter. The difference isn't huge though, and in practice we use both methods.

Gas

Butane, propane, or a mixture of the two called LPG or Autogas is used in a motorhome for cooking, water and air heating and running the fridge. The gas is stored in liquid form in bottles or in a tank fixed underneath the vehicle. The butane or propane 'boils' in the bottle, changing from liquid to gaseous form in the space above the liquid. It's at too high a pressure to be used at this point, so a device called a 'regulator' is used to lower the pressure to something useable by your gas hob, water heater and so on. A high pressure hose called a 'pigtail' connects the bottle to the regulator (unless the regulator is connected directly to the bottle).

When travelling in the UK it's normal to use gas bottles from Calor (*www.calor.co.uk*). These bottles are colour-coded: red for propane and blue for butane, and they're widely available at garages, garden centres, supermarkets, caravan dealers and so on.

You have to ensure you have the correct regulator for the type of gas being used. Butane regulators drop the pressure to 28 mbar, and propane regulators to 37 mbar. Euro Gas Regulators work with both types of gas (and with LPG), dropping the pressure to 30 mbar (our van has this type of regulator). Some older American and German vans need a 50 mbar supply. While butane is more efficient than propane, it can't be used below around -1°C, as the gas freezes. Propane can be used down to around -42°C, so most folks use propane or LPG in winter.

With Calor-type bottles, you cannot safely refill them yourself. Instead you take the empty bottle back to a dealer and swap it for a full bottle, or actually an 80% full bottle, as 20% of the capacity has to stay free to keep them safe. Bottles are sold by weight: a bottle marked '6Kg' holds 6Kg worth of gas when full. Combined with the weight of the bottle, a full 6Kg cylinder actually weighs about 16Kg. To roughly work out how many litres of gas this bottle holds, multiply the marked Kg value by two, so a 6Kg bottle of gas holds around 12 litres of gas.

How long will your gas last? Obviously, this depends on many things, such as: how much you run your heating, how many hot showers you have and whether you're using mains hook-up to power your fridge. We have a 17Kg LPG system (around 34 litres of gas) which lasts around seven to 10 days in freezing conditions, and six weeks or more in summer.

There are tons of gauges which try to work out how much gas is left in a bottle, from scales which weigh the bottle, to pressure gauges, to magnetic stick-on gauges. Some bottles are even see-though, so you can visually see how much gas is left (see *www.safefill.co.uk*). We've tried a few of these, and eventually gave up although we're sure there are accurate gauges available. Instead of relying on our gauges, we have a two-bottle refillable LPG set-up (one 11Kg and one 6Kg bottle, both from *www.gasit.co.uk*) with a 30-mbar regulator and an auto changeover valve, which switches between the two bottles when one is empty. The change-over valve has a green/red band around it showing when one bottle is empty. We make a quick visual check when we switch off the gas bottles for driving, if one bottle is empty, we get an idea how quickly we're burning through gas and can get that bottle refilled when convenient.

A full discussion of gas systems is beyond the scope of this book. The Calor website (*www.calor.co.uk*) has helpful articles on buying and using their products, but here are a few hints and tips:

- Calor gas isn't available outside the UK. If you plan to tour Europe, think about getting a refillable LPG system. These refillable systems also allow you to buy gas more cheaply than Calor, see *Self-Refillable LPG Tanks* on page 161.

- We turn our gas bottles off every time we drive, to reduce the risk of fire in the event of an accident. You can get valves that automatically do this for you.
- If a gas appliance in your van's malfunctioning, it might create Carbon Monoxide (CO) gas, which has no colour or smell, and can be deadly. Fit a CO or combined CO and smoke alarm to detect it and get your gas appliances tested each year.
- You can use some soapy water on any suspected leaks around your gas tank and hose connections to check for bubbles. If in doubt get a Gas Safe Registered plumber to check it for you (see *Safety* on page 37).
- Vans have floor-level gas drop out vents to allow any leaking gas to leave the motorhome. These have a wire mesh to stop mice getting in. Don't block them up, for obvious safety reasons.
- Vehicles powered by LPG aren't allowed on Eurotunnel (Channel Tunnel) trains. You can take your domestic gas (butane, propane or LPG) bottles onto the train, but you must turn them off before boarding. You also have to turn them off on ferries, so plan for an empty fridge and freezer on long crossings.

Heating

Motorhomes have air and water heating systems which are usually manufactured by Truma (*www.truma.com*), Whale (*www.whalepumps.com*) or Alde (*www.alde.co.uk*). Our motorhomes both had Truma combined water and air heaters (combi systems) powered by gas. They were installed in the bottom of the wardrobe and controlled using a small panel on the outside of the wardrobe.

Water Heating

Some water heaters are instantaneous; as soon as you start them up and run a tap or the shower, hot water comes out. Ours were based on a boiler, so we needed to wait a few minutes after turning the water heater on before we could get hot water. The systems easily heated enough water at a time for a shower or two.

We use our water heating extensively when we're touring. The system works fine, although there are a few points to be aware of:

- Our current system has a safety valve ('frost control', or 'dump valve') which dumps the water from the boiler outside if there's any risk of it freezing. This has never happened to us because we always leave the water heater on overnight in cold or sub-zero temperatures. Some people place a clothes peg onto the small valve, preventing it from dumping the water, with the obvious risk the boiler might freeze and be damaged as a result.

- The safety valve will also dump the water if the 12V system fails, like the leisure batteries being drained. This happened to us on the edge of the Sahara Desert where water is scarce. Fortunately, we identified the loose wire causing the problem, and abundant sunshine recharged everything using our solar panel.
- Some systems can heat water on electrical hook-up or even diesel. These would have been useful, especially where we couldn't easily refill our LPG system, such as in ski resorts in winter, or in Finland and Morocco which have no LPG refill stations.

Air Heating

Both our motorhomes had blown-air heating systems. The hot air was created by the Truma heater which uses an electric 12V fan to blow the air through wide ducting pipes inside the seats and in between the double floor and into the bathroom, kitchen and main living area.

This keeps the van comfortably warm, even at temperatures below -10°C, and ensures the water tanks and toilet cassette don't freeze. In cold weather we leave the heating on low overnight, relying on our carbon monoxide alarm to alert us to any problems.

Powering the fan for the blown air heating needs about 10 to 15Ah a day, so we have to be careful not to deplete our leisure batteries as well as keeping an eye on our gas bottle levels.

When our leisure battery gave up in our campervan on a cold night in Skegness, the heating also stopped working. We woke to a layer of frost on the duvet and the idea of using the gas cooker hob to heat the van was very tempting. However, it's a bad idea. The ventilation needed to remove the waste gasses is fine for the relatively short time needed for cooking, but vans aren't designed to cope with the hob burning away for hours.

Cooking

Motorhome kitchens are small, but perfectly usable long-term! Some have a gas oven, some have a microwave, but most only have a gas hob with two or three burners. Space for preparing drinks and food is very limited compared with a kitchen in a house, and yet somehow it always seems to be enough?

Our motorhome doesn't have an oven, but there are several alternatives you can buy:

- **Double Skillets** (*thedoubleskilletpancompany.com*) these are two deep pans which clip together, forming a cylindrical metal box. By heating the box before placing food in it and using a diffuser to spread the gas flame across the base of the lower skillet, you can simulate the cooking effect of an oven. They're not perfect, but we've had some lovely roast chicken dinners from ours.

- **Remoskas** (*remoska.co.uk*) these use 230V AC so either need hook-up or a suitably-sized inverter. They consist of a metal dish on a stand, on top of which you place a lid with an electrically-heated element inside. They're very good at roasting food but be careful handling the lid which gets very hot and is awkward to put down anywhere other than on the dish.

- **Slow Cookers** (*www.roadpro.co.uk*) you can get 12V slow cookers for trucks and motorhomes. To be honest we didn't rate ours. Even if it was on for ten or 12 hours it would struggle to cook vegetables fully and placed a steady, long drain on our leisure battery. Other folks love them though, so we may have had a poor example.

- **Thermal Cookers** (*mrdscookware.co.uk*) with these cookers, you heat up your raw food for a short time and pop it into a thermally insulated container for a few hours, where it's kept hot and slowly cooks. We've never used one of these, but they need no power, and we've heard good things about them.

Depending on where you're parked you may also be able to cook outside. Gas BBQs are great on campsites (the Cadac Safari Chef is a popular gas BBQ range), but not so great if you stay on aires or free camp a lot, as they're often difficult to use without falling foul of 'no camping' laws. We use a camping gas stove which runs from a small gas canister. These can easily be carried away from your van to a more suitable spot on a beach or picnic table.

We found the simple recipes in The Camping Cookbook (by Love Food, ISBN: 1407562509) to be easy to make using just our hob, and we also pick out the non-oven recipes from 'one pot' cookbooks. Otherwise we generally make it up as we go along. Our top cooking tip has to be that you can make decent toast by heating up a frying pan with no oil, and placing the bread in it, flipping it over to stop it burning.

The Fridge

Most motorhome fridges and freezers don't work like those at home and weirdly need a source of heat to work. The heat comes from:

- **Gas** when you're parked up and not connected to mains electricity.
- **12V electricity**, but only while driving as it would quickly flatten your leisure batteries if used without the power from your van's engine.
- **230V mains electricity** while you're hooked-up.

As there are three ways to power your fridge, they're called '3-way' fridges, or absorption fridges. Some motorhomes have compressor fridges which only run with 12V electricity, but they tend to be expedition vehicles which have numerous solar panels and a big fat bank of batteries, as they use a lot of power.

Here are a few lessons we've learned using our 3-way fridge:

- Unless your system automatically switches between heating sources, you'll quickly get into the habit of changing them over. The fridge and freezer will stay cool for a few hours if you forget. We forgot to switch ours over for 5 hours once. It was 18°C outside but everything was OK.
- These fridges like to be level. If you're on a significant slope, they don't work as well and will warm up, especially if it's hot outside.
- If your fridge isn't cooling on gas, and you've plenty of gas, then it could be an issue with a blocked burner. Small bits of dust can stop the gas flame working properly. You can access the burner from behind the external fridge vents and gently clean it using compressed air. Our first van's fridge wouldn't stay cool on gas and needed a new burner as the old one was over 10 years old. It wasn't an expensive replacement and was done by a dealer in northern France.
- The instructions for our fridge say we should only put pre-frozen food in the freezer. We've popped plenty of cold (but not frozen) items into our freezer without any issues.
- If the outside temperature gets above around 30°C 3-way fridges struggle to stay cool. Some folks install one or more fans which help move the heat out the vents on the outside of the van. We've never done this, but we try to park the fridge out of the full glare of the sun, and cool down freezer blocks in the freezer overnight before shifting them to the fridge during the day (we also do this before catching a ferry when we know the gas bottles have to be turned off).
- In low temperatures below about 6°C external vent covers will help the fridge to work efficiently (they have gaps to allow fumes to escape properly).

Cleaning

Clearly, it's faster to clean a motorhome than a house, as you'll be living in a space about the same size as a big bathroom. We have a carpet in the lounge part of the habitation area in winter, but not in summer as it's easier to brush out sand than hoover it. We keep the kitchen carpet-free, as this makes it easier to clean up food spills and mud/sand from boots as our kitchen is by our habitation door. The carpet's removable, so when we're on a campsite or somewhere quiet, we can take it out and give it a good beating. Otherwise we use a good quality 12V hoover to keep it clean.

Our van has seat covers on the driving seats and arm rests, and throws on the sofas, which are easy to remove and wash. We've also washed the sofa cushion covers on a cool wash in the machine and line-dried them. We were concerned they may shrink, but they went back on with no problems. We use antibacterial wipes for cleaning the bathroom, and microfibre cloths and sponges for cleaning elsewhere (different coloured cloths for different cleaning jobs). A scourer (not a metal one) comes in handy for scrubbing stubborn stains from the metal hob.

Some folks carry a long brush for washing the outside of their van, some use the 'lance and brush' car washes, others simply choose not to bother washing it. We have a tendency to fall into the latter camp, although we're careful to make sure the lights, windscreen and number plates are always clear.

Laundry

Most campsites have a washing machine and sometimes a tumble dryer, so we find ourselves using sites sometimes just to get our bulging laundry bag under control.

If the weather's good, we hang our washing out to dry on a campsite, which you can only do on in a limited way on an aire or when free camping (a few items on a small rack or a hanging sock/peg dryer). We always keep a stash of pound or one-euro coins for washer and dryer machines and take our own liquids to the machine as often they aren't included. If we're using a dryer, we pop in a couple of tumble dryer sheets to keep it all smelling fresh.

When we can find them, we use laundrettes, but they're not as common as they used to be in the UK. Searching the internet helps but be aware some of the results will be dry cleaners. There are a number of laundrettes popping up at petrol stations and supermarket car parks in the UK, a common sight in France.

Some motorhomers do all of their washing by hand, or by placing their washing in a box with water and washing liquid, fitting a tight lid, and then driving. We know one couple who have a laundry spinner in their motorhome's garage and hang their washing on a line around the cab window to finish drying (*ourbumble.com*), which saves them the cost of using campsites and launderettes.

We used to take our big fluffy towels from home with us in our motorhome, but they took forever to dry and often smelled musty. We swapped to micro-towelling ones (not micro-fibre as we didn't like how they feel when drying ourselves). Micro-towelling towels dry much faster, but they can't be tumble-dried. We've sewn loops onto two corners of each towel and hang them from suction hooks across the bathroom to dry. This works really well.

Travelling with a Pet Dog

Charlie, our King Charles Cavalier Spaniel, travelled with us in our motorhomes for over four years. His final journey took him into the French Alps where his heart finally gave up and he was put down by a local vet. Rest in peace Charlie, enjoy sniffing that mountain air our little man.

Charlie enjoying motorhome life

Luckily for us, Charlie was a good traveller. He slept most of the time when we were driving, and we tried to keep journey times short for him. While driving, a barrier went between the cab area and the living space, and his water bowl was topped up just enough so it didn't spill. Charlie would install himself on the floor alongside his bed, wedged in so he didn't roll around, and went to sleep. Legally, dogs should be restrained with a harness or crate in some countries, to stop them bothering the driver, or being flung around in the event of a crash.

As we arrived somewhere, Charlie would know we were getting close and go a little mad barking. This made parking a more tense experience than normal. Once he'd had a sniff around outside, he was completely calm again, like he needed to check we've not arrived in a cat-dominated society! Not all campsites allow dogs, or limit the size, breed or number of dogs you can bring, so check before you travel.

Charlie brought his usual bed when he travelled and slept in it at night initially on one of the benches, but in his later years on the floor so he had access to water at all times. His bowl stayed in the kitchen, held in place with a piece of lino with a hole cut for the bowl's base. You can get specialist no-spill water bowls, but we had no trouble with our standard bowl. He would have his own cupboard with food, treats, balls and the non-fun things like old towels and tick removers – see the packing checklist in *Appendix A* starting on page 219.

Out and about, having a dog does restrict what you can do. Museums, restaurants, cafes, public transport and attractions often don't allow dogs in the UK. Fortunately, they are more accepting of dogs in Europe, so he's been in many a restaurant and shopping centre.

One big upside to having a dog with us was the instant ice-breaking affect our friendly pooch had. We found ourselves chatting with lots of interesting people and being immediately befriended by children.

We could leave Charlie in the van when the weather was cooler, with the skylights open, but if it was warm this wasn't possible. Air conditioning would be an answer to this (roof-mounted or you can get units which hang over the side windows), but we chose to stay with Charlie when it was hot, with windows and door open, or head to a campsite where we could create shade with the awning, and he could retreat under the van to keep cool.

If you plan to take your pet outside the UK, you've been able to do this for some years without quarantine. You need to comply with the rules of the Pet Travel Scheme though (PETS), as described in *Taking Your Pet* on page 99.

Internet Access

Before we started out on our first long European tour in 2011, we remember being incredulous at the idea of being able to access the internet and work from a remote beach. We'd been reading the fantastic dry-humour of Catherine and Chris' three-year motorhome tour of every country in Europe - *www.theworldisourlobster.com*. Chris, a finance director at the time, worked from the van for the first two years using a satellite-based internet system. We'd read in envy as he roamed to wonderful places in his mobile office, including some fantastic-looking beaches!

We too ended up doing some 'digital nomad' work on the road, setting up websites, producing promotional videos, blogging, writing books and articles. This needed internet access, which we had almost everywhere. The cost of satellite internet was out of our reach at roughly £3000 for a roof-mounted system and another £300 to £800 a year for the data contract. Instead we opted to use WiFi wherever possible, plus we had a small amount of daily data on our phone. We used a unidirectional WiFi booster antenna to help us connect to networks from the van, some of which could be over a mile away (across water for example).

As the years rolled by 3G and 4G cellular (mobile phone) networks have become available almost everywhere, and newer 5G networks are now being rolled out in towns and cities. The cost of data has also steadily come down. As a result, we have found cellular internet to be much more convenient than WiFi, as it just works. There's no need to worry about WiFi passwords, we're not limited to one or two devices, we don't need to be parked near campsite reception and we're not sharing the same connection with lots of other folks (which sometimes makes it unusably slow).

The big disadvantage of cellular internet has historically been the cost of data. Unlike WiFi, you pay per megabyte (MB) or gigabyte (GB, where 1GB is the same as 1024MB) of data, and you pay to both upload and download. However, several providers now sell SIM cards with unlimited data, although fair use policies apply (restricting you to admittedly-massive amounts such as 1000GB a month), but you're usually much more limited when roaming outside the UK. This reduction in cost makes 3G/4G/5G the obvious choice, unless your budget constrains you to seeking out free WiFi networks.

If you don't want to pay for an unlimited contract, be aware it's very easy to quickly eat data! Watching standard definition video gets though around 0.6GB an hour, and high definition is around 1GB an hour. If you have apps set to auto-update on your phones, and laptops set to automatically download updates, these can also take up a lot of data without you even noticing.

When it comes to buying a SIM card and data contract, the usual considerations are the cost of data (unless you buy unlimited data), network coverage (although all the major networks are very widespread now), and whether we want to buy a 12-month (or longer) contract or to buy a pay-as-you-go or 30-day contract SIM. We also prefer contracts which allow us to tether, as outlined below.

We have lots of devices which we want to connect to the internet: smart phones, a laptop, tablets, Kindle eBook readers, internet TV sticks and so on. None of these are locked to a network, so we're able to pop in any SIM card we like and it should work. There are a couple of ways we can connect this little lot to the internet using the cellular networks:

Method 1: Use one of our smart phones as a personal WiFi hotspot, so our other devices can connect through it. This phone needs a SIM card and contract which allows cellular internet access, the hotspot feature and the contract must allow tethering. Once set up, this feature shares the phone's internet connection with other equipment via a password-protected WiFi network.

Method 2: Use a dedicated personal WiFi hotspot device, sometimes referred to as a MiFi. This has a SIM card in it and works in the same way as the smart phone in the first option, sharing out its internet connection using a private WiFi network.

We normally use the second method as it has these advantages for us:

- It can be connected to a permanent roof-mounted unidirectional antenna, which boosts the 3G and 4G signals it receives (and sends). The metal shell of our motorhome does an effective job of blocking these signals, and before we fitted the antenna, we would find ourselves placing a phone on the roof, which isn't ideal when it's raining.
- The MiFi is connected to the van's 12V system, so it is always charged up.
- We can easily take the MiFi with us when we're out and about, so can have internet access on both of our smart phones although we only need to pay for one contract.
- The MiFi has a built-in feature which tracks all the data we've used that month and shows it on the front, so we always know how close we are to using all our allowance.
- Also, the system works while we're driving.

The diagram below illustrates how our motorhome internet system works. You can find all this equipment and get advice on what will work best for you from *motorhomewifi.com*.

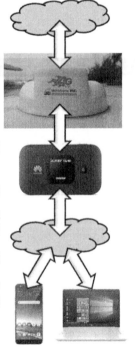

3G/4G Cellular Internet
(Broadcast from terrestrial cell masts)

4G Roof-Mounted Antenna
(Optional but improves signal strength, Unidirectional so doesn't need pointing at the cell mast)

Personal WiFi Hotspot (MiFi)
(In our wardrobe, attached to the antenna with wires, remaining bandwidth shown on front, contains a SIM card)

Personal WiFi Network
(Created by the MiFi, password-protected Extends throughout the van and a short distance outside)

Our Internet Gadgets
(Up to ten devices can connect at a time)

Our current motorhome internet-access system

As noted above, 5G networks are now starting to appear. There are a few reasons we're not looking to start using them, at least for a year or two:

1. 5G is currently restricted to towns and cities. When we're in the van, we're unlikely to often be in locations with a 5G signal.
2. 4G typically gives us 10Mbit/s download and 5Mbit/s upload speeds. This is easily enough for streaming HD video, which requires around 4Mbit/s download speed (although we stick to SD video, which needs only 2Mbit/s).
3. Although 5G is much faster than 4G (5G should be 100Mbit/s or more), we don't need the speed. The main limitation with 4G for us is the cost of downloading and uploading data, which isn't helped by faster networks.
4. We'd need to buy new 5G-capable equipment (a new antenna and MiFi), but we're happy with our current kit.

Handling Weather Extremes

Being in a motorhome, you're much closer to nature than you are in a house, so you'll really get a sense of the weather! If it's blowing a hoolie, you'll know about it, as you will if it's raining, snowing, hailing, or baking hot outside. Some tips for handling the weather:

- If strong winds are forecast, get your awning and outside furniture in, close the windows and skylights, park facing into the wind if you can and lower your motorhome's steady legs if you have them. If possible, get alongside another van, wall or building to shelter you from the full impact. Look around and see what might fall on you from above – trees, signs and so on, and try not to be under them.
- When getting in and out of the van in strong wind, be careful to avoid the habitation or cab doors either whipping open or slamming on you. We've broken two door hinges this way so we know from experience how easy it is to happen.
- In very wet weather, don't park on grass as you may sink. Also, check for water courses around where you're parked which might flood.
- In very hot sunny or cold weather, external thermal windscreen covers (silver screens) can be used to wrap around your windscreen and side cab windows to help insulate them. These are also good for reducing morning condensation inside the cab windows.
- In very hot weather, work out the path the sun travels across the sky and park so your windscreen is as shaded as possible. Use your awning to shade the side of the van if you can. When we can't use our awning, or for the window on the other side of the van, we peg a towel over them to create shade and help keep it cool inside.
- If you plan to head to a hot country and need to be sure you can cool your van down, for children or pets for example, consider fitting air

conditioning. You'll need mains hook-up for this, so budget for campsites; systems which work on 12V don't cool the van down by much. As an alternative to fitting a roof-mounted air condition system, there are units which fit over a side window such as those from *coolmycamper.com*.

Habitation Repairs and Maintenance

Every year you're supposed to get a habitation check carried out on your motorhome, ensuring your gas and electrical systems are safe and efficient, your water systems are all working as they should, your smoke/carbon monoxide alarm is functioning and so on. We've never personally had a full habitation check done on our motorhome, but we do get gas safety checks carried out by a Gas Safe Registered engineer every year or two. Habitation checks do of course make sense, especially if the van is new to you, or if you aren't using it daily, so you can spot things not working as they should. We've also heard that some insurers insist on a current habitation check, although ours have never asked for one.

In terms of maintenance, we like to do some of the jobs on our motorhomes ourselves, rather than paying for someone else to do them. Over time we've installed a solar panel, installed a roof-mounted 4G internet antenna, replaced a skylight, replaced leisure batteries, installed a SOG unit, fixed a damaged bumper and installed refillable LPG bottles. Facebook also has groups set up for specific makes of motorhome too, which again are heaving with fantastic amounts of information. Instructional videos on *youtube.com* are invaluable if you want to watch someone else do the DIY job before you attempt it.

If you're not confident doing a job yourself, or just don't have the time, you can outsource the job. Once you've had a motorhome for a while, you'll get to know the best dealers for installs and repairs. To start off with though, or if you're away from home, an internet search on 'motorhome dealer', 'motorhome habitation check' or 'motorhome service' will throw up a list of companies to try. Bear in mind you may have to drive some distance, and it may be a few days before a repair can be done. Forums like *outandaboutlive.com*, *motorhomefun.co.uk* and *motorhomefacts.com* are packed full of helpful information and recommendations for tradesmen.

Condensation

Boiling kettles, hot showers, wet towels and clothes, washing up and even breathing all release a fair bit of moisture into the confines of our van. In warm weather this isn't an issue and having windows and skylights open keeps the habitation area fresh and clear of condensation. Come the cooler days and nights though and waking up to a soaking wet windscreen becomes the norm.

The simplest solution to this is to invest in a rechargeable Kärcher Window Vac (or a similar alternative) from *www.kaercher.com* and use it to hoover up the water from the inside of the windows each morning. Fitting external silver screens also helps reduce the level of condensation, as do other precautions like running the extractor fan when you're cooking or boiling the kettle and opening the windows for a short while for fresh air during the day.

Vehicle Repairs and Maintenance

Our local garage can cater for our 3.5 tonne, 3m high, 6m long motorhome, and we use them for all our servicing and for repairs when we are in the UK, only making small repairs ourselves. The kinds of things we get them to do include:

- **Servicing the engine and chassis.** Our garage follows a standard servicing process which maintains the van's full service history.
- **Replacing the cambelt.** Having experienced a broken cambelt on a previous vehicle, resulting in a wrecked engine, we make sure we get the cambelt replaced when our garage recommends it.
- **Making repairs to the suspension.** We've had front struts and coil springs replaced on one motorhome to lift up its front end and had a rear leaf spring mount replaced on another due to rust.
- **Issuing MOTs.** Our vans have all been much older than three years, so need a yearly MOT. These can only be issued in the UK. We always come home once a year to keep our MOT valid or have it done early, losing a few months, so we can be away when it is due.
- **Replacing consumables such as tyres and exhaust.** We fit motorhome-specific M+S-marked tyres (see the *Tyres* section on page 163), and have had a section of exhaust made up from stainless steel, as the standard Fiat exhaust wasn't wide enough for our motorhome.

Storage and Mothballing

We don't live permanently in our motorhome, and don't tend to use it very much when we're in the UK. With nowhere to park it at our house, we pay for storage at a local farm where the van sometimes sits all winter. The farm is CaSSOA-accredited, meaning it meets certain security criteria, which helps keep insurance premiums down (*cassoa.co.uk*).

Having learned how not to do it, by freezing and damaging our campervan boiler twice, we now follow the steps below to mothball our motorhome when it's being parked up for any length of time, especially in winter:

- Wash and wax the van.
- Some folks cover external vents to stop leaves and insects getting in.

- Empty the fresh and grey water tanks, the water heater and water pipes. Instructions specific to your motorhome will tell you how to do this. Ours says we're supposed to use air to blow water through the pipes, but we've never done this and, so far at least, haven't had an issue.
- Some water systems have an inline filter which needs removing to stop it freezing up.
- Empty the loo and pop a drop of olive oil on the blade to stop it sticking.
- Turn the gas bottles off.
- Empty and dry the fridge and freezer.
- Leave the fridge and freezer doors slightly open.
- Leave the cupboard doors open to allow air to flow in and out.
- Close the curtains to keep sunlight out.
- Remove batteries from your CO/fire alarm, wall clocks and so on.
- Close the skylights and check all the windows are closed.
- Take out any food to avoid issues with mice. Some folks leave a small piece of chocolate biscuit on the floor and if it disappears place traps to catch the mice (you can get humane ones which don't kill the mice, but you will have to check them frequently to release any captives).
- Take out the bedding and leave the drop-down bed in the sleeping position, to get air to it.

We nip to the van every few weeks to check the solar panel is charging the batteries, to let some fresh air inside and check for damp. We also run the engine for a few minutes and move our motorhome a little so different parts of the tyres bear the weight of the van.

Checking on Zagan in his storage space during the winter

Part Two: Your First Time Abroad in a Motorhome

A while back we met a couple who'd bought their first motorhome in the UK, and immediately travelled south, all the way to the spot on the Moroccan Atlantic coast where we stood talking with them. We were amazed. It took us years of travelling in the UK before we plucked up the courage to cross to France, never mind Africa! Our guess is more people are like us than our adventurous friends, so we've included this part of the book to ease you a little more slowly into continental European travel.

Official motorhome parking by a marina in France

Why Go Abroad?

Apart from satisfying a personal sense of adventure, why would anyone want to head out of the UK in their motorhome? These reasons spring to our minds, you may know of others.

Exposure to the New

Just on the doorstep of the UK, Europe presents us with an incredible range of countries and associated cultures. Foods, languages, architecture, climates, histories, landscapes, wildlife, fiestas, sporting events, even the alphabets can vary dramatically from what we're used to at home. By taking the plunge and heading off to Europe in your van, you'll get to discover all of these from the comfort of your own home on wheels.

Quiet Roads

If you're used to driving in the UK, roads on the continent can seem eerily free of traffic. With the possible exception of the Netherlands, which seems pretty packed with traffic too!

Away from large cities and main lorry routes, motorways in particular are often devoid of traffic. This could be related to the fact many countries charge tolls to use their motorways, unlike most of the UK network. But even the non-toll roads seem a lot less congested than the UK. In France lorries don't, as a rule, travel on Sundays, making it a great day to make some progress across the country.

Low Cost Overnight Stops

The prevalent method of overnight stop in the UK is a campsite. When we started wandering in our motorhome, we had no idea there was anywhere else to stay but campsites. Since then we've enjoyed staying on hundreds of free or low-cost places across over 20 countries.

Parked on a Stellplatz by the Rhine in Germany

Aires, Stellplatz and Sostas

For reasons we don't really understand, many countries in continental Europe have a different approach to motorhome overnight stops to the UK (or England and Wales at least). Sure, there are campsites, but there are also motorhome-specific parking areas called 'aires' ('stellplatz' in Germany, 'sostas' in Italy). Some are dedicated to motorhomes, while some are shared with other vehicles. Some are privately run, while others are run by the local authorities.

Some aires are little more than a car park, and you are expected to use the shower and toilet in your motorhome. Many have service points, also called 'bornes', for filling with fresh water and/or dumping grey and black water. Some have electricity, although most of these are limited to an hour or two for battery charging. A few aires have campsite-like facilities such as a shower block and can be thought of as being more like 'motorhome campsites'.

A popular aire at Capbreton in France. This one even has a daily bread van

You can't book your place on an aire: they're first-come, first-served. Outside peak season (July and August in summer, and school holidays in winter ski resorts), there's normally space available. Arriving mid-morning is our tried and tested technique for getting a place, but it pays to have a back-up aire or two in mind just in case your preferred one is full.

The great advantages of aires are:

- **They're official.** Aires don't constitute 'wild camping'. They officially designated by the local authorities, private businesses or individuals for motorhomes to use. You're welcome to stay in them, and you can be there guilt-free, as long as you stay within the rules, without fear of being moved on by the police.
- **They're cheap.** There are thousands of aires, many are free, some cost a few euros, and even the most expensive ones close to cities or 'big ticket' attractions tend to cost only around €20 a night.
- **They often have great locations**. Aires tend to be located close to villages, beaches, towns, rivers, mountains and cities, often in walking or cycling distance of attractions, shops and so on.
- **They're available in quantity**. There are a serious number of aires, especially in France and Germany, but also across most of Western and Southern Europe and Scandinavia. In France alone, you could literally stay in a different official aire every night for ten years, and you still won't have seen them all.
- **They have rules, but no rule book**. You can arrive and leave at what time you like, although it's polite not to drive around when everyone's asleep. There's no need to check in, show your passport, fill in forms, sign your life away or read a rule book. The rules are fairly basic – see the following list.

The obvious disadvantages of aires are:

- **They're not campsites**. Usually you won't be able to put out chairs and tables, have a BBQ, hang your washing out and so on. This is probably the biggest downside of aires for us.
- **Parking spaces can be tiny**. We squeezed into the last spot in a French Atlantic coast aire, which left us about 2cm space after opening our habitation door. They're not all that tight, but they can be.
- **You can't book in**. If you arrive and the aire is full, you either have to wait for a space, or go find somewhere else.
- **Some are shared**. Some aires are part of larger car parks, with a designated area for motorhomes. In busier places, cars and vans ignore the motorhome-only restriction, or drive around at all hours.
- **They're mostly self-regulated**. There's no warden to ask people to adhere to the sign-posted, or implied rules, which means you might find your ears being assaulted by someone's generator running half the night.
- **Some are poorly-located**. Aires next to busy roads or all-night train lines don't tend to score too well as great places to sleep.
- There's usually a **limit on the number of hours or nights** you can stay. Limits between 24 hours and 5 days are fairly normal.

For more information see *Using Service Points (Bornes)* on page 123. One important point about aires: be very wary of those on motorways. Personal and anecdotal evidence reveals aires as a rule to be very safe places to stay. However, there are plenty of warnings on forums, and reviews on websites, suggesting this isn't the case for aires located directly on motorways. Best to steer clear of them.

France Passion

As well as the fantastic aires network, you can also take advantage of the France Passion scheme (*www.france-passion.com*). The forerunner to Brit Stops (see page 50), France Passion operates using a book which lists over 2000 French businesses who've agreed to allow motorhomes to stay for free.

This is a great opportunity to get a closer look at 'the real France', and chat with the locals. Among others, we've stayed at various vineyards, an olive oil farm in sight of the snow-capped Pyrenees, a goat farm on the Loire, a lavender farm in Provence and an auberge (farm restaurant, with delicious meals) in the Vosges Mountains near Germany.

The businesses always have something for sale. In theory you don't need to make a purchase, but, the scheme does require you to go see the hosts to say hello. We always buy something, maybe we are too polite! The goods and services tend to be high quality, and a little more expensive than supermarkets, but still great value for money for a unique experience.

Each year a new book is issued, along with a new windscreen sticker to show you've bought the latest edition. In reality, no-one has ever looked at our book or sticker, or even checked if we had one, but the locations do drop in and out of the scheme. Without the latest book you risk a wasted trip to find a business has left the scheme, as we had once near the Canal du Midi in France.

We can highly recommend France Passion. Not every stop will gift life-long memories, but some will. If you speak a few words of French, these places are also an excellent opportunity to practice the local lingo. Similar schemes operate in the UK, Spain, Germany, Switzerland, Sweden, Denmark and so on, you can find details at: *www.france-passion.com/en/france-passion/similar-networks*.

Free Camping, Free Parking and Wild Camping

In this book we've used the term 'free camping' to cover off overnight stays away from official campsites and aires. We sometimes use 'free parking' or 'wild camping' in conversation, as do most people. The terms are inter-changeable, but here we're using 'free camping', as there's not really much 'wild' about the luxury of motorhome travel.

Although it varies between countries, seasons and even parts of a country, you can often stay overnight across Europe in car parks or spare ground. This opens up a massive range of unusual and stunning opportunities across Europe as a whole and offers options for low-cost stays out of touristic areas.

Free camping overlooking the French Alps

If there's a sign which makes it clear you can't stay overnight, then you should park elsewhere. If there is no sign though, working out where you can and can't stay is something of an endless learning curve. Most countries have laws limiting or prohibiting free camping, but the definition of 'camping' can be vague. If you park up your motorhome, cook and eat inside, and sleep in it, is that 'camping'? Often it isn't, but as soon as you put a steady leg down, wind your awning out, drive onto a ramp or place a chair outside, it is.

So, while it's often called free camping, you can't usually 'camp' with chairs out, BBQ, washing line and so on, without risking upsetting the locals or attracting the attention of the law. Of course, there are exceptions. In the far reaches of the Arctic, we found spots where we were utterly alone with no sign of a living soul. No-one was bothered that we were sat under our awning cooking freshly-caught fish in this isolated paradise.

Enforcement of overnight parking laws is also highly variable. In Croatia you're likely to get a knock on the door from the police and escorted to a cash point to pay a fine if you free camp anywhere too obvious on the coast. In Spain you might get fined along the south coast where hundreds of motorhomes sometimes congregate in winter, but inland may find you can free camp in an endless number of places without issues. In rural Scotland you're likely to be able to free camp unless you push your luck and try to stay somewhere for days on end. In Greece free camping is generally prohibited, but widely overlooked and often encouraged by local businesses. Also, attitudes change: a place which was fine for free camping one season might be actively policed the next.

Free camping for a night near Woodhenge in the UK

Our approach has generally been to use official parking places initially when we first entered a country. We then see what other motorhomes are doing and check with tourist information offices or the police if we're not sure about free camping. On some occasions, the attitude on the ground is very different to the official one, and we've had police happily advising us where we can free camp for a night or two in countries where it is technically illegal.

As with aires, there is a general assumption with free camping that you'll leave no trace of your passage. Take all of your rubbish with you or pop it in suitable bins, never dump your toilet cassette anywhere other than a sewer or suitable toilet and don't drop grey water unless down a drain. The locals, and owners of motorhomes who travel after, you will thank you for it.

Low Cost Campsites with ACSI

There are thousands of good quality campsites available on the continent. We personally shy away from using campsites in high season (July and August) as they're often very busy. As we only use sites out of season we use the ACSI Camping Card scheme (*campingcard.co.uk*) – not to be confused with ACSI campsite guides which cover all campsites, not just those in the discount scheme.

The ACSI scheme gets you access to cheap, out-of-season camping at over 3500 sites in over 20 countries. The sites all agree to charge one of a set of fixed prices, which includes the motorhome pitch, electricity, hot showers, a dog, two adults and VAT. You'll pay extra for additional members of your group, and possibly if you have more than one dog. Local tourist taxes can also add a few euros a night in some countries.

You need to buy the ACSI discount card books, which list details of all the sites and contain your discount card on the inside cover. You need to present this card when you check in at a site to get the reduced rates. The scheme runs January to December each year, and we find that we easily get the cost of the books back after a few nights camping per year.

Each site decides what 'out of season' means, so you need to check the dates the scheme applies to in the books. Some sites also offer discounts for longer stays, so you might only pay for six nights when you stay for seven, whereas others won't let you stay on the best pitches using the ACSI rate or have specific ACSI card pitches.

In lower-cost countries, you can sometimes get sites for less than the ACSI rate. So, it pays to find out the going rate before assuming the sites in the ACSI scheme will be the cheapest.

Camping Key Europe Card

Officially, some campsites, particularly those in Scandinavia, require you to have a Camping Key Europe Card (*campingkeyeurope.com*). The card includes liability insurance in case of any accidents while on a campsite, offers discounts and supposedly simplifies checking into each site. The card only costs a few euros, but in practice we found than none of the sites we've used have ever asked for it, so we never bought it.

Where to Go on a First Trip Abroad

With a motorhome, you can go where you like, given the time, freedom from obligations back home, and money. The simplest option is to head for France. Arriving in Calais, Boulogne or Dunkirk, you can have a great week pottering around the Normandy towns and beaches to the south-west, or the Champagne region around Reims to the south-east without long driving days.

Or you could 'turn left at Calais' and nip over the border into Belgium, visiting Ypres, Bruges and Ghent.

The vineyards of Champagne

If you've more than a week, or are happy with longer drives, you could choose to travel across to the French Atlantic coast around La Rochelle, perhaps returning via Brittany and a ferry home from St Malo or Roscoff. Or perhaps head east into the Netherlands or follow Germany's Romantic Road, Moselle or Rhine routes

More time or longer drives open up access to Provence, the French Alps and Le Midi (the French name for the South of France). From Eastern France you could nip across the border into Germany and tour the Black Forest. We've met fellow travellers who, by using Germany's and Austria's fast motorway networks, have made it to Croatia in just a few days. The ferry across the Bay of Biscay to Bilbao or Santander takes a day or so and opens up Spain and Portugal to those with a couple of weeks available. Our advice would be to pick an area you like the look of, grab a Rough Guide or Lonely Planet book and explore.

For more inspiration, have a look at some of the many motorhome blogs published on our Fellow Travellers page at: *ourtour.co.uk/home/fellow-travellers*.

Planning your Trip

It pays to do some basic planning before you head off to foreign parts. There's not a huge amount of effort needed but give yourself enough time to prepare. If you intend to take your pet dogs or cat, you'll need to allow a few weeks for them to get their pet passport and have an inoculation for rabies, so it's best to speak to your vet as soon as possible.

Quick Checklists

This quick checklist covers off the most critical things you'll need to consider.

Motorhome Paperwork Checklist.

☐ **MOT** needs to be valid for the duration of your trip.

☐ **Original V5C** vehicle registration document (log book) needs to be with you.

☐ **Vehicle insurance** certificate showing you are covered for all the countries you intend to visit for the duration of your trip.

☐ **Breakdown cover** - if you have it, make sure it covers you in the countries you intend to visit for the length of your trip and is suitable for the age and size of your vehicle.

☐ **Ferry or Channel Tunnel tickets** if you have pre-booked.

Motorhome Preparation Checklist

☐ **Lights** – these need to be legal to drive on the right as you leave the ferry or Channel Tunnel, the easiest way is to use headlight deflectors.

☐ **Tyres** - are they in good condition? If you plan to travel in winter, you may need all-weather (M+S) tyres or winter tyres, and snow chains if you're heading to the hills.

☐ **Service your van** and consider getting a habitation check done if one is due.

☐ **Gas** bottles are different in each country, so make sure you've enough gas for your trip unless you have a self-refillable LPG system, or plan to use a local bottle.

☐ **GB Sticker** - if you don't have an EU number plate.

☐ **Local Legal Equipment** for all the countries you are visiting. Such as one or two warning triangles, a high visibility jacket for each passenger, a fire extinguisher, first aid kit, a red and white bike rack rear warning sign and so on. See page 230 for links to more information.

☐ **Low Emission Zone Stickers** – Crit'air for France, Umveltzone for Germany - it's worth applying for these stickers at home unless you're sure you're not going to the areas which need them. See page 119 for more details.

☐ **Satnav and Paper Maps**. If you plan to use your satnav while abroad, make sure it has the maps on it for the countries you intend to visit. We'd also advise taking paper maps for route planning and as a back-up.

Personal Travel Checklist

☐ **Passports** need to be valid for the duration of your trip.

☐ **European Health Insurance Card (EHIC card)** for each person travelling.

☐ **Driving Licence** – must be full, not provisional, in date and allow you to drive the correct category for your motorhome.

☐ **Medication** - enough for the duration of your trip.

- ☐ **Glasses** - If you need them for driving it makes sense to carry a spare pair (some countries legally require this).
- ☐ **Credit and debit cards**– check what charges you'll incur paying for goods or getting money out abroad and ensure they won't run out while you are away. Consider telling your card issuer of your travel plans.
- ☐ **Local Currency** – you can take it out at a cash point, but it's handy to have some with you when you set off.
- ☐ **Mobile phone** and **Internet** may need to be set up so you can 'roam' (use abroad) with your network provider before you leave the UK.
- ☐ **Sports Medical Certificates** – if you intend to compete in sporting events in France, Italy or Spain, you may need one of these. Check with your event organisers.

Pet Travel Checklist

- ☐ **Valid pet passport** for each pet.
- ☐ **Medication** – ensure you have enough for the trip, including tick, flea and worming treatments.
- ☐ **Vaccinations** if their annual boosters are due while you are away, you can easily get this done abroad, but you may want to bring them forward slightly and get your own vet to do them (especially the rabies vaccination because it is only valid for one year if done in Europe).

Brexit Checklist

In the event the UK leaves the EU without a deal at the end of the transition period (or even if we do leave with a deal, some of these may be necessary), include these additional checks:

- ☐ **Green Card** – obtain this document from your motorhome insurers.
- ☐ **IDP** – obtain International Driving Permits for each driver which cover the countries you plan to visit from the Post Office.
- ☐ **Pet Passport** – even if you have an EU Pet Passport you'll likely need to replace it with a UK Pet Passport or other documentation. See page 103 for more information and talk your vet to understand the implications.
- ☐ **GB Sticker** – you'll need one of these even if you have an EU number plate.
- ☐ **Travel Insurance** – the EHIC may not be valid in all countries so ensure your travel insurance includes pre-existing conditions.

Trip Preparation

The following sections take a more in-depth look at planning your first trip abroad.

MOT

Your MOT has to be valid for the duration of your trip, or your motorhome won't be legal abroad (or in the UK, unless you're on your way to a pre-arranged appointment at your MOT station). You can't get an MOT for a UK-registered vehicle outside the UK (not even in Gibraltar), so if your vehicle is over three years old, make sure the MOT will be in date when you return.

Your V5C

Make sure you have the original paper V5C (log book) for your motorhome with you. Photocopies don't go down well, even colour ones, as we discovered trying to use one to leave Ukraine going back to Poland (they let us out in the end, phew, but were less than happy).

Motorhome Insurance

There are plenty of companies who'll cover your motorhome for travel abroad. Some of the more commonly-used motorhome insurers are listed in *Appendix B* starting on page 230. You'll need to ensure that your specific policy covers you for the duration of your journey and all the countries you plan to travel in. You'll also need to carry a copy of your motorhome insurance certificate with you when you are abroad, so it's a good idea to print it out.

Some insurers won't cover motorhomes over a certain age or will limit the amount of time you can be abroad for each trip, so ring around a few. If your policy includes breakdown cover, check the level provided – see below.

Breakdown Cover

Some insurance policies include European breakdown cover. If not, you may need to purchase a separate policy. Check this covers your van's age, weight and dimensions as well as the number of days you plan to be away (some limit the length per trip, some the total number of days you can be outside the UK per year). Also check whether the policy will put you up in a hotel while repairs are made and if it will recover all members of your party, including pets, back to your home or garage in the UK if your van is unrepairable abroad.

Even with breakdown cover, be aware you might be vanless while repairs are undertaken, as most garages won't let you stay in your motorhome overnight on their premises. We found ourselves in a hotel in Narbonne, France for four nights while our clutch was repaired. Friends whose motorhome clutch also broke while on a two-week holiday, found themselves being repatriated as it couldn't be fixed while they were away. Their van was eventually returned to the UK, but they didn't see it for weeks.

We have breakdown cover included with our motorhome insurance. We also have cover from ADAC as they include any vehicle we drive, not just our motorhome. They are the German version of the AA and provide excellent cover at a low cost across all of Europe. Sadly, in October 2017 ADAC stopped taking new members not based in Germany, but if they open their doors again in the future we would recommend them.

EHIC Cards

Until the end of the transition period EU law applies to the UK. This means UK residents can apply for a free European Health Insurance Card (EHIC) using this website:

www.gov.uk/european-health-insurance-card

According to the NHS (*www.nhs.uk*):

"A valid European Health Insurance Card gives you the right to access state-provided healthcare during a temporary stay in another European Economic Area (EEA) country or Switzerland.

The EHIC covers treatment that is medically necessary until your planned return home. Treatment should be provided on the same basis as it would to a resident of that country, either at a reduced cost or, in many cases, for free. For example, in some countries, patients are expected to directly contribute a percentage towards the cost of their state-provided treatment. This is known as a patient co-payment. If you receive treatment under this type of healthcare system, you are expected to pay the same co-payment charge as a patient from that country."

While the EHIC covers pre-existing conditions, the NHS also makes it clear the card isn't a replacement for travel insurance. If you need repatriating to the UK, it won't cover the cost for example. We buy either an annual multi-trip policy using a comparison site, or a year-long back-packers policy depending on what types of trips we have planned to ensure we have adequate cover. We've used Alpha Insurance (*www.alphatravelinsurance.co.uk*) for long-term trips. Make sure your policy includes any 'unusual' activities you plan such as skiing or hiking at altitude.

Driving Licence and International Driver's Permit

Almost everywhere in Europe accepts the UK EU photocard driving licence. Make sure yours is in date and that you have it with you. If you're travelling after the Brexit transition period is complete or you're off anywhere unusual, like Albania (or if you're not an EU citizen), you might want to get an International Driver's Permit (IDP) to be doubly sure you don't have an issue at the border or while dealing with the local police. The RAC website has a useful list of countries which require or recommend having an IDP, which you can buy at the Post Office in the UK:

www.rac.co.uk/drive/travel/driving-abroad/international-driving-permit

Local Safety Equipment

Each country has its own list of things you must carry in your vehicle, such as red warning triangles, first aid kits, high visibility jackets etc. France technically has a requirement for breathalysers, but to date hasn't agreed on any penalty for not having them, so we personally don't bother with them.

If you have a bike rack on the back of your motorhome you'll need a red and white striped warning board fixed onto it for travelling through Spain and Italy (where the sign has to be metal). The AA website keeps an up-to-date list of everything you need to take for each European country you intend to visit:

www.theaa.com/european-breakdown-cover/driving-in-europe/what-do-i-need

Taking Your Pet

For many years there's been no need to place your pet in quarantine upon returning the UK. EU legislation, referred to as the PETS Travel Scheme (*www.gov.uk/take-pet-abroad*), allows you to take your pet dogs, cats or ferrets between EU member states.

You'll need a valid Pet Passport for each animal, which can be issued by your local vet, but make sure you visit them well in advance of when you plan to travel as your pet will need:

- a microchip to be fitted,
- to be vaccinated against rabies,
- a blood test to confirm the rabies vaccination worked (only if you plan to visit certain countries outside the EU, called 'unlisted countries').

Once these are done, your vet can issue the pet passport, but bear in mind:

- You can't go abroad until 21 days after the rabies vaccination.
- The rabies vaccination is not for life, your pet will need a booster injection every three years if administered in the UK, or every year if done

elsewhere. As long as the booster is administered before the previous jabs expiry date, the blood test won't have to be done again,

- Your dog must visit a vet on the continent before returning to the UK, for a tapeworm treatment. This has to happen between 24 hours and 120 hours (5 days) before re-entering the UK and has to be recorded in the pet passport.
- The details of the Pet Passport scheme will change when the Brexit transition period is complete.

The rules around the pet passport scheme are fairly simple, especially if you only plan to travel to other EU countries and back into the UK. However, they do change from time to time and the UK departure from the EU will also affect some of the details. We strongly recommend discussing your travel plans with your vet as soon as possible.

Before going abroad make sure your pet's yearly vaccination booster jabs are all up to date. While you can easily get them done abroad, you may want to bring them forward and get your own vet to do them (especially the rabies vaccination, because as mentioned above, it's only valid for one year if done in Europe).

Charlie had us visiting a number of vets in several countries while on his travels. His visits ranged from routine pet passport treatments (see *Visiting a Vet* on page 143) and annual booster vaccines, to an allergic reaction to something he sniffed in Slovenia and a panic-stricken trip when he ate rat poison in Sicily. He liked to keep us on our toes! One thing we learned during these visits was that most vets speak English. If they don't there is often someone around who will translate. All the ones we visited took very good care of Charlie, but be prepared, vets abroad have a slightly different 'bedside manner' towards the owners compared to those in the UK, so if your pet is overweight you'll be told so in no uncertain terms.

If your pet takes prescribed medication, ensure you have enough for the duration of your trip as you may not be able to obtain it abroad. We found that for non-prescription items such as ear drops and flea treatments, most pharmacies either have it in stock or can get it in a day or two – take in the old packaging so they can match it.

If you plan to visit countries bordering the Mediterranean check with your vet about tick and flea treatments that cover leishmaniosis as it is endemic in this area. We would buy Charlie a 'Scalibor Collar' online before we left the UK, which provides protection for four to six months. His first collar was bought from a vet in Spain, so we got advice to ensure he had the right size and we had fitted it correctly. The vet warned that some dogs are allergic to the collars, and suggested an alternative is regular Advantix Spot On treatments. Fortunately, Charlie wasn't allergic to his and wore it all the time.

If your pet is partial to a particular brand of food or has specific dietary requirements, bear in mind you may not be able to get buy it abroad (assume you can't). You'll need to either take enough food, treats and so on, for the duration of your trip, or be prepared to swap your pet to other makes of food. Before we first set off Charlie was on hypoallergenic dog food. Assuming we wouldn't be able to get this everywhere (we were right) we asked his vet what to use as an alternative. She said to buy the cheapest dry dog food we could find as it had the least additives in it, especially colourings. It worked a treat and saved us a fortune!

We ensured Charlie always had his normal dog collar on whenever he was out of the van, and that its dog tag had both of our mobile phone numbers etched on it. We ensured 0044 (the UK dialling code) was included at the start of each number (remember to drop the leading 0 if you do this), so we could be easily contacted if he was found while abroad.

In some countries like Italy, dogs, especially bigger dogs, have to wear a muzzle when on public transport. We had a muzzle for Charlie with us but were never asked to put it on him. That said, most countries are much more relaxed about dogs than the UK. In a small busy city centre restaurant in Bologna, Italy the owner peered over the counter at Charlie, nodded his head and waved him in. He sat beneath our table among the other diners and no-one batted an eyelid, he also sat under our seats as we floated around Venice on a 'vaporetto'. In France we once ate with a cat watching us from the next table, and most restaurants seem to allow well-behaved dogs.

Charlie also had his own section on our packing list, see *Appendix A* starting on page 219.

Checking Foreign Office Travel Advice
Before heading off and while you're on the road, it's worth having a look at the UK Foreign Office's travel advice for the countries you're heading to: *www.gov.uk/foreign-travel-advice*. Keep the advice in perspective though; any points about terrorist activity for example should be compared with current levels in the UK itself.

ETIAS Authorisation
UK citizens will still be able to travel visa-free as tourists to EU countries after Brexit (with some restrictions, see *Impact of the UK Leaving the EU* on page 102). However, from 2021 (assuming the transition period isn't extended) we will need to apply for ETIAS authorisation before travelling to an EU country. ETIAS stands for European Travel Information and Authorisation System and

will be a new website where we will need to provide details of travellers. There will be a small cost for each request, and authorisation will last for three years at a time. For more information have a look at *www.etias.info*.

Blogging

One great way to keep a record of your travels, and to keep your friends and family up to date with where you are, is to write a blog. A blog is simply a website which you can load 'posts' to, with text, video and images as a diary of your travels.

There are plenty of free blogging sites available, which don't need any technical ability and can be set up very quickly. Some of the biggest free blog providers are *wordpress.com*, *blogger.com* and *weebly.com*. If you don't fancy the idea of blogging, another option is to set up a specific Facebook page about your travels and post updates on there.

If you do want to start a blog, have a look at the above sites and, if you want a hand on how best to use them, search YouTube for tutorials (*youtube.com*). The sites often have a 'premium' version, which lets you have a domain name (URL) without their website name embedded in it.

There are loads of folks out there blogging about their motorhome travels. Check out the Fellow Travellers page on our blog for some inspiration:

ourtour.co.uk/home/fellow-travellers

Potential Impact of the UK Leaving the EU

Unless you've been living under a rock, you'll be aware that the UK is in the process of withdrawing from European Union (EU) membership. This will have some impact for UK citizens wanting to travel to Europe in their motorhome, although exactly what will change remains a moving target. It seems certain we'll see some increased restrictions and red tape, but nothing unsurmountable, especially for trips lasting less than three months.

Until the UK has agreed a long-term relationship with the EU, the exact details for motorhome travellers will remain unpredictable. However, the fact the UK government has now ratified a Withdrawal Agreement has firmed things up:

- Nothing will change until at least the end of the transition period, which is currently 31 Dec 2020, and we can continue to tour as EU citizens.
- At the end of the transition period, the UK will either leave with a deal or without one. It's only at this point we'll feel any impact of leaving the EU. This section runs through what look to be the main implications, but we suggest keeping an eye on the official government website for the latest situation (*www.gov.uk/visit-europe-brexit*).

Even though some European countries are not in the EU, Brexit will still affect our travel to them. Iceland, Liechtenstein and Norway are in the European Economic Area (EEA). Switzerland is in neither the EU nor the EEA but is in the EU single market. These four countries have freedom of movement of EU/EEA citizens between other EU/EEA countries. Once the transition period is completed, the UK will almost certainly halt freedom of movement, which will be reciprocated by the EU, EEA and Switzerland, and the '90-day rule' described on page 152 will kick in.

Other European countries are in neither the EU, EEA or single market, including some Balkan States (Turkey, Albania, Bosnia and Herzegovina, Kosovo and North Macedonia) and Belarus, Ukraine and Russia. For all these countries we already have to consider our motorhome insurance (obtaining a Green Card through your current provider if possible or buying insurance at the border) , checking our breakdown cover applies and checking our mobile phone and internet SIM card roaming rates (or buying a local SIM). Along with Morocco, these countries might start to feature more in the itineraries of long-term UK motorhome tourists as we seek to work around the 90-day rule.

Passport Validity

During the transition period UK citizens can travel to Europe on the basis our passports are valid on the day we return to the UK. If the UK leaves the EU at the end of this period with no deal agreed, then the requirements for your passport will depend on which countries you plan to visit but will broadly speaking you'll need at least 6 month's validity on all passports, and they'll need to be less than 10 years old. You can use the government website to check whether your passport will be valid for travel:

www.passport.service.gov.uk/check-a-passport.

Pet Passports

During the transition period the EU Pet Passport will remain valid and you can travel to and from continental Europe with your cats, dogs and ferrets under the rules of the current scheme (outlined on page 99). After the transition period the UK will become a 'third country' under the EU Pet Travel Scheme. There are three categories of third country:

- **Unlisted** – the UK would only likely become an unlisted third country if there is no agreed deal at the end of the transition period. In this case your EU Pet Passport(s) will become invalid. For new pets you'll need to follow a process of rabies vaccination and testing which takes at least four months, and then visit a UK vet to obtain an Animal Health Certificate (AHC) each time you travel, which is only valid for re-entry to the UK for four months, and present your pet and their documentation upon arrival in the EU. It's not clear what happens to pets which already have a Pet Passport with a proven rabies vaccination.

- **Part 1 Listed** – you'll need to apply for a UK Pet Passport (which remains valid for the life of your pet) to replace your EU Pet Passport. This scheme would then be very similar to the EU Pet Passport: you'll need your pet to be microchipped and vaccinated against rabies at least 21 days before travel, and to have your dog tapeworm treated.
- **Part 2 Listed** – again you'll need your pet to be microchipped and vaccinated against rabies at least 21 days before travel, and to have your dog tapeworm treated before leaving the UK. You'll also need to visit your vet for an AHC prior to each trip abroad.

We recommend talking to your vet about your travel plans as early as possible and keeping an eye on the UK government website for the latest information: *www.gov.uk/guidance/pet-travel-to-europe-after-brexit*.

European Health Insurance Cards (EHICs)

EHICs allow you to receive state-provided healthcare for new and pre-existing conditions in any EU country, or in Switzerland, Norway, Iceland and Liechtenstein, and can be obtained for free. The cards will stay valid during the transition period, and some countries may continue to accept them even if no deal is agreed, assuming the UK reciprocates. The general advice being given by the UK government is to buy comprehensive health insurance, covering any pre-existing conditions you have, so you're not reliant on the EHIC.

Green Card Insurance

In the event the UK leaves the EU without a deal at the end of the transition period, you'll need to contact your insurer a few weeks before you leave and ask for a Green Card to be posted to you. This is a simple paper document which proves your insurance is the legal minimum for the countries it covers.

Roaming Internet and Mobile Contracts

During the transition period EU law will continue to apply to the UK, so you can continue to use your UK-issued mobile SIM cards for making calls and accessing the Internet in the EU countries without incurring 'roaming' charges. After this period, it remains to be seen whether UK-based mobile operators will re-introduce roaming charges in some form, although several have already stated they have no plans to do this.

Remember that this EU law includes a 'fair use' clause, and if you spend months at a time roaming in Europe there's still a chance your mobile operator will cap the speed on your SIM or even block it. In our time roaming Europe, we've only had this issue once with a Three SIM card, after 8 months of continuous travel in Europe, and we've had no issues with Vodafone SIMs.

International Driving Permits (IDPs)

As a withdrawal agreement is in place, there is no need for UK citizens to obtain an IDP for driving in EU countries during the transition period. After the transition, it's possible we'll need to go to the post office before leaving the UK and buy up to three IDPs per driver, depending on which countries you plan to visit. For more information, see: *www.gov.uk/drive-abroad*.

GB Stickers

If your number plate shows Euro symbol and GB national identifier on the left-hand side, you don't need a separate GB sticker, at least until the end of the transition period. After that, it's likely you'll need to buy and display the white sticker on the rear of your motorhome, if you don't already have one.

Bringing Alcohol and Tobacco Back to the UK

Prior to leaving the EU, we can effectively bring back unlimited amounts of alcohol and tobacco into the UK for personal use without paying UK duty. This will continue through the transition period but may not be the case afterwards. If you're reading this after the transition is complete, please check what your duty-free allowance is before buying large amounts of alcohol to bring home to the UK. For the latest information, see: *www.gov.uk/duty-free-goods*.

Border Controls

Once the transition period is over, travelling through borders into and out of the EU might change. It's possible our passports will have entry and exit date stamps, used to enforce the 90-in-180-day rule. We may have to answer questions about the purpose of our visit, and potentially prove we have access to the funds needed to sustain ourselves while in the EU (a credit card for example). So, nothing huge, but worth being aware of.

Working in the EU

As UK citizens, our right to work in the EU, EEA and Switzerland without a work permit may be removed once the transition period is over. This might complicate life if you plan to do paid or unpaid work while you travel. We're not qualified to provide advice on this subject so can only suggest you keep this restriction in mind and do research for your specific situation.

One point to consider: if you do digital nomad work in Europe, such as writing and self-publishing books or maintaining an ad-funded travel blog, you could technically be breaking the law, although there's little anecdotal evidence of people being prosecuted for working in this way in other parts of the World.

Booking a Ferry or the Eurotunnel (Chunnel)

There are two ways to get your van off our islands and over to mainland Europe – a ferry or the Channel Tunnel. Here are our thoughts on the pros and cons of each.

Booking a Ferry

There are various ferry routes between the UK and (among other countries) Ireland, Spain, France, Belgium and the Netherlands. Ferry costs for motorhomes vary depending on the dimensions of the vehicle – usually the length and height, not the vehicle's weight. Costs also vary with time of sailing; typically, being cheaper in the middle of the night, but that will mean arriving in the dark which isn't ideal for a first time abroad.

You can either book direct on the ferry companies own website or use a broker site. By playing around with a few of these sites you'll get an idea how much your crossings are likely to cost.

- *www.aferry.co.uk* – brokers for ferry routes worldwide
- *www.directferries.co.uk* - brokers for ferry routes worldwide
- *www.ferrysavers.com* - brokers for UK-Europe ferry routes
- *www.dfdsseaways.co.uk* – direct with DFDS for UK-Europe routes
- *www.poferries.com* - direct with P&O for UK-Europe routes
- *www.brittany-ferries.co.uk* - direct with Brittany Ferries for UK-France and Spain routes

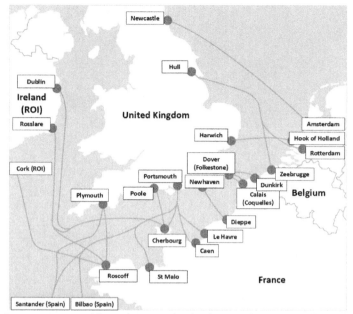

Ferry routes to and from the UK and Ireland, image from *maps.dft.gov.uk*

If you have pets, you'll pay an additional cost per animal. Your pet will have to stay in the motorhome during short crossings. On longer crossings there will be kennels on the ferry. Some crossings have pet-friendly cabins close to a dog walking area on deck, but you'll need to book early if you want one. If you book a pet-friendly cabin on your way out, ensure you have one booked for the return too as we found ourselves trying to smuggle Charlie into a standard cabin when the boat from Tunisia to Italy was swapped for one with no pet-friendly cabins (pampered pooch didn't do kennels!).

We used to leave Charlie in the motorhome for any crossings less than four hours, ensuring he had food and water, and had been exercised before boarding. We would also open the skylights for ventilation while on board. Returning to the motorhome at the end of the crossing Charlie would wake up, so we suspect he had happily slept for the duration. Staying with your pet in the motorhome on a closed car deck is forbidden by the ferry companies for safety reasons.

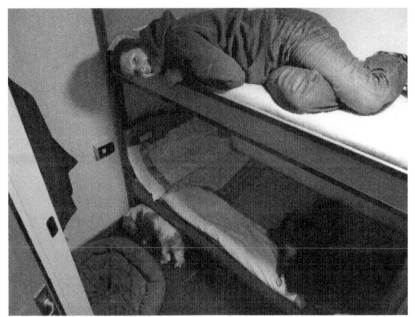

Charlie having a sniff around the pet-friendly cabin from Italy to Croatia

Booking the Channel Tunnel (Eurotunnel)

If you don't like the idea of leaving your pet alone in your motorhome when crossing to France, you can take the Channel Tunnel, officially known as the Eurotunnel (*www.eurotunnel.com*) or more informally the 'Chunnel'. The Chunnel is generally more expensive than getting a ferry, but it's faster (around 35 mins versus maybe 90 mins for a ferry) and avoids issues with weather and sea-sickness.

We have found that the Chunnel makes leaving the British Isles more clinical than ferries. While being on a ferry departing across the sea can bring on a feeling of 'leaving', starting a journey, or of your holiday or tour really beginning, the Chunnel whisks you underground and pops you out in France without any of this sensation.

You book your Chunnel tickets direct through *www.eurotunnel.com*. Make sure you correctly state the height of your van, so you don't have to try to squeeze it into a car carriage. Like with the ferry routes, Chunnel tickets are cheaper late at night or early in the morning and booking in advance can get you a cheaper deal. If you plan to go abroad regularly there is a frequent traveller scheme where you buy 10 crossings at a time. Eurotunnel currently accept Tesco Clubcard vouchers (*www.tesco.com/clubcard*), so by collecting these you could get your crossing for free.

You can use the Chunnel if you have self-refillable LPG tanks, or Calor-type gas bottles which are used for habitation only, but they must be turned off during the crossing. However, you can't use the Chunnel if your van's engine runs on LPG.

Setting Off: Getting to the Continent

The day's finally arrived, and you're heading off to the continent! Here are a few lessons we've learned from our time traveling to foreign parts.

The Dartford Crossing

If you use the Dartford Crossing on the eastern M25 motorway between 6am and 10pm, make sure you pay the toll charge the day before or by midnight the day after (*www.gov.uk/pay-dartford-crossing-charge*). If you forget, you'll be fined. We pay for two trips at the same time, so our return journey is covered too, and then write it in the diary so we don't forget we've already paid.

Overnight Stays Before Leaving the UK

We live in the East Midlands, so tend to travel most of the way to the ports the day before and then get the ferry/Chunnel the following morning. For those travelling from further afield, a well-placed campsite, aire or Brit Stop can be handy to bed down for the night.

The motorhome aire at Canterbury Park and Ride (GPS: N51.26232, E1.10247, post code: CT1 3EJ) is a good stopover option about 25 minutes' drive from Dover and Folkestone. The aire, which is at New Dover Road Park and Ride, has a service point, so you can fill up and empty your grey tank/cassette and the price includes a bus to Canterbury. It costs only a few pounds (see *www.canterbury.gov.uk*), but you'll need to pay for two days at the pay machine, as the payment for each day lasts until midnight. The gates are open for arrivals between 6:00am and 8:00pm, but you can leave at any time.

In the past we've stayed overnight parked on the roadside on Marine Parade at Dover, which is just a few minutes from the ferry and is free overnight. We now prefer to stay at the Canterbury aire for additional peace and quiet. Brit Stops also have a few places in the area, and there are of course plenty of campsites.

Getting On and Off the Ferry

To get to the port, we use the 'car ferry' points of interest in our satnav, although they're also well sign-posted on all the main routes. Your ferry company should tell you when you need to arrive – usually 30 to 45 minutes before the sailing. We always end up being early and if there's an earlier ferry with space they might place us on it, otherwise we get directed where to wait. On one occasion we were several hours early so we were redirected out of the port and had to find somewhere on the roads outside to wait.

Once we're at the port, we never fail to get a little nervous. Ferry ports always seem to be a maze of lanes and signs, although they invariably manage to funnel us to the right place with help from a passenger on 'sign lookout' duty! It's a good idea to check your ferry company's website for details about the process at the port you are leaving from as they all vary slightly.

You may get a 'spot check' at immigration, we've had this a couple of times. We were asked to drive into a large hanger where two officers checked under the motorhome while another one got inside for a look around. They asked us a few questions, including a slightly comical one about whether we had any knives on board, and we were on our way in just a few minutes.

At the ferry company's booth you need to hand over passports for everyone in your vehicle, including pets. They'll hand back a boarding card which hangs from your rear-view mirror and tell you a lane number to head for. If you have a dog with you, it's worth asking where the designated dog walking area is located, so they can stretch their legs before the crossing.

Once the barrier is lifted you drive into the port and follow the signs to your lane. There can be hundreds of lanes but if you forget which one is yours it should be written on your boarding pass. Once you've found your lane, drive down it and queue up behind anyone already in it. If you're first, stop at the end of the lane, turn your engine off and wait. At this point we tend to flip the fridge back onto gas, walk the dog, stick on headlight deflectors, change our satnav units from miles to kilometres, make some snacks and drinks to take on board, and start to get excited.

At some point the ferry staff will indicate you can start boarding, or you'll notice the vehicles in your lane (or the one next to you) start moving. We turn the gas off at this point if we haven't already, turn the fridge onto 12V (so it's ready when we leave the ferry) and transfer frozen cool blocks from the freezer into the fridge. We then follow the port staff's guidance onto the ferry. There is often a ramp up onto the ferry, so it can be worth hanging back a little if you are in a queue, so you don't have to stop and start on the ramp.

Once on board, a member of the ferry staff will direct you into a lane and direct you to drive close up to the vehicle parked in front of you. Keep going until they tell you to stop, which is usually just that bit closer than you think you can get. Turn off your engine, leave the van in gear and pull the handbrake on. At this point we would open the skylights for Charlie, close the blinds or curtains, make sure he had plenty of water, and grab our snacks before heading upstairs. Remember the deck number you're parked on and, on some ferries, the colour of the stairwell, so you can find your van again!

Parking space can be a tad tight on ferries!

When you arrive at your destination, an announcement will be made in several languages, including English, to let you know when to head to the car deck. This often seems to be made after the ship has docked. Follow everyone else down the stairs and return to your van. Start up your satnav and wait for the ferry doors to open. Staff will indicate when it's your time to drive out. There's no need to start your engine until the vehicle in front of you is moving, as you may be waiting a while for the lanes around you to clear first.

There are no checks when you get off the ferry (unless you've taken a long ferry to Spain), so you'll be driving straight out of the port and onto the local road network. Having your satnav on and programmed, helps it gets a signal quickly once you're out of the ferry. Follow everyone out into the port (or the road signs if you are at the front), remembering to keep in the right-hand lane if there is one, to let faster folks overtake. Then just follow your satnav or look for signs to the road you need. The fear of messing this part up is always there for us, but trust us, it's easy. Before you know it you'll be cruising along, although most likely still concentrating hard!

Using the Eurotunnel (Channel Tunnel)

Getting to the Channel Tunnel is simple: drive down the M20 southbound and follow the signs for passenger traffic (not freight). The GPS co-ordinates are: N51.093389. E1.119278, and the address is:

Eurotunnel Le Shuttle, UK Terminal, Ashford Road, Folkestone, CT18 8XX

Aim to arrive between 45 minutes and two hours before your train is due to leave. Have the debit or credit card you booked with to hand, plus your reservation number. You'll be stopped by a barrier next to a machine. If you paid online your registration plate will be automatically read by the check-in machine, otherwise, check yourself in using the machine.

Eurotunnel enables you to take an earlier train if there is space available. The machine will show you the train times and any additional charge if applicable. Select the train you want and the machine will print out a boarding pass for you to hang from your rear-view mirror. You can now drive to the waiting area, where you'll find toilets, shops and a dog walking area, or head through British and French passport and customs controls. At these booths you may be directed to one side to ensure that your gas bottles are switched off, so make sure they are before you go through the final barriers and queue for your train. As you won't have access to gas on the train, now is a good time to make a brew and pop it in a flask to drink on your journey.

Once the barriers raise, about 25 minutes before departure, follow the directions and head onto the train. Take your time at the entrance to line yourself up. Drive forwards through the carriages, leaving a gap so you don't end up reversing if the carriage in front is full. Park so you're up close to the vehicle in front of you, turn your engine off, leave the van in gear and pull the handbrake on.

Ju enjoying a lack of sea-sickness on the Chunnel

Some folks have mentioned to us that the carriages on the Chunnel are too small and claustrophobic. We've found there was easily enough room to drive a 2.2m wide motorhome into the carriage, get out and walk up and down. It was also great to be able to stay in our motorhome with our pooch. The crossing seemed to take about 8 minutes, OK, it was 35 minutes, about a third the time of a Dover to Calais ferry, but sadly, you can't see the water during the crossing, but there are small windows so you can see when you're not in the tunnel.

There are no checks when you get off the train, so you'll be driving straight out of the station and onto the local road networks. Have your satnav on and programmed, so it gets a signal quickly once you're off the train. Follow everyone out into the station, or the signs if you are at the front, remembering to keep in the right-hand lane if there is one, to let faster folks overtake. Then just follow your satnav or look for signs to the road you need.

Driving in Europe

Once your wheels touch down on foreign tarmac, the following sections should help you get safely to your first destination and beyond.

Driving on the Right

We (the UK) drive on the opposite side of the road to everyone else in Europe apart from Eire, the Channel Islands and the Isle of Man. The thought of driving on the right has frankly terrified us in the past, but the experience itself has always been more exhilarating than fearsome. Being sat in the van waiting to get off the ferry, we always have to remind ourselves which side of the road we need to drive on and set up satnav to nag us about it too.

We found roundabouts are surprisingly easy to navigate on the right, as there is usually plenty of signage and other traffic to follow. We got the hang of them almost straight away. One point to be aware of though: vehicles often use the outside lane to turn left at roundabouts, unlike in the UK where we use the inside lane when going right.

The hardest part for us is at 'change points', such as a single carriageway road becoming a dual carriageway, where we might forget whether the left or right lane is the slow one. Or when we turn out of a one-way street into two-way traffic, we have found ourselves on the left for a moment. This rarely happens on day one, when we're concentrating hard on getting it right, but after a few days when we're more confident and less alert. We've never had an accident in this way, perhaps as we only get the lane wrong when there's no other traffic.

Road Signs, Signals and Laws Across Europe

Aside from the obvious requirement to drive on the right, much of European driving is like driving in the UK. Road signs are often familiar and vehicles tend to follow fairly similar rules regarding giving way and overtaking.

There are, however, a whole bunch of weird driving laws to be discovered while wandering about the continent, such as 'la priorité à droite', France's 'give way to the right' rule which means cars joining the main road from some, but not all, side roads on the right have priority - we mainly see this in action in villages and car parks with few road markings. At least you might do: we were woefully unaware of almost all of these over the years, and still didn't manage to crash or attract the attention of the law.

We have been caught out by a few things such as traffic lights where a flashing orange light is used in place of a green one (we now call these 'go if you dare' lights). It's also worth checking up on the laws for alcohol limits, speed limits (as there are speed cameras everywhere and tickets now find their way back to the UK), and if you need to drive with dipped headlights during the day.

In some countries white road markings are replaced with yellow ones in road works. This can be helpful in working out when the works have ended, so you don't do what we did, when we accidentally drove down a stretch of freshly-laid tarmac in the Vercors region of France.

OK, you do spot the odd weird sign out and about on the continent!

The RAC website has useful reference guides for each country, so you can check before you cross the border what basic requirements are in place: *www.rac.co.uk/drive/travel*. Not every country takes the same approach to enforcement of the minor laws as the UK by the way. We're not suggesting you do the same, but half the population in some countries seem to ignore many of the more minor rules. Yes, Italy, we're thinking of you.

Crossing Borders and the Schengen Area

Twenty-six countries in Europe are part of the Schengen Area (*en.wikipedia.org/wiki/Schengen_Area*) and often have no passport or other controls at their borders. Crossing between these countries is usually very simple: you just drive across from one to the other. Unless you've got your eyes peeled, you might even miss the blue EU sign for the country you're entering! For most motorhome trips you won't find any borders more complex than the UK border.

That said, there are sometimes checks in place, even between 'borderless' Schengen countries, and on the odd occasion you might encounter a queue as passport checks are put in place. It's worth having your passports, pet passports, insurance certificate and your van's original V5C document to hand when crossing any international border. Three other important points to note about the Schengen:

- Once the UK has completed the process of leaving the EU (at the end of the transition period), UK citizens will be restricted to spending a maximum of 90 in a rolling 180 days inside the Schengen Area. See page 152 for more information.
- Some Schengen countries aren't part of the EU, like Norway and Switzerland. These countries can apply significant restrictions on imports of alcohol, tobacco, certain foods, medicines and so on. Norway is a particular case: although motorhome travellers frequently carry large amounts of alcohol into the country, there are potentially serious fines for anyone caught not declaring this at the border, even if it's for personal use.
- Some EU countries aren't yet part of the Schengen Area, like Croatia. These countries will enforce passport checks on their borders, so you may find yourself queueing for an hour or more at busier times.

Re-entering France, with no border post, just a lonely sign

The 26 Schengen countries are: Austria, Belgium, Czech Republic, Denmark, Estonia, Finland, France, Germany, Greece, Hungary, Iceland, Italy, Latvia, Liechtenstein, Lithuania, Luxembourg, Malta, Netherlands, Norway, Poland, Portugal, Slovakia, Slovenia, Spain, Sweden and Switzerland.

The Schengen Area Countries (in black) as of 2020

As well as passport and customs checks, here are some other points to consider when travelling across international borders:

- Most countries have specific laws about the equipment you need to carry. For example, if you have bikes on a rack when you cross into Spain and Italy, you'll need a red and white striped 'warning board' attached to the back.

- Some countries require use of dipped headlights even in broad daylight, so you may need to turn your lights on as you cross the border.

- If travelling in winter, some countries require winter or 'M+S' (mud and snow) tyres. The legal tread depth can also vary between countries, so tyres legal on one side of a border might not be legal on the other.

- Remember your SIM cards in your phone and internet equipment. In general SIMs designed to roam between countries shouldn't need reconfiguring and shouldn't cost more in the new country but check before you use them.

- Fuel costs can vary significantly between neighbouring countries. Plan ahead and fill up before entering a more expensive country.

- If driving into a country which has toll roads, you may need to buy a vignette (or mileage-based toll box at the border if over 3500Kg MAM), such as Slovenia, Austria, Switzerland and Hungary. If you're not on a toll road at the border and can avoid using the tolls, you'll avoid this cost.

- Some mountain borders can be crossed using tunnels, which are especially handy in winter. But if you use them, you may need to pay for the privilege.

- If you're re-entering the EU, the border authorities should check your pet passport(s) and scan their chips. They don't always do this, but you should make sure everything is in order in case they do.

- If your vehicle insurance doesn't cover the country you're entering (only likely for North Africa and some eastern European countries such as Ukraine, Albania, Bosnia and Turkey), have your V5C and driving licence ready, and be prepared to buy third party green card insurance at the border. We've done this for Bosnia and Morocco, and it's worth checking what the cost should be before you reach the border so you can question the first figure you're quoted.

Using Toll Roads and Vignettes

If you want to use the motorways in Europe, and some bridges and tunnels, you may need to pay for the privilege (Germany, Luxembourg and Belgium being obvious exceptions, where the motorways are free). In return you'll get access to well-maintained, empty stretches of road which speed you across large expanses of country with little stress.

When you're planning your routes, most paper maps show which roads are toll. The symbols are sometimes hard to spot, but they're there - have a look in the map key. Some satnavs have the options to exclude toll roads, but ensure your satnav is up to date if you rely on this.

How you pay for a toll depends on which country you're in (have a look at *www.tolls.eu/europe*). In Croatia, France, Italy, Portugal and Spain you pay at toll booths in cash or with a credit card, with the amount charged depending on the road, the distance you drive and your vehicle class. The French motorway company website has an English version and provides all the information you should need: *www.autoroutes.fr*.

Portugal (*www.portugaltolls.com*) and Norway (*autopass.no*) have an automated payment scheme, which you must sign up to before you hit their roads or as you enter the country. Others, like Slovenia (*www.dars.si*), charge by the length of time you're in the country, requiring you to buy a sticker (called a 'vignette'). You buy your vignette just after the border from a garage or special booth and stick it on the inside of your windscreen. Also, some countries offer an 'e-vignette' which lasts for a defined length of time like the window stickers, and which you can buy in advance. Finally, some sections of toll road (like the M50 near Dublin) require you to go online and pay for each use.

Switzerland also has a vignette system, but the sticker is for a full year, for example the 2020 vignette is valid from December 2019 to end of January 2021. If your vehicle is over 3500Kg in Switzerland you pay an initial amount then a daily rate (*www.ezv.admin.ch*). Other countries charge per km using an electronic tag to track the distance you've driven: Austria (where you'll need a GO-Box, *www.asfinag.at*), Czech Republic (Billien box, *mytocz.eu/en*) and Slovenia (DarsGo, *www.darsgo.si*). Having chatted with friends who were fined a few hundred euros in Austria for not having a GO-Box, it pays to know how each country charges for tolls.

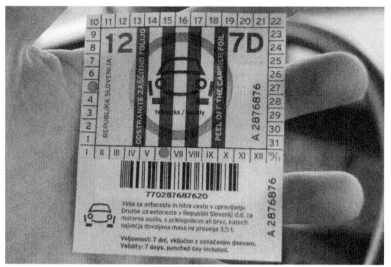

A toll road vignette for the Slovenian motorway network

In most countries you can avoid the toll roads by using roads which follow similar routes. This is pretty easy in France as nearly all toll motorways have an A road running alongside. These roads are much slower as they go through towns and villages, have roundabouts, and are often bumpier. In mountainous areas, non-toll routes may ride up and down the sides of surrounding hills while the motorway ploughs straight through and over them with tunnels and bridges. We tried to replicate our money saving success from France in Hungary a few years ago. It cost us a few grey hairs as the A roads we were driving along would have signs at seemingly random points saying they were now toll, at least that is what we think they said! In the end, we gave in and bought a vignette to lower our stress levels.

The Caravan and Motorhome Club also has a good article summarising the toll rules for motorhomes by country and whether you're under 3500Kg or over:

www.caravanclub.co.uk/overseas-holidays/planning-your-route/motorway-tolls-and-vignettes

Low Emission Zones and ZTLs

Like London, most countries in Europe have at least one low emission zone (LEZ). These restrict access to certain vehicles, sometimes at different times, in order to try and protect the air quality. Breaking the rules, whether by accident or on purpose, can result in a fine. *urbanaccessregulations.eu* and *www.green-zones.eu* are good resources for understanding these schemes, mapping them out and showing what restrictions there are. Italy has a specific type of restricted area in the centre of old towns and cities, called Zona a Traffico

Limitato (ZTL). The following sections briefly outline the LEZ and ZTL schemes in France, Germany and Italy.

France

France has the Crit'Air system, which issues one of several levels of vignette (windscreen sticker) depending on the type and age of your vehicle. Several cities require you to have a vignette to drive in the centre, and over time will probably ban the older/dirtier classifications of vehicle. Some French regions can also issue temporary driving restrictions on some classifications of Crit'Air vignette, in case the weather causes heavy pollution. Yes, it's complex, and confusing, but the vignette only costs about £4 and if you are planning to go to France it's worth applying for one for peace of mind. *www.certificat-air.gouv.fr* gives more information and enables you to buy a vignette before you leave.

Germany

Called 'umweltzonen', there are over 50 LEZs in Germany. If you drive into one without having a special plakette (windscreen sticker), you're liable for a fine, although German friends told us this is only likely if you actually park up inside the umweltzone. You can buy the plakette online before you set off on your trip from various sites, like *www.dekra.de/de/feinstaubplakette* and *www.umwelt-plakette.de*.

We've found ourselves accidentally in one or two umveltzones without a plakette. When we got our second motorhome we went into a car dealer in a small town in Germany and asked for a plakette. After firstly saying we didn't need one, then followed much consternation, head scratching and inspection of our V5C. Eventually they handed over a level 4 (green-coloured) plakette, which was for the cleanest category of vehicle. We very much doubt our 2001 Fiat Ducato-based van would be clean enough to really deserve this sticker, but he wears it with pride!

Italy

In Italy LEZs are called *ZTLs* (Zona Traffico Limitato) and are often monitored with cameras. You can't get a sticker for these, so if you stray into one, you'll likely get hit with a fine. However, you'd have to be a little mad to want to drive into them, as they're often the cramped medieval centre of a town where your motorhome would almost certainly get jammed stuck in a jiffy.

What to Do if You Break Down

As well as a tyre blowout in Spain, we've had clutch and wheel bearing failures in France. That's three fairly serious mechanical issues, but they were spread across four years of touring and we use motorhomes which are at least 15 years old, so we expect and budget for some problems like this.

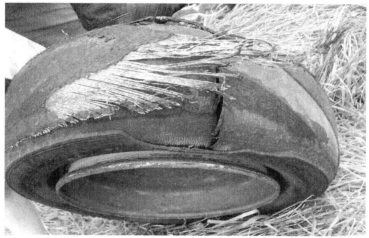

Our tyre after a blow out on a Spanish motorway

With a well-maintained vehicle, hopefully you won't experience any major issues while abroad, but if you do, here are some thoughts based on our experiences:

- If the breakdown hasn't left you stranded and the vehicle's safe to drive, consider resolving the issue yourself. We used the internet to find a nearby garage when our wheel bearing started to fail. This might be a quicker way to get the problem fixed but could mean you miss out on cost-saving options offered with some breakdown policies, like paid-for nights in a hotel during repairs.
- If you can't drive the vehicle, call your breakdown company and go through the process of being recovered. Our satnav has a 'Get Help' feature which pinpoints our exact location; useful when we're somewhere unfamiliar, which is most of the time.
- If you go to, or are recovered to a local garage and there is a language barrier, Google Translate can really help with basic communication.
- Agree a price up front for the repair, so there are no unexpected shocks at the point you come to pay.

Below is a summary of the AA's advice on personal safety during a breakdown (*www.theaa.com/breakdown-cover/advice/what-to-do-if-you-break-down*):

- Get your vehicle off the road or onto the hard shoulder if possible.
- Put your hazard lights on.
- Put your reflective jackets on (in France you must do this before you leave your vehicle, so they need to be stowed somewhere accessible).
- Get out of the van and wait behind a barrier.
- Put your warning triangle out at least 45m away (but not on a motorway).
- Use your mobile or a roadside emergency phone to call for assistance.

Day-to-Day Travelling Abroad

This section covers a few topics you're likely to encounter as you spend your days travelling in your motorhome abroad; obtaining money, using service points, motorhome etiquette and so on.

Finding a First Stop in Europe

These days we try to arrive on the continent during daylight, and to have a couple of places lined up not too far from the port where we can get settled in. We use the resources suggested below to identify a couple of nice places about an hour's drive away from the port. Having a back-up overnight place lined up is generally a good idea, in case one is closed, full, we can't find it, or we don't like the look of it.

When we first ventured abroad in our campervan, we pre-booked our first campsite, even though it was out of season and very quiet. If you are going out of season, it's worth getting the ACSI discount card and pre-booking a campsite (see page 93) so you know where you are going on your first day, and can relax when you arrive. We would certainly recommend booking in advance if you want a campsite in July or August. Some folks will book a campsite for every day of their trip, either just one as a base and explore the surrounding area, or several to work their way around the country.

You can get information about campsites and aires, such as their location, price and facilities, from a number of books, websites and phone apps. The books are great to flick through, are sometimes in English and obviously don't need the internet, but they are heavy and bulky and have no user reviews, so they start to go out of date as soon as they're printed.

Apps and websites are cheaper than books, more up to date, and have user reviews, but they need a gadget to access them, sometimes have poor quality locations included, sometimes need the internet, and aren't as much fun for dreaming your way along the road!

Books

- **All the Aires**, English language books listing details of thousands of aires. The two 2018 France books combined cover 3562 inspected locations (*www.vicarious-shop.com*).
- **Camperstop Europe**, the 2018 edition covers 10500 motorhome stopovers in 27 countries (*www.camperstop.com*).
- **The ACSI Camping Card**, these campsite discount books list over 1500 sites in France alone (*www.campingcard.co.uk*).
- **Vicarious Books** also sell a broad range of other campsite and aires books (*www.vicarious-shop.com*).

Websites and Apps

- *campercontact.com* - Includes a huge number of campsites, aires and businesses which allow overnight stays. The website and app are both free, but there is a subscription charge if you want to download the information to use offline. Reviews are usually in various languages.
- *park4night.com* - Like CamperContact but also includes car parks (some are daytime-only) and free-camping locations. Once again, the website and app are both free, but there is a subscription charge if you want to use it offline. Reviews are usually in various languages.
- *camperstop.com* - The website is free and has the same data as the Camperstop book. It also includes user reviews and more photos. You can pay a yearly subscription to get offline access to the app, saving your internet data.
- *search4sites.com* - Lists tens of thousands of aires, car parks, campsites, service points.
- *eurocampings.co.uk* - Not to be confused with the ACSI discount scheme mentioned above, this website and app list almost 10,000 campsites across Europe, each of which is inspected every year.
- *campingfrance.com* - Over 9000 campsites in France.
- *ioverlander.com* - To get your imagination really fired-up, check out this worldwide database of parking places. For Europe, it's nothing like as good as the others above, but is fun to browse.

Motorhome Aire Etiquette

Waving to fellow motorhome drivers is an established part of etiquette across Europe, which even extends to drivers towing a caravan in Finland. That is until you're in a spot where every other vehicle seems to be a motorhome and your arm would fall off trying to greet every single oncomer.

Aside from that, here are a few other things worth knowing about to get in the good books of your fellow motorhomers if you decide to stay on aires (campsites tend to have their own rules which will be posted somewhere on the site):

- Try and park so your habitation door is on the opposite side to your neighbours. This gives each of you that bit more privacy.
- Follow any posted rules for aires. If camping isn't allowed, keep your chairs and awning away, cook inside, don't hang your washing out. Checking what the majority of other folks are doing on the aire is sometimes a good way to get an idea what's acceptable at that particular location (but it could still land you all in hot water).
- Don't stay on aires for more than the number of hours/nights allowed. Move on, make space for newcomers.
- If there are 20 spaces left in an aire, don't park right next to someone else, unless you have to for some reason.
- Keep noise down in the morning and evening. If you've a van with a sliding door, think about how much noise it makes or if you run a generator, be considerate to your neighbours and turn it off at a reasonable hour.

Using Service Points (Bornes)

A Service Point or 'Borne' is a place where you can empty your cassette toilet (black water), empty your grey water and load up on fresh water. Some also allow you to hook-up to electricity for a limited time, so you can charge your leisure batteries.

Using a commercially-made motorhome service point in France

On the continent, especially in France and Germany, service points are often commercially-made machines. Some are free to use, but most have a small charge, usually €2 to €4. Many service points in France used to use tokens called 'jetons', which you had to buy from the local shops. There would be a sign on the machine directing you where to go. They don't do that so much these days and more often they take cash or a credit card. Make sure you've a stash of €1 and €2 coins for these machines. UK-issued credit cards will usually work, but a few service points want a French card. In this case try a different card, if you have one, ask a local to pay in exchange for your cash, or find another service point.

The commercial machines also vary in design. If there are any instructions, read them as best you can. The critical question of where the toilet gets emptied isn't always as simple to answer as you'd hope. We usually go and have a look before carrying the cassette over. Most have a dedicated drain, clearly marked out, along with a dedicated water tap which you can use to wash out the cassette (don't not fill up your water tank with this tap).

We tend to keep a stash of antibacterial wipes available, so we can clean the water tap before taking water on. Even at service points which have separate taps for fresh water and loo cleaning, you'll get to witness lots of folks using them the other way around. If you're not sure, the fresh water tap usually has a screw thread while the black water one may not have.

The taps at some aires are turned off over winter (marked as *hors gel* in France) to avoid frost damage, so plan to visit several locations or research ahead, don't assume the water will be available.

In some aires, the service points are made by local craftsmen (they're sometimes called 'artisanal'), and their designs can vary massively. Some of the hand-made service points use the grey water drain for the black water too, with a gap in the grate. This is unusual though, so only pour black water down the grey drain if you're 100% sure that's where it should go.

At busy aires it often seems that everyone wants to use the service point at same time and will sit in their driving seat sometimes with the engine running, while you use the service point. We start the grey water draining as soon as we arrive at the service point, then connect the water pipe and then empty the loo. That way the water in-out processes are happening in parallel, and we're finished faster. If you don't want to feel rushed, wait half an hour or so for most folks to leave.

Internet Access When Abroad

Getting access to the internet when abroad is fairly straight-forward, but sadly it's not always as easy as hooking up to your WiFi at home. There are basically three ways to get at the internet while on the road:

- 3G, 4G and 5G networks (used by mobile phones)
- Local WiFi
- Satellite Internet

3G, 4G and 5G Networks

This is our favourite method, and you need nothing but your (ideally unlocked) smart phone or tablet and a suitable SIM card. Turn on data roaming on your phone, and perhaps on your provider's website too in your account settings, and you're away. 3G (HSDPA) and the faster 4G networks are now available almost everywhere, while 5G networks are currently limited to parts of towns and cities. The biggest problem with 3G and 4G is getting the right SIM card to avoid high data costs. There are thousands of ever-changing offers available. Should you buy a SIM card in the UK and 'roam' with it in Europe? Or should you buy a SIM card in the country you're visiting? Should you pay on a contract, or use a pay-as-you-go (PAYG) SIM card? How much data should you get – will 5GB a month do the job, or do you need 24GB a month?

Before it all gets a bit overwhelming, this is the solution we usually use, which might help give you an idea what will work for you. We have a pre-paid 4G SIM card from Vodafone (*vodafone.co.uk*). We pay around £15 to £20 a month and can cancel the SIM with 30 days-notice (helpful for us as we don't use it for more than a few months at a time). The SIM automatically connects to foreign networks in 48 European destinations (everywhere except some of the Balkans). We use the SIM in our MiFi device (see *Internet Access* on page 80), which shows exactly how much data we've used on a display on the front, plus we can 'log into' the MiFi from a smartphone and check how much data we've used. This way we can avoid using more than our allowance, although we've also used Vodafone's website to set our account to stop working if we exceed our monthly data, to avoid high out-of-allowance costs.

In addition, we have a couple of pay-as-you-go (PAYG) SIM cards with a fixed amount of data which can be used over a period of up to one year after activation. The '3' company offers such a SIM, called 'Internet with Legs' (*www.three.co.uk*), and EE sell a similar product. It works in most European and some other countries. Three's PAYG offering has been, on balance, the best for us over the past few years, but is now our back-up to the Vodafone SIM.

Some lessons we've learned when buying a UK data SIM for use in Europe:

- Check in the terms and conditions if it allows smart phone tethering (if you intend to use it that way), or whether it can be used in a personal WiFi hotspot device.
- Check it can be used abroad, and how long it can be used abroad for (if a SIM can only be used for a few months, and you'll be away longer, consider buying two or more and swap them over).
- Also check whether there are restrictions on data use abroad. Some contracts are unlimited in the UK but are limited to 20GB per month outside the UK, for example.
- Unless you have unlimited data abroad, ask if there is a way to cap your monthly data use, so there's no risk of paying higher 'out of plan' costs.
- Check if the data expires after a month or rolls over from month to month.
- Ask how you can top the SIM up when the data expires.
- Full roaming SIM cards will connect to whichever is the strongest network wherever you are abroad. This gives you the best possible network speed, but not all SIM cards work in this way. Some, like those issued by Three, only connect to a selected number of 'partner' networks abroad, which can leave you with slow connections at times.
- Make sure your SIM fits in your device (there are three different sizes of SIM card, although usually you can just 'snap out' the correct size).
- Check if it works on both 3G and 4G. It's not a massive issue if it doesn't do 4G, unless you intend to watch internet TV or stream other video.

If we are in a country not covered by our UK data SIMs, or if we plan to stay in the same country for several months, we buy a local SIM card. Offers change on a regular basis, so we use this website to find out the latest deals: *prepaid-data-sim-card.fandom.com*. This site also indicates how you can top up the SIM, and any gotchas such as not being able to buy credit using a UK card.

A selection of the prepaid SIM cards we've used across Europe

Local WiFi

The great advantages of 3G and 4G networks are availability and convenience. The biggest disadvantage is cost, which is where Local WiFi networks come in.

If we're staying on a campsite which includes WiFi in the cost, then we turn off our 3G/4G connection, and use the campsite WiFi instead. These types of connection aren't metered, so don't charge you per MB or GB unlike most 3G/4G networks. They can sometimes (but not often) be fast enough to make video calls back home, watch internet TV and the like. Sometimes they're unusably slow, so we just go back to our 3G/4G system.

Nearly all tourist offices have a free WiFi network for you to use, some also have a PC that you can use and enable you to print things out. McDonalds, larger shopping centres, libraries and many cafes, restaurants and bars also offer free WiFi, so it's always worth a quick search when you arrive somewhere to see if you can get connected.

One disadvantage of Local WiFi network is that they're too local! The further you are away from the broadcast antenna (called an Access Point), the weaker the signal and the slower the speed until it becomes unusable. You can buy boosters which are very good at increasing the speed of the network, or helping you connect to networks which are (literally, if nothing's in the way) a mile or more away. Adam and Sophie at *motorhomewifi.com* helped us ensure we had the right equipment and sell their popular WiFi iBoost system.

Finally, the forerunner to local WiFi was the Internet Café, remember these? Little shops with rows of PCs where you could pay per hour to access the internet. There are a few remaining, but not many. Ask around to track one down. These can also be useful if you need to print something off.

Satellite Internet

If you're planning on working while wandering, and need always-on internet, everywhere, no matter what, then satellite internet may be for you. A dish on the roof lifts itself skywards, locks onto a satellite and kit inside your van shares an unlimited data internet connection with your laptop and other devices. As long as you've sight of the sky, you should have a connection. The downsides:

- It's not cheap, maybe over £3000 to buy and install a roof-mounted system (plus something like £500 a year for the data connection). Tripod-mounted systems can be picked up for half this amount, but need manual alignment, somewhere to stand outside the motorhome and are harder to secure.
- The satellite footprint might not cover everywhere you plan to visit, especially if you're heading into Northern Scandinavia, the far south of Spain and Portugal or anywhere in North Africa.
- You can't use it in all weathers. If it's too windy to have the dish up, you can't get on the internet, so may want to use a combination of internet access methods if you absolutely, definitely must have connectivity.
- There's an inevitable delay in sending data into space and back, which can drop the quality of time-sensitive stuff like internet phone calls.

We've never used satellite internet, so can't comment on how good it is. 3G/4G networks are available almost everywhere now, so we wouldn't consider using satellite internet in Europe (or North Africa either, where cellular networks are very good).

Virtual Private Networks – VPNs

Some websites and applications check which country you're in, the BBC iPlayer being a notable example which only works if you're in the UK (*www.bbc.co.uk/iplayer*). If you're using a SIM card issued by certain UK-based providers, they make it look like you're in the UK even when you're abroad, so iPlayer and other 'geo-locked' services continue to work. However, with most SIM cards, or when using WiFi, you'll have to use a Virtual Private Network (VPN) to access these services. A VPN is software which makes it look like you're in the UK (or whichever country you want to make it look like you're in).

You can load a VPN app onto your smart phone, tablet, laptop, Amazon Fire TV Stick and so on, and you simply start and connect the VPN before trying to use geo-locked services. You'll pay a monthly charge for VPNs which will include unlimited data (but bear in mind you'll still have 3G/4G/5G data costs to pay if using them). Sites like Tech Radar can help you find the best current VPN service (*www.techradar.com/uk/vpn/best-vpn*).

Obtaining Money

We have a combination of methods for obtaining cash and buying goods and services abroad. By having cash plus different types of card (credit and debit), and cards issued by different agencies (MasterCard, VISA), we feel it's far more likely we'll have a working method of payment in any given situation.

- **Foreign Currency Pre-Paid Card.** We use a CaxtonFX MasterCard (*www.caxtonfx.com*). Which is a pre-paid card. We top it up online with funds from our bank, and can carry over 20 currencies on it. It isn't a credit card, so we can't over-spend. We mainly use it for cash machine withdrawals as it doesn't charge a transaction fee. This means we can take out relatively small amounts at a time, so we don't carry more cash than we want to. We've found it works almost everywhere for payments too, but we avoid buying fuel with it from self-service petrol stations as they tend to 'reserve' an amount of money on the card which isn't released for some days. If you're driving and filling up a lot this can mean most of your funds become inaccessible.
- **Credit Card.** We use a Halifax Clarity MasterCard for general purchases including buying fuel and shopping (*www.halifax.co.uk*). This doesn't charge a fee for purchases abroad, but does charge interest on cash withdrawals, so we rarely use it to obtain cash.
- **Bank Debit Cards.** We carry our bank debit cards as a back-up. Each withdrawal and transaction is charged, so we avoid using these cards unless it's an emergency.

Buying Diesel and Petrol

Buying diesel and petrol abroad is pretty much the same as in the UK, but there are a few things to know which can be helpful. Perhaps the most useful difference to be aware of is simply the name used abroad for your type of fuel:

- Petrol, or unleaded is called *SP95* (*sans plomb* 95 octane), *SP98* (98 octane, sometimes also called *super*), *A95*, *A98*, *essence*, *benzene*, *motorbenzin*, *βενζίνη Αμόλυβδη, gasoline sem chumbo* or just *petrol*. Unleaded fuel is also shown as E5 or E10, with 5% or 10% biofuel, the numbers shown in a circle.

- Diesel has an equally impressive array of names: *gasoil, gasolio, gaz-oil, gasóleo, nafta, mazot, motorina, Дизел* or just *diesel*. Diesel is also labelled B7 or B10, with the numbers shown in a square.
- Thankfully the pump handles are almost always colour-coded to help you pick the right fuel: unleaded are green, and diesel are either black, orange or yellow.
- Some stations also sell ethanol, paraffin and LPG, so don't be too surprised to see an array of prices and pumps for these other fuels. Blue handle: *superethanol*, or E85, again shown in a circle.

DIESEL TYPE OF FUEL   PETROL TYPE OF FUEL

European standard fuel pump labels for diesel and petrol

Like in the UK, fuel on motorways and major roads tends to be more expensive than that found in supermarkets. Diesel is usually, but not always, cheaper than unleaded too. Websites like *www.fuel-prices-europe.info* give an idea of average fuel prices in a particular country, which is useful for budgeting or deciding which side of borders to fill up.

For help finding the cheapest station on your route, have a look at websites like *www.prix-carburants.gouv.fr* (for France) and *es.fuelo.net* (for Spain and other countries). Our approach is simply to avoid running low on fuel and filling up when we see a cheap station as we drive. If you've a smartphone, there are free apps to help you find lower-cost fuel.

In most countries, you're expected to fill up yourself. Italy's a notable exception, where two prices are shown for each fuel type: one for self-service and a more expensive one for attendant service. Pull up at the correct set of pumps (easier said than done) for self-service if you don't want to pay the extra. If you find yourself at an attendant pump in any country, knowing the local word for 'full' is useful. Since we hardly ever know this, a bit of comical miming usually works, or just have the notes ready for the amount you want to spend, and show them to the attendant.

When it comes to paying in cash at an exit booth, we find it much easier with one of us walking and the other driving, as the cashier window is usually too low to pay from the cab. Whoever's paying doesn't need to know the local lingo; just pointing at the van or holding up the number of fingers for the pump we used always works.

And finally a few hints and tips we've picked up over the years:

- Some stations are tight to drive around in a motorhome, particularly in France. We try and have a look at the station before we drive in, and if it looks too tight just find another one. On one occasion a high concrete plinth trapped our exhaust under the van, requiring help from a hammer to help us exit. On another we spent five minutes edging back and forth with one of us outside the van checking the van roof wouldn't hit anything before we could get out of a tight filling point.
- Some countries have lower fuel prices on certain days of the week, and even different times of day. Trying to work out the cheaper days and times can keep us entertained for weeks.
- Luxembourg has fixed fuel prices across the country, so all stations are equally low-priced compared to the surrounding countries. Andorra has low-tax fuel so is cheap compared with France and Spain, and Gibraltar is cheaper than Spain, but beware of long border queues to get in and out.
- In Switzerland, prices are often shown in both Swiss Francs and Euros, with signs rotating between the two currencies.

Buying Food

Getting food and drink while you are abroad is very similar to how it is at home. The simplest option is to head to one of the many supermarkets, most of which have a huge car park and hardly any height barriers so you can guide your motorhome in easily. At the supermarket and you'll find aisles of familiar products and brands to keep your cupboards stocked up. In the larger supermarkets you'll probably even find an English aisle or section with baked beans and HP sauce. It may be a treat to find them, but they will be priced at a premium.

In some countries your fruit and veg needs to be weighed and labelled before you get to the check-out. Keep an eye out for weighing scales, or a small counter with a member of staff to do it for you. If there just are weighing scales, you'll need to note the reference numbers for your items (it's usually on the information panel with the price). At the scales, pop each type of produce on the scales and select the number. The scales will print out a price label with barcode for you to stick onto your veggies, ready to be scanned at the check-out.

While we can happily spend hours wandering around foreign supermarkets, you can't beat a street market for shopping fun. Most towns and villages will have a market once a week where you can stock up on fresh fruit and veg and they'll do the weighing for you. If you don't speak the language, smiling and pointing has worked very well for us. One of our favourite market day treats is a freshly cooked chicken from one of the stalls. We choose the van with the longest queue and if they ask if we want sauce or gravy, the answer is always yes, as it's the tastiest stuff.

Small shops in towns and villages seem to have survived better than they have in the UK, especially in France where even the tiniest of villages has a 'boulangerie' (bakers) for your daily baguette, and even sometimes a 'boucherie' (butchers).

Cold Weather Travelling

Heading into the mountains at any time can be a wonderful experience in a motorhome. In winter it's quite possible to tour resorts skiing or snowboarding, while staying in your motorhome in perfect comfort throughout. Winter campsites (sometimes called *caravaneige*) are usually on the ski bus route and offer heated boot rooms to dry out your kit. Many have wellness spas and some even have a heated bathroom on each pitch. Our experience of this has been fairly limited, spending just a few days in aires high up in the Alps, but we quickly learned a bunch of things we were getting wrong! Here are a few pointers if you plan to head up into the snow and ice:

- Fit mud and snow (M+S) or full winter tyres before setting off.
- Get a set of snow chains for your driving wheels, and practice fitting the fiddly things before you have to put them on for real. Don't put these on unless the road is covered in snow or ice. There are special 'aire de neige' alongside the road which you can pull into to fit chains.
- To avoid your diesel gelling up (resulting in your engine not starting in the deep cold) try and top up with fuel from a station which is near the hills. If needs be, ask if it has anti-gel additive in it. If you're concerned, buy and take some diesel winter fuel additive.
- Check when the local school holidays are: if you arrive just after they've started, you may find there is no room at the inn, or every electrical hook-up point has a full complement of cables plugged in it.
- Get some external silver screens for your cab windows to try and keep some of the heat in.
- If your van doesn't have one fitted, carry a ladder and brush. You'll need to clear your roof each morning of fresh snow, or it'll build into a thick ice sheet which might cause an accident when it comes off.
- Take a shovel. Aires are cleared frequently by snow ploughs, but they can't get to the area between vans. Each morning experienced winter motorhomers clear around their van to stop the snow building up.
- With temperatures dipping at night to -10°C or -15°C, and not getting above freezing during the day, you'll need your air and water heating on

all day and night. Make sure your gas tanks are full, unless you're able to use a local bottle which might be available in-resort.

- Make sure you can either hook-up to electricity or your leisure batteries are full. You can't guarantee solar PV charging when your panel keeps getting snowed on. Some folks use generators in ski resorts during the day to recharge leisure batteries.
- Be prepared for stuff freezing up: windscreen wipers, external locker locks, door hinges, your ramps freezing to the floor, ice building up on any flattish surface, you name it. One fellow traveller reported their awning being forced away from the side of their van by a build-up of ice.
- If your grey tank isn't winterised, leave the tap open and leave a bucket under it to catch the water as it comes out. Ideally fit tank heaters and insulation to any water tanks slung under your van.
- Take some pegs with you. These can be used to keep your wipers off the windscreen and attaching one to your heating exhaust outlet will mean any water condensing from it will freeze away from the side of your van.

If you are thinking of heading for the slopes in your motorhome the Facebook group 'Motorhome & Ski' has lots of useful information.

Mountain Driving

Large parts of France, Spain, Norway, Switzerland, Italy and Austria are mountainous. While mountainous areas can present testing driving conditions, the majority of the routes are possible with some preparation.

- Mountain roads follow contours across the side of a valley, using hairpin bends to come back across the hill, ascending and descending at typically a steepness of 6% to 10%. The highest point of one of these valley-to-valley roads, is called a pass, or col and is often marked by a sign.
- If you're heading for the mountains from late autumn to spring, having 'mud and snow' or 'full winter' tyres, plus a set of snow chains, makes sense. This may also be a legal requirement; see the *Tyres* section on page 163.
- Being at altitude, many mountain passes close in winter, either for the whole season or until a snow plough can clear the fresh snow. Road signs leading to the pass will tell you if your chosen route is currently open, and snow gates close off access to snowbound roads. Some passes stay closed until late summer, we once found ourselves stuck at the bottom of the Col de l'Iseran in France, waiting for it to open in late June. *www.alpenpaesse.co* is a good resource to check whether mountain passes are open.
- Some mountain passes have tunnels which can be used to bypass the very highest part of the road, although you'll miss out on the sense of 'topping out'.

- If you want to avoid the mountain roads completely you can sometimes do this using tunnels like the Mont Blanc tunnel between Chamonix in France and the Aosta Valley in Italy. You'll often need to pay for these, and be aware of strict speed limits, use of dipped headlights, mandatory gaps between vehicles that the fact tunnels may be closed for maintenance.

- There are also 'car trains' in Switzerland where you drive your motorhome onto a train and sit in it while it ploughs through the mountains, speeding up an otherwise hilly crossing. Refer to this website for more information: *www.myswissalps.com/car/cartrains*.

- If you don't take the tunnels, there are some very long and relatively steep descents to handle. You can find yourself heading downhill for many miles, and if you try and use your brakes all the way down there's a good chance you'll 'cook' them. We did this once in Austria, with the brake pedal feeling progressively spongier until it felt like the brakes weren't working. We pulled in to a safe area and let them cool down for an hour before carrying on (throwing water on hot brakes is a bad idea). Now we 'engine brake' using roughly the same gear to go down a hill as we'd use to drive up it. (for example, if we'd have needed 2nd to drive up the hill, we use 2nd, or even first gear, to go down it). We then use the brakes from time to time to scrub off speed, rather than have a foot on the pedal the whole time.

- Although our motorhomes are slow, they have always made it up and over the high passes. From time to time we've needed to stop part way up, like on the miles-long ascent of Mont Ventoux in Provence, to allow the engine to cool down a little. Being only 6m long, we've never had an issue negotiating hairpin bends or with front end traction. If you've a longer vehicle or have weight loaded on the back of a front wheel drive motorhome, then you may have some issues on ascents.

Keeping Safe and Healthy

While we all want new experiences on our travels abroad, being blunt, none of us want to get hurt in the process. Our safety, that of our party and the people around us is paramount to us all. This section gives our personal thoughts on some areas to consider to ensure you have a safe holiday or tour.

Drive a Well-Maintained Motorhome

A few weeks into our first tour a rear tyre on our motorhome blew itself apart. We were driving at about 55mph at the time on the inside lane of a Spanish motorway. An almighty bang, followed by the back end of the van dropping and a cloud of dust billowing up inside the van had us both thinking we'd snapped our motorhome in half.

Once on the hard shoulder we found the entire tyre tread had ripped off, whipped around, smashed the wheel arch and badly damaged the habitation door step, a seat and our fresh water tank. We were recovered by roadside assistance and found a fantastic repair shop in Santander who made the van like new, but it could have been a different story.

The tyres on the motorhome were at least five years old when we bought it (probably much older), and showed signs of cracking. We'd ignored this as the van passed an MOT a few weeks before, and had lots of tread depth left. Clearly this wasn't the brightest of moves. We've learned our lesson and we make sure we've good quality tyres these days.

We fit new tyres whenever the old ones are getting low on tread, well before the 1.6mm legal limit. If we're heading into snowy areas in winter, some countries require a 4mm minimal tread depth (*www.theaa.com/european-breakdown-cover/driving-in-europe/snow-chains-winter-tyres*). As we tend to drive a fair bit, the tyres wear out before they get old.

Out and about we check tyre pressure periodically, although probably not as often as we should. An ex-police driver we know checks his tyre pressures once a week and records it in a notebook to help spot slow punctures. We get advice from our tyre fitters on what pressures to use. Some folks contact the tyre manufacturer with their axle weights to get more accurate figures.

We see motorhome maintenance as one of the key things to concentrate on when preparing for a tour. We use a local garage and make sure they know we're going abroad and want everything inspected and well prepared: suspension, brakes, oil, coolant, starter battery and so on. Anything which is borderline, we ask them to replace. It's not cheap, but it's worth it for the peace of mind.

Things we can do ourselves to keep safe include: making sure we're not overloaded by using a local weighbridge, and making sure the lights all work, the horn works, the windscreen is clean and the mirrors are adjusted. Our current van has small convex mirrors mounted above the standard ones, which are very helpful at slip roads, or when overtaking on motorways.

Traffic Accidents Abroad

In the unlikely event you're involved in an accident while abroad, it might be simple enough to sort out, depending on how serious the incident was. In our years of touring we've only had a couple of minor accidents, clipping wing mirrors in France and reversing into a car in Slovenia. For the French incident the other vehicle's driver produced a *constat à l'amiable* form which we both completed and sent to our insurers, although no claim was ever made on either side. In Slovenia we agreed a cash amount for the repair to his car and the insurers weren't involved.

If you want to be better prepared than us, you can download and print off a European Accident Statement (or EAS) form, or ask your insurer to send you one. This, like the *constat à l'amiable* form, is a standard way of the parties recording what took place in the accident and is widely used across Europe. Be careful to only sign the form if you agree with what the other people have written on it. The EAS form has advice on what to do in the event of an accident. In summary, it advises this:

- Stay calm, be polite and don't admit liability.
- Call 100 to contact the police and ambulance, if the severity of any injuries justifies it.
- Photograph the scene. Make sure you include the number plates of all vehicles involved.
- If you're blocking traffic, move the vehicles once you've taken photos. If necessary, mark the corners of the vehicles with chalk before moving.
- Make some notes and a drawing of what happened.
- Get names and address of witnesses if you can.
- Exchange your insurance details with the other parties involved.
- Contact your insurer and send them the EAS or similar form if you complete one.

Obviously if you're unable to continue your journey, you'll need to contact your insurer and breakdown recovery. As you might be without your vehicle for some time while it's repaired, we'd suggest using any time spent waiting to find a hotel, pack clothes, toiletries, computer, chargers, food and so on. Also have a think about what to do with food in your fridge and freezer, as this might have to be turned off in a repair shop.

Staying Safe on Foot

There's already loads of travel advice in books like the Lonely Planet series for staying safe when out on foot in unfamiliar places abroad. We won't try and repeat it all here, but lots of it is common sense and stuff you would do at home too:

- Even if we have them, we don't wear expensive clothes, jewellery or watches when out and about.
- We carry only small amounts of cash.
- We expect pick-pockets in busy places. Don't put anything in your back pockets. When it gets very busy, we walk with our hands on purse/wallet and phone in our front pockets, zip them into an inside pocket, or carry them at the bottom of a rucksack.

- Carry a fake wallet in places you're particularly cautious of. When we caught the tube in Rome, a notorious pick pocket location, Ju put an old purse packed with old receipts and old cards on the top of everything in her rucksack. A group of thieves managed to quietly surround her and unzip the rucksack on her back before stealing the wallet without her noticing. They dropped it as they left the train once they realised it was worthless and we lost nothing.
- If we're concerned, we ask which areas of towns and cities might be best avoided. Some places are OK during the day but less so at night.
- We try to work out where we are and where we're going before we leave the van. While very helpful for avoiding getting lost, we try to avoid walking about staring at a phone app or a map in busy areas. We feel this marks us out as folks not familiar with the locality, when ideally we want to blend in.

Finding Medical Help if You Need It

Apart from needing to seek out vets in various countries, we've been lucky and haven't needed much medical help abroad. We both have EHICs (European Health Insurance Cards) and travel insurance (the latter includes cover for repatriation). Whenever we've needed long-term medication, we talk to our doctors to ensure we can take enough with us to cover the entire time away.

If we need medical help and it's not an emergency, we normally head for a pharmacy, campsite reception or tourist information to ask for advice. Failing that, we search the internet for local dentists, opticians or doctors. The EHIC only provides free treatment at state hospitals, not private ones, so you need to ask where you're being sent.

In the event of an emergency, and there was no-one we could quickly ask around us, we would call our travel insurers to get help. Having a local map handy at this point would probably be essential: *maps.me* is a great smartphone app, or Google Maps is very good if you have internet access.

When we did need medical help after Ju fell over in Spain, we made our way to the local medical centre. We took our smartphone and mifi so we would have internet access, this enabled us to 'speak' to the doctors using Google translate as our Spanish was pretty much non-existent.

Keeping Your Motorhome and Belongings Secure

It's a fact of life that there are bad folks who'll pinch your stuff if they can. Travelling by motorhome is, in our opinion, as secure as any other form of travel, but with some preparation you can hopefully avoid the stress and hassle of a break-in.

Hope for the Best, Prepare for the Worst

Our campervan and motorhome travels have seen us sleep in around 900 different places to date, and we've had nothing stolen. Even so we always work on the assumption one day we will be broken into. In practice this means:

- Before leaving the UK, we take photos (or photocopies) of all our critical documents and email them to ourselves: passports, driving licences, insurance certificate and contact details, V5C, travel insurance certificate and contact details, breakdown cover details etc.
- We don't take anything of sentimental value with us. If it does get broken into and things stolen, we make sure it is just stuff that can be replaced and means nothing to us. The exception to this rule was our dog Charlie, and we took care not to leave him in the van when we weren't confident it was safe.
- We carry a small portable hard drive with us when we are out and about. This contains a back-up of what is on our laptop in the van, so if that is stolen at least we won't lose our photos.
- While asleep in the van, we make sure everything is put away. If a thief manages to sneak in, they'll at least have to open and rummage through cupboards to find stuff.
- When leaving the van, we make a call on how secure we think the location is. If it's a leafy campsite with lots of people about and away from built-up areas, we would tend to leave our passports hidden in the van. Otherwise we carry them with us, at the bottom of a rucksack with lots of stuff on top of them.
- We carry a spare key with us, which opens the habitation door and lockers. We also have a spare set of keys hidden somewhere on the van so we can get at them if the ones we have are lost or stolen.

Our Second-Hand Experience of Break-Ins

As we've not been broken into, we have no first-hand experience of it. But we've some experience gleaned from chatting with fellow travellers:

- Motorhome windows are a weak point. They can fairly easily be prised open, breaking the plastic catches, and are often large enough for someone to climb through. There's not a great deal we can do about this other than get a motorhome with small windows, or fit bars, which would make us feel like we were in prison. Our view is this: even with an alarm, immobiliser, wheel locks and umpteen locks on doors, a determined thief will get in through the windows, so we don't try to turn our van into Fort Knox.
- Break-ins tended to happen in built-up areas. One was parked at the side of the road in a Norwegian town (a country which felt remarkable safe to us), one in the car park of a tourist attraction in Portugal, one alongside the

road in the French Riviera, and another parked near a museum in Spain. One chap we met returned to his van on a campsite in Poland to find it had been ransacked. There wasn't much in common between these other than the fact they were in towns and cities.

- One couple we met were woken in the night by their cab light coming on. They discovered someone had quietly bypassed the lock on their C Class motorhome cab door and opened it. They loudly shouted some choice words to make sure the would-be thief knew they were awake, and never got to see whoever was after their belongings. Owners of C Class motorhomes (which still have the original cab doors) tend to chain or strap the front doors together at night, to prevent them from being opened.

Fitting and Using Additional Security Measures

Although we can't make our motorhomes (or cars or houses for that matter) 100% secure, there are a few measures we have in place to deter thieves:

- Both our motorhomes had a deadlock fitted to the habitation door in addition to the standard manufacturer's lock. This means we have to use two different keys on two different locks, but it also means the relatively flimsy standard lock has a more secure one to back it up.

- Originally, we were worried the van might be stolen with all of our documents, cards, cash and paperwork in it. Since then we've learned vehicles seem to very rarely be taken, and opportunistic thieves usually try to make off with anything valuable lying about inside.

- Our current motorhome has an alarm, which also covers the external lockers and apparently has a feature so we can disable the internal sensors while inside, but we've never worked out how to use it. As our dog was often asleep inside, the alarm was hardly used when we had him, but we now use it most times we leave the van (we leave it off if we have an electric heaving fan running inside, as this sets it off). The alarm has an LED fitted to the front bumper, which flashes away when it is armed.

- We've considered fitting a safe, but never have partly because of the additional weight, but mainly because we've a routine worked out where we don't have much cash and carry passports etc. with us.

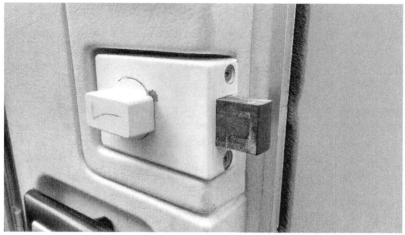
The deadlock fitted to our habitation door

Sneaky Tips and Tricks, Which May or May Not Work!

As well as the additional lock on the habitation door, we use a few tips and tricks which may well have no effect whatsoever, but here are they anyway:

- We were once issued a 'dog inside' sticker by our ferry company, with a silhouette of a large pooch on it. We've left this in the windscreen, as it gives the impression there is a huge guard dog inside. For a while we put 'Beware of the Dog' signs in the windows, written in the local language, but we've given up on that.

- We always close all the blinds and curtains when we leave the van. Some folks leave theirs all open, but either way everyone makes sure there is nothing of value left in sight. The idea is there's nothing to attract a thief and, if someone does break in, they'll need to spend time hunting around for anything of value.

- We return the habitation step to the 'up' position when we go out and at night. As our existing van's quite high up, the thinking is the bad guys would have a slightly harder time getting inside.

- We've been known to leave our cab blinds or curtains open a little and lower the drop-down bed, to make it look like someone's asleep inside. A few pillows arranged like a person under the duvet helps with the illusion. At least we like to think it does. One friend of ours had a plastic mannequin's head, which he'd place in the bed to give a more realistic effect!

Choosing Safe Places to Park

Probably the single biggest thing we can do to avoid being broken into is choosing the right places to park. Always staying on campsites, and not leaving your van parked up anywhere else, is likely the most secure way to overnight in a motorhome.

Whenever we feel unsafe, which is typically around large cities, we stay in a good quality campsite and walk, cycle or use public transport to get into the city. Some folks are very happy only ever using campsites, but we enjoy staying in aires, free camping and France Passion-style locations too. This means we have to make more of an assessment of whether these places are secure.

With access to so much information through databases and smart phone apps, we can often get a feel for a place even before we get there. These are the kinds of things we look for:

- Any negative reviews about break-ins or noise at night. Even if these exist and there are lots of other positive reviews we'll go and see the place in the hope the problems were one-offs.
- Does the area look popular with other motorhomes? If it does, having neighbours provides a kind of informal Neighbourhood Watch scheme, as we're a curtain-twitching lot.
- Is there evidence of us intruding on the domain of bored teenagers? Doughnut tyre marks, beer bottles or cans, graffiti, or even just a large parking area with no cars in it can all spell a few slightly nervous hours at night listening to banging tunes, squealing tyres or un-translatable shouting.

As a couple we've agreed that if one of us isn't happy with a location, we move on. At one otherwise-idyllic spot above a cove in Greece, broken glass and graffiti had one of us spooked while the other loved the place. As agreed we moved, without much grumbling – honest!

Exaggeration, Urban Myth and Reality

We've tried to give a fairly balanced view on motorhome security, while not scaring the wits out of you and ensuring your van never leaves UK soil. Yes, bad things do happen abroad, as they do in the UK too. The reality is, in our opinion, that motorhoming abroad is a safe and secure way to travel, especially if you take some of the basic precautions we've mentioned.

There are also some stories which spread and blow out of proportion, as well as urban myths which perpetually travel around the motorhome grapevine, despite the fact they're simply untrue. Again be aware of these stories, but don't let them instil unnecessary fear. Here are a few of 'em:

- **Aires and wild/free camping are unsafe.** Instead of adopting a blanket idea that a particular type of parking's unsafe, we try and judge each spot on its own merits. That said, we do avoid motorway aires as we've heard lots of tales of break-ins on them.
- **Migrants will stowaway on our van.** There's a steady stream of stories of people trying to sneak into/onto/under motorhomes as they return to the UK. Personally, we've had no experience of this, but common sense says it must be happening, although probably in a very small way. As news coverage of this has increased, we now plan our last overnight stop to be away from ports and coastal aires by the port. Before setting off, it doesn't take long to check your van to make sure no-one's hiding in the bathroom, on the bed or clinging crazily to the grey water tank.
- **"We've been gassed!!!"** This comes from folks waking up to find they've been robbed, then claiming they must have been knocked out with gas. Regardless of whoever tells you they know someone this has happened to, it has never been proven to have taken place. The cost alone of using gas, regardless of the massive difficulty in safely and effectively applying it under such uncontrolled conditions, means it's infinitely more likely the occupants simply slept through the break-in, even if they don't want to believe it.

Returning Home

Sadly, all too soon, it's time to end your adventure and return home to plan the next one. Coming back into the UK's pretty simple. Here are a few things to consider before heading back.

Visiting a Vet

Currently, if you have a pet dog with you, you'll need to visit a vet to administer a tapeworm treatment to your pet and complete a section in your Pet Passport to say when it was done. This time/date has to be between 1 day (24 hours) and 5 days of the point you arrive back in the UK (*www.gov.uk/take-pet-abroad*). As we've said earlier in this book, once the transition period for withdrawing from the EU has ended, the pet passport rules may change. Speak to your vet or check the Government's website for the latest information *www.gov.uk/guidance/pet-travel-to-europe-after-brexit*.

We would arrange a vet appointment somewhere in Northern France for an afternoon two days before we caught a morning ferry home. This allows the 24 hours to elapse but means if the ferry is delayed due to bad weather, we have a few days' grace. Vets anywhere near the ferry ports are all well aware of the Pet Passport scheme, and generally speak some if not fluent English, although their receptionists might not.

We've used the Clinique Vétérinaire du Haut Pont vet in Saint Omer and can recommend them (GPS: N50.756190, E2.259662). The vets speak English and do a thorough check of your pets before issuing the worming treatment and completing the passports. They're not the cheapest, but they do a good job. You'll need to make an appointment in advance.

There is a motorhome aire nearby on Rue de la Gaiete (GPS: N50.75643, E2.25952), although we've just parked on the roadside or in the town for the hour or so needed to complete the job.

Clinique Vétérinaire du Haut Pont
5 Rue de Belfort, 62500 Saint-Omer, France
Tel: 00 33 3 21 88 87 54
cliniqueveterinaireduhautpont.chezmonveto.com
www.facebook.com/cliniqueveterinaireduhautpont62

We've also used Clinique Vétérinaire du Faubourg in Amiens, which are cheaper than the St Omer vets, and located a short distance from a Lidl where we could park our motorhome, and again they spoke good English:

Clinique Vétérinaire du Faubourg
328 Faubourg de Hem. 80000 Amiens, France
Tel: 00 33 3 22 66 28 99
www.cliniqueveterinairedufaubourg.com

Stocking Up
Some things we like either aren't available in the UK or are far more expensive. Wine and beer are one obvious example, so we tend to head to a hypermarket to stock up a day or two before we cross the channel. We also like to grab some of our favourite tinned foods but have to bear in mind the additional weight all of this stuff adds to the van.

Getting the Ferry or Tunnel Home
Our satnav has car ferry ports and the Channel Tunnel entrance as points of interest, which is useful when planning a route to the port. If you're using the Tunnel, the GPS co-ordinates for the Calais terminal are: N50.936315, E1.814964.

Your company will tell you when they expect you to be at the port or tunnel, usually 30 minutes to an hour before you're due to leave. The process is roughly the same as the one you took when leaving the UK. If you have a pet, the authorities will usually hand you a scanner to scan your pet's microchip as you check in, to ensure it matches that in the passport.

Guided Tours Abroad

If, after reading all of this, you'd like more support or company on your first trip abroad, you could consider a guided tour. The Caravan and Motorhome Club, for example, offers 'First Time' tours which start at campsites in the UK before taking you to campsites abroad and finally back to the UK. They include ferries, a course on driving on the right and a pack of essentials like high vis jackets, headlight adaptors and the like. See *www.caravanclub.co.uk* for information on prices and to book.

Part Three: Your First Long-Term Tour

The idea of a spending months or even years touring Europe in a motorhome appeals to lots of us. Why wouldn't it? If you can make the time and generate the funds, then Europe will reward you for it. Our continent is a diverse, historic and beautiful place to travel, and exploring it at your own pace is, for many of us, a dream come true. This part of the book discusses the ultimate of European motorhome travel: the year-long tour.

Why Tour Long-Term?

Everyone's reason to leave home and travel will be different. We've been privileged to meet lots of fellow travellers, and many of them were spurred into action by a reminder of their own mortality. Either they'd had a health scare, experienced the death of a loved one, or had a chronic illness of their own. Health is definitely a driver for many of us to get past whatever blockers there are to following a dream.

Some people simply feel they've done enough work for two lifetimes, perhaps their children have grown up and flown the nest, and they want to experience what the continent has to offer while they can. Others just want to avoid the cold and gloom of Northern European winter.

The 'reasons' below are just some indicators of what you can expect from a long-term tour. They're there to fire your imagination, not to try and describe what will, in all likelihood, be an indescribable and deeply personal experience.

To Have an Adventure

Many of us crave personal adventure, and a long motorhome tour offers as much of it as you can take. Speaking a new language. Driving over a mountain pass. Eating a meal in an unfamiliar country. Snorkelling in a calm sea. Seeing a famous art gallery, or archaeological museum. The opportunities are endless.

To Chase the Sun

British winters have a well-deserved reputation for their grey, drab, wet, coldness. The feel of daily sunshine in winter is a joyous sensation, and plenty of long-term motorhome travellers enjoy it year-in, year-out. Andalusia in Spain, the Peloponnese in Greece, Sicily in Italy, all have much better winter climates than the UK and all see motorhome-dwellers sitting chatting over a glass of wine, eyes shaded with sunglasses in the middle of January.

To Escape

Go where you want, when you want, and stay as long as you want. There are no deadlines to meet. No reports to submit to the boss. No need to listen to endless bad news stories on the radio (even if you can understand the local language). One day you might be in France, the next in Switzerland, or Italy. Taking off in a motorhome is a very effective means of escaping the daily grind.

Freedom! Relaxed on a beach near Trogir, Croatia

To Learn

Europe's old! There's a lot to learn about the place, whether you're interested in the World Wars, Spanish fiestas or Sicilian cooking, it's all out there, at your fingertips. We were surprised to find ourselves interested in architecture after a visit to the Sagrada Familia in Spain. Touring our continent has enabled us to see everything from wooden huts in Norway and Finland built to protect from the Arctic winter, to baroque villages in Italy where we gawped at the incredible ability of stone carvers.

To Experience Natural Beauty

Living in a motorhome places you closer to nature. Opening the habitation door for a first-class view over a beach, fjord, mountain range, river or lake is one of the enduring wonders from our tours to date.

Rainbow watching in the Norwegian Fjords

To Meet New People

Doctors, airline pilots, retired Champagne makers, haulage company owners, B&B owners, policemen, IT managers, teachers, paramedics, drummers, you name it – we've met them all in their motorhomes. Encountering folks from outside your normal social circle exposes you to new ideas and concepts, which in turn can help steer your life in a new, unexpected direction.

To Live More Simply

Motorhome life is a life stripped back to the basics. Heating, washing, cooking, getting access to water and offloading waste all take up more of your thoughts than they do at home. This should be a hassle, but it's not. By replacing our thoughts with these simpler, more manageable challenges, the more complex, vague and unsolvable questions posed by modern life get pushed out. This has a pleasant, cleansing effect.

Long-term tours also generate masses of opportunities for simple walks, cycles, long slow meals, swims in the sea, time to read, learning a new (small) musical instrument, fishing, crochet, anything and everything.

To Live in Low-Cost Luxury

Motorhome life may be back to basics, but with your own bed every night, your own kitchen, wardrobe, heating, hot showers and cold beers in your fridge, it is a luxurious way to see the continent. Most couples spend less than £20,000 on a year's tour, some much less. Around £800 per person per month for touring across tens of countries is, in our opinion, pretty good value for money. For more on costs, see *Long-Term Living Costs* on page 203.

To Eat Good Food

On all but the tightest budgets, you can experience some delicious local grub. Spain's *menú del día* was a particular favourite of ours; get one in a less touristic spot and you'll be treated to three courses of quality food, including wine, for about €12 a head.

Gelato – Italian ice cream – surely the best in the world!

Italy and France fight it out for top spot when it comes to taste bud tingling. They are more expensive, but the quality's arguably higher. They do have some cracking lunchtime offerings in France, look out for a *menu du jour*. Croatia's food is simpler but sitting eating fresh baked fish against the azure Adriatic is just wonderful.

Is Long-Term Touring for You?

It's a common question for anyone pondering a long trip in a motorhome: is it for me? In the end, only you can answer that question, and perhaps the only way to find out is to give it a go? But before you rush off to buy a motorhome and head off into the sun, hold fire. Here are a few considerations from our personal experience, which might help you with the decision.

Small Space Living

A defining element of motorhome life: you'll be living in a very small space. Even the largest motorhomes are a fraction of the size of most bricks and mortar homes. Our current motorhome is 6m long by 2.2m wide, and that includes the wing mirrors and bumpers. The living space, which includes the kitchen, bathroom, lounge and bedroom, is roughly the size of a large family bathroom.

How will you get on in such a small space? We got on surprisingly well, perhaps partly because the restricted living area is offset with an unlimited amount of space outside. When the weather allows, there are loads of options for spending time out and about, which limits the amount of time in the van. When parked somewhere where 'camping behaviour' is allowed, we extend our living space outside with a camping table and chairs.

Splash Showers and Washing Machine Hunting

Unless you intend to stay exclusively on campsites, you'll need to make use of your motorhome's facilities. With a maximum of 100 litres or so of water on board, showers tend to be a 'get wet, stop water, shampoo and wash, rinse, stop water' type of affair, rather than a long, lingering hose-down. The water's hot though, and with blown-air heating we can warm the bathroom to a nice temperature.

Washing clothes is a bit trickier than at home. Hand washing or seeking out a washing machine becomes a periodic chore. But given the fact you've almost unlimited time on your hands, it won't feel too much like one.

Do You Have Children?

We've met plenty of people travelling with their children in a motorhome across Europe. Most home-school their kids while they're on the road, and report their children gain a real sense of the world they're a part of. As we don't have children, we're not qualified to discuss what it's like to travel with them. Instead, here are two of the best blogs we've come across written by people who motorhome with their children:

- *lifeinourvan.com* – loads of information from teachers Catherine, Richard and their girls Lottie & Libby on a multi-year tour of Europe.
- *tincanfamily.com* – another extensive blog about four family members travelling Europe and North Africa in an old Hymer.

Even if your children are grown up, you may still not feel you can leave them for a long-term trip. We've met lots of people who do several shorter loops, over a long period of time. This enables them to pop back to see their children and usually more importantly, their grandchildren.

Do You Have Pets?

Charlie, our King Charles Cavalier Spaniel, went everywhere with us on our travels. He spent over a third of his life travelling and, we like to think, enjoyed the vast majority of it! Fortunately for us, he travelled well in a motorhome, and we very much enjoyed having him with us.

We've met long-term motorhome dwellers with huge dogs, multiple dogs, cats walked on leads and even a parrot complete with a cage occupying half the lounge. Long-term motorhome travel with a pet is entirely possible, although obviously you'll experience a few restrictions such as not always being able to travel on public transport with them. In Spain, for example, you can't take your dog on the bus or train unless it's small and in a carry case.

Staying a UK Tax Resident

Tax and residency laws are complex and we're not qualified to offer advice on them. The following information is very much our personal opinion only.

Being UK citizens, we knew that travelling abroad for a year or two wouldn't alter our ability to come back, live and work in the UK. However, we were unsure what other implications there might be. Research turned up the HM Revenue & Customs Statutory Residence Test (SRT). HMRC use the SRT to determine if you're a UK resident for tax purposes. Using this test it was ambiguous as to whether we were UK tax residents, but as we were already completing UK self-assessment tax returns, we continued to do so, declaring all of our income on them. For more information search *www.gov.uk* for SRT.

Another area to think about is benefits. We don't receive any but check *www.gov.uk/claim-benefits-abroad* if you think you might be affected.

Finally, we were letting out our house in the UK through an agent, and once they were aware we'd be away for over six months they had to go through a formal 'Non Resident Landlord Scheme' process. This advises HMRC of our plans and could have resulted in the agent having to withhold tax from rent payments to us, but the HMRC allowed us to pay our tax through self-assessment returns instead.

Renting a Motorhome for a European Tour

An obvious option for shorter tours (a few months perhaps) is to rent a motorhome in a European country, rather than buying and selling. We've met Australians, New Zealanders and South Africans in rented German and UK registered motorhomes. The main downside to renting is cost, and also you cannot modify your vehicle. One couple were keen to fit an additional lock to their habitation door but they were nervous about this causing an issue when they returned it. Take a look at *www.mcrent.eu* for an idea of motorhome rental prices across Europe.

Getting a Motorhome for Free

What? Is this really possible? Yep, sort of. Some motorhome manufacturers lend out one of their vans for free, for months! The deal is normally that you need to promote their brand by writing a blog, recording and publishing videos of your travels and so on, so you will have to do some 'work'. David and Karen (*thegreygappers.co.uk*) and Hannah and James (*www.winterised.com*) both used Elddis motorhomes for free for several months in this way (*www.elddis.co.uk*).

Visas and Other Issues for Non-EU Residents

Plenty of Australians, New Zealanders and other non-EU residents come to Europe to tour in a motorhome. You can often spot them in a UK-registered motorhome, but with kiwi insignia, or Australian flags proudly showing their resident's true heritage. If you don't have an EU passport, check your home country's government advice on travel to the EU, and read the information on *europa.eu*. Here are a few points to consider before setting out:

- **Rent Versus Buy** – renting is the simplest option, removing the need to worry about insurance, servicing, repairs and registering the van in your name. It also removes the need to sink a large amount of capital into the vehicle. On the other hand, renting quickly gets expensive, provides a limited choice of layouts and removes the option to customise the van. Some travellers suggest only considering renting for trips of three months or less for this reason. If you do choose to buy, you could consider looking for a dealer who will provide a buy-back option, to provide some peace of mind around how much you'll get for the van when you sell it.
- **Storage** – if you plan to return home without selling the motorhome then you'll need somewhere secure to store it while you're away. UK storage locations are typically used for caravan storage, but will accept motorhomes too if they have space.
- **Visas** – EU residents don't need visas to travel between the EU countries (or for most other non-EU European countries). However, if you're not an EU resident, you need to check and understand the Schengen Zone visa-free travel restrictions. For some nationalities, visa-free travel allows 90 days of travel in the Schengen countries in any 180 days, for example. If you want to stay longer in the Schengen zone, or if you're not from a country which allows visa-free travel, you officially need to apply for a visa. We've met some folks who ignore this restriction (with the risk of being fined or banned from the Schengen countries), others who get around it by spending three months at a time in non-Schengen countries like the UK or Morocco and one couple who delved into their family tree and found they had grandparents from Malta so applied for and gained dual nationality.

- **Passport** – this needs to be valid for at least 3 months after the date you leave the EU and must have been issued in the last 10 years.
- **Driving licence** – EU residents are issued with an EU driving licence which can be used almost everywhere across Europe. Coming from outside of Europe you may need to apply for an international driver's permit or licence in your home country.
- **Non-resident insurance** – many motorhome insurers in the UK will not cover non-residents (we don't know if the same is true in other European countries). If you choose to buy your motorhome in the UK you may be limited to specialist companies for insurance (*www.duinsure.com* and *hertsinsurance.com/walkabout* are frequently mentioned), which are more expensive than normal UK insurers, and may limit the number of European countries they cover.
- **Breakdown Cover** – if you have cover in your home country, check whether they have reciprocal agreements with breakdown companies in the countries you want to travel to.
- **Registration address** – you'll need a local 'residential' address (not a PO Box) to register the vehicle to. Ideally a friend or family member in the country you buy your motorhome from could let you use their address.
- **Money transfer** – unless you have the funds in a local bank account to buy the van, think about out how to transfer the money from home. Any fee and the exchange rate will feature in your decision, as well as ensuring the money is safe during the transfer.

The 90-in-180-Days Rule

There is an important Brexit-related point to be aware of if you're planning to tour continental Europe for several months (or years) at a time. After the transition period is over, UK citizens will only be able to spend 90 days in any 180 days (3 months in 6) travelling as tourists in the 26 Schengen Area countries without applying for a visa (under EU Regulation 2018/1806). From 2021 we're also likely to need an ETIAS Schengen visa waiver (see page 101).

We'll be able to make multiple entries into the Schengen Area, but the total number of days in the area cannot exceed 90 days in 180. An important point: the 180 days is a rolling period, it doesn't get reset when you leave the Schengen Area. For example, if you travel to Spain for January to March, then you'll have to leave and remain outside of the Schengen Area for three months before you can travel to any other Schengen country.

Are Long-Term Tours Still Possible?

In a word, yes. If you plan a long trip to Europe, then the simplest way to work within this restriction on a year-long tour is to plan to leave the Schengen Area for a few weeks or months at a time, travelling to non-Schengen countries such as the UK, Morocco and Turkey. The example tour on page 197 illustrates this approach. Eire, Serbia, Croatia, Cyprus, Bulgaria and Romania are also currently outside the Schengen Area, and comprehensive motorhome insurance for these countries is easy to get (see the map on page 116). Croatia, Bulgaria and Romania are all legally obliged to join the area at some point in the future, so keep an eye on the latest status before planning to use them as 'waiting countries'.

You could also spend time in some of the lesser-visited countries in Europe or North Africa. You'll almost certainly have to buy 3rd party border insurance for several of these countries which will probably limit the length of time you can stay without spending a small fortune, such as Tunisia, Albania, Montenegro, Bosnia and Herzegovina, Russia (which also requires visas) and Ukraine.

Another option will be to apply for a long-stay visa in one of the Schengen member states. Be aware these are national visas though, and don't confer the right to spend longer than 90 days in any 180 in the other Schengen Area countries. Obtaining a long-stay visa for a Schengen country like France (*france-visas.gouv.fr*) might enable UK motorhome travellers to use France as a base, from which we could tour for three months at a time in the surrounding Schengen Area. It's difficult to see how the restrictions could be enforced for someone with a long-stay visa who stays within the Schengen Area, but bear in mind border controls can be enforced at any time, as they were in recent years as a result of large-scale migration, so you could be caught out trying to return to France (for example) having spent over three months outside the country.

There is much discussion on Internet forums around how tightly the 90-in-180-day rule is currently enforced (it already applies to US and Australian citizens, for example). There are stories of people overstaying their allowance by weeks or even months with consequences ranging from none, to a fine, to having 'illegal immigrant' stamped in their passport and affectively being banned from re-entry to the Schengen Area. These same forums indicate some countries enforce the rule much more rigidly than others. Our approach will be to work within the 90-in-180-day rule, at least until the situation has settled down and it is clear what legal alternatives there are, other than becoming resident in a Schengen country.

Planning to Leave

Leaving an established life in the UK to travel for months or years is never easy, at least not for us. Each time we do it we experience what we call 'the hump': the challenge of shifting from an entrenched, comfortable existence to a more adventurous nomadic one. This section runs through some of the topics we've dealt with when gearing up for a long time away.

MOT for a Long-Term Tour

If your motorhome is over three years old it will require an MOT each year to keep it road legal, and your insurance valid. You can only get an MOT issued in the UK, so if you are on a long-term tour you will need to factor this into your route plans.

If our MOT was due while we were away on a tour, we would get it done the week before we left, giving us a full 12 months before we had to return. You can also get your MOT done up to a month in advance and still retain its renewal date, giving you 13 months before you have to return. There is nothing to stop you getting an MOT in Dover, turning around and heading straight back to the continent.

Insurance for a European Tour

You'll need the right policy to ensure you're covered for your long-term motorhome tour. Consider these points when searching for insurance:

- Buy comprehensive motorhome insurance. Third-party won't cover costs to repair your vehicle in the event of an accident, so you could lose your entire motorhome's value.
- Check all the countries you plan to visit are covered by the policy. Some European countries probably won't be covered, like Albania, Turkey and Bosnia (and maybe Morocco if you plan to head for Africa). If you plan to visit these countries, ask if the insurer will issue a 'green card' – some may offer it for free while others may charge. This is a separate certificate which you can show at the border to demonstrate you have insurance for that country.
- If you can't get a green card for a country, you'll have to buy insurance at the border. This may limit the number of days you can stay, will be expensive per day, be indecipherable to you, and will almost certainly be third-party only. We've done this in Morocco, Ukraine and Bosnia, but have never had to claim on it.
- If you have rented out or sold your house in the UK, you'll probably need to buy a full-timing policy. This will be about double to three times what you'd pay for a '365 day' policy, which lets you travel for a full year at a time on the basis you MUST have an address you can come back to at any time.

- Check the small print on your motorhome insurance policy to ensure repairs can be done abroad.
- Check the small print on your motorhome and personal travel insurance to ensure there are no limit to the number of days per year you can be abroad.
- Some personal travel insurance companies require you to have been in the UK for six of the past 12 months, to consider you as a UK resident. If you plan to be outside the UK for over a year, consider buying a two-year policy to avoid or at least delay the impact of this restriction.

Getting Over the Hump

Whatever your motivation for hitting the road, you'll likely have your own 'hump' to climb to break away from 'normality'.

Maybe you need to rent your house out and sell or store your belongings, perhaps you have fears of being abroad without the immediate support you'd have from an organised holiday, and maybe you're concerned about living in such a small space with your loved ones. Everyone's got their own 'hump': the only support we can give is this: the hump is invariably worth climbing. At some point in your journey it will sink in: when you pull off from home, sat at the port, on the ferry or at your first overnight stop on the continent: you've done it. You're free. An entire continent awaits.

Selling a House

If you have a house in the UK, and don't want to rent it out, one option is to sell it. This isn't something we've opted to do, although we have gone through much of the process of downsizing it involves. If you do sell your house, you'll have these challenges to handle:

- **Selling almost everything**. Yes, you could pay for storage to keep some furniture, books and the like, until you buy another house somewhere, but you may find the costs exceed the value of the items stored. Selling and giving away a lifetime's things sounds romantic: our experience of it was anything but. It's hard work.
- **Needing a UK address**. You'll need a UK residential address to register the van, use for your driving licence and so on. A family member might offer to help.
- **What to do with the money.** We can't recommend selling your house to fund your travels, but of course it's your money. At the time of writing bank interest rates bobble along at roughly nothing, so if you keep the money in cash it will depreciate in real terms year-on-year as the cost of living increases. Some folks choose to invest the money in something else, perhaps a rental flat, bonds or share funds.

Renting Out a House

As an alternative to selling, you've the option to rent your house out while you're away. This could help cover the mortgage or, if you don't have a mortgage, provide you with an income. We've rented out houses in the UK for the past ten years, which now fund as much travelling as we choose to do, so the following information comes from direct experience.

Pros and Cons of Renting Your House Out

Whenever the subject of renting out your house comes up on forums, there always seems to be a steady series of comments decrying the whole idea. It's unclear how many of the commenters have actually rented out a house. While we'd agree that there are definitely downsides to being a landlord, they should be taken in context. Here are the main pros and cons we see as sometime travelling landlords:

Pros of Renting

- **Income** - this is obviously the main driver. After costs we see an income of around 3% of the value of a paid-off house.
- **House stays occupied** – leaving your house empty for months or years risks the garden going jungle, pipes freezing and bursting, vagrants moving in and the like. By having tenants, there's someone living in the property to keep an eye on it and help maintain it. This avoids problems with home insurers limiting your time away too.
- **Less permanent than selling** – you can let your house on an AST (assured shorthold tenancy) for six months. After that you could move back into the house with a couple of months' notice (we'd suggest giving as much notice as possible though) without needing to go through the cost and inconvenience of the selling and buying process.

Cons of Renting

- **Legal implications** – becoming a landlord makes you legally responsible for the safety of your house, and any deposit you take. You'll need to understand the implications, like gas and electrical safety checks, and make sure you take care of your obligations. A good letting agent will help with this.
- **Tax returns** – if you're not already completing a tax return, you may have to when you start letting your house out. You'll have to contact HMRC and tell them your plans, and they'll decide if they want a return each year. If the house is joint-owned, you can split the income which might reduce your tax liability, but this will mean completing a tax return each.
- **Mental association with 'home'** – having someone else living in your home can be a hard thing to handle. You'll need to think of your house as an asset to fund your adventures, and not your home, at least for the time you're away.

- **Resolving issues** – if you get a call while you're in Southern Italy telling you there's a water leak in your house, you need to be able to sort it. We use a letting agent who handles these calls for us, sourcing tradesmen and co-ordinating with the tenants to get repairs done. The agent also pays the tradesmen and gives us evidence of the costs for our tax returns.
- **Possibility of bad tenants** – some tenants may not take care of your house the way you would, and some will fail to pay the rent. In a decade of renting, we've not had this experience. We make sure we respond to any issues quickly, treating the tenants the way we'd like to be treated. Our letting agent vets tenants, takes references, and periodically checks on the properties for us. All of this perhaps helps us avoid bad experiences.

How Much Can You Earn?

In our area of the UK, a two-bedroom semi-detached house in good condition will cost around £120,000, and rent out for around £500 a month, or £6,000 a year (www.zoopla.co.uk is a good place to get an idea of these numbers). Keeping things simple and assuming no mortgage, that's a gross return of 5%. In reality, our experience as 'amateur landlords' saw a return closer to 3% of the cost of the house after we've paid letting agent fees, repairs, void periods (when the property is empty), maintenance and insurance. So, the same £120,000 house really returns around £2,400 to £3,600 a year, before income tax.

Your situation could be very different, so you need to do your own sums. If you budget for repairs and maintenance, you'll be more likely to make them quickly, which makes for a far better relationship with tenants. The point is costs will eat into your return, and it pays to be realistic in terms of what you'll actually see for spending on diesel, campsites, eating out and wine.

Using an Agent

A good letting agent is, in our experience, nigh-on-essential for anyone considering being a travelling landlord. They'll cost you about 10% plus VAT of your monthly rent but will handle critical tasks, enabling you to concentrate on hairpin bends rather than gas boilers while you're driving over the Alps. We avoid national agencies and use local agents with a dedicated letting manager, as we find the service is much better.

In return for your money, a good agent should provide these services:

- Give you a realistic estimate of the rental value of your house.
- Source tenants, take and check references and carry out credit checks.
- Ensure a legal agreement is in place between you and the tenant, normally an Assured Shorthold Tenancy.
- Take a deposit and legally store it.

- Ensure that the electrical and gas systems in your house are legal before the tenancy starts.
- Arrange for yearly checks on the gas appliances.
- Periodically check on the property for any repairs needed, and to ensure the tenant is keeping the property in good condition.
- Arrange for tradesmen to make repairs to your property while you're away.
- Carry out end-of-tenancy checks and return the deposit to the tenants.
- Most importantly, they are the first point of contact for any issues the tenant has and will deal with emergency issues, like a tenant getting locked out and needing a locksmith.

Knowing that we may be uncontactable sometimes, we agreed with our agent to make repairs estimated at less than £200, without getting our go-ahead. This helps to ensure small repairs and issues are fixed quickly.

Handling Snail Mail

For a home UK address, you can pay the Royal Mail to redirect your mail to another address for up to 12 months (*www.royalmail.com*). If you're away for longer, you'll need to contact the people sending the mail and change the address to that of a friend or family member who's happy to handle it for you. Alternatively, you could use a 'virtual address' service, where you get your mail sent to them and they scan it so you can read it on the road (*expatpost.uk* or *www.ukpostbox.com*). We've never used these services so can't comment on cost, security and so on.

Packing for a Year on the Road

Working out all the stuff you'll need for an entire year's travelling is, ah, fun. You'll likely see every type of weather, every type of water tap on this Earth, every kind of terrain. We've included *Appendix A* starting on page 219 to give you a starting point on what to pop in your cupboards.

Long-Term Travel with a Pet

We've met lots of folks travelling with pet dogs (some of them huge!), cats and even a parrot in their motorhome. It's entirely possible to take your pet with you, and it's worth having a quick read of these hints and tips while you're preparing to go:

- Each pet will need a pet passport (see *Taking Your Pet* on page 99).
- If you plan to travel outside of the EU check the Pet Passport status of each country you will be visiting. Countries such as Morocco are classed as 'unlisted' so your pet will require a blood test to prove the rabies vaccination was effective. The blood sample needs to be taken at least 30 days after the vaccination, and you'll need to allow time for the results to come back and a possible retest, so visit your vet to talk about your plans

as early as possible. If you want to do further research before talking to the vet you can refer directly to the EU regulation: search the internet for: Regulation (EU) No 576/2013.

- Research the countries you plan to visit for border restrictions for pets. On our tour around Scandinavia we found out that Charlie would need a tapeworm treatment from a vet before he could enter Norway (the same as you need before returning to the UK). As Norway and Finland have an agreement, it meant he would need the treatment before we entered Finland, so we found a vet in Estonia who sorted it for us. In reality if we'd found this out at the Norwegian border we could have turned around and driven to a vet in Sweden or Finland. If we had discovered it at the Finnish border it may have meant an expensive ferry ride back to Estonia to comply with the regulations.
- You can get annual vaccinations done abroad. We took our dog's vaccination history with us, and got his boosters done in Spain, Portugal and Italy on various occasions. The vets all spoke English, didn't expect us to make an appointment, completed his vaccination history sheet and pet passport and were highly professional. We made sure his rabies boosters were always carried out in the UK as having them done here means they last for three years as opposed to one year if done abroad.
- Our dog needed medication, so we packed enough for the tour. Where the medicine was prescription-only, we bought prescriptions from our vets so we could get more abroad if necessary.
- We used either Advantix or Scalibor flea and tick treatments which also protected against sand flies, and leishmaniasis.
- In Italy we struggled to buy the 'pro-active' type of worming tablets we use in the UK (they re-actively treat dogs once they have worms). After that we made sure we had enough worming tablets for a full year's travel.
- Despite being treated for ticks, our dog still picked up a few. We took O'Tom tick removers (one large, one small) and read up on how to use them.
- We found it impossible to consistently buy the same food as we travelled between countries. We took an initial supply of our dog's food and treats, and then got used to swapping him between local foods, depending on what was available. We weighed the different foods to ensure he got the right amount.
- We took on some jobs which we'd normally outsource when in the UK: we bought fur clippers which we ran on our 300W inverter. It was useful to trim his fur to help keep the van clean and keep him cool in hotter countries. Our vets also showed us how to empty his anal glands (a task which was hated by all involved, but necessary).

- We carried a travel water bowl, which folded up and dried quickly, when walking out and about, so we could make sure our dog was always hydrated.
- Dog poo bags are widely available, but not everywhere, so we made sure we had a good supply with us when we left the UK.
- Some countries require a muzzle, especially on public transport. Our dog refused to wear one, but we had one in our pocket just in case. In practice no-one challenged us, although he was a toy breed which helped.

Travelling with our pet dog sometimes limited the beaches, restaurants and attractions we could visit, but we wouldn't have changed it for the world. As we wrote on *ourtour.co.uk* back in 2017:

"Travelling with a dog is a heart-warming, endearing and fun experience. He's an endless source of hilarity and loyalty, and acts as a fantastic ice breaker. He's introduced us to a massive range of people, dog lovers in the guise of Tunisian kids, the Venice Port Authority, a gift shop owner on the side of Mount Vesuvius, a retired airline pilot in Greece and a huge range of other fascinating folks."

Checking your Passports
British adult passports expire every ten years, so check yours won't run out while you're on the road. Some countries require at least 6 months validity on entry, and some need blank pages, look through the 'Entry Requirements' sections on the UK Foreign Office website (*www.gov.uk/foreign-travel-advice*).

Seeing Your GP, Dentist and Optician at Home
If you are due a check-up at the dentist it might be worth going in case there are any issues. If they are like our dentist it may be worth asking them to hold off making any future appointments until you return, so you don't get charged for not turning up. It's also a good idea to visit your optician, and make sure you get a copy of your prescription, if you need one, so you can order more glasses or contact lenses from abroad if you have to. Ask your optician to make a note of your interpupillary distance if you wear glasses, as this isn't part of the prescription but you'll need it to buy glasses online.

If you've any issues your GP isn't aware of, now is a good time to go and see them. If you take regular medication you may need to see your GP and explain your plans to ensure you have enough medication to cover your trip. It's best to see your GP early, as some will only provide up to three months of medication, if this is the case you'll need to discuss alternative options with them.

There are no vaccinations recommended for Europe, other than routine ones for MMR, Tetanus and so on. When at your GP you may want to ensure your routine vaccinations are up to date.

Van Modifications for Long-Term Touring

Aside from the bits and bobs you need to do to make your van legal on the continent, like headlight deflectors, you should consider making the following modifications for a long-term tour.

Self-Refillable LPG Tanks

There's no standard propane or butane gas bottle across Europe. Once your UK Calor gas bottle runs out in France, you won't be able to get it refilled (at least not easily). A bottle bought in France won't be refillable in Spain, and so on.

One approach is to buy new bottles and pigtails (the pipe which connects the bottle to your regulator) and potentially regulators in each country. One couple we met were travelling with three part-used gas bottles stored under a bench, as they'd not been able to refill them once they crossed into new countries. This is obviously a pain, costs money and is potentially very wasteful if you can't return the bottles.

Most long-term multi-country tourers get a self-refillable LPG system instead. These are usually sourced from GAS IT (*gasit.co.uk*), Alugas (*www.alugas.eu*), Gaslow (*www.gaslowdirect.com*) or Safefill (*www.safefill.co.uk*). This allows you to buy gas from thousands of petrol stations across Europe. Look out for signs for LPG, GPL, GLP or Autogas - they're all names for the same thing – a mixture of propane and butane.

We opted for a GAS IT system and installed it ourselves. We went for one 11Kg and one 6Kg bottle, as the bulkhead regulator position prevented us from installing two 11Kg bottles (and we couldn't use an under-slung tank as the van is too low). In hindsight, we'd have moved the regulator to increase our capacity from 17Kg to 22Kg, but the lower capacity's not been an issue for us, and we've saved a few kilograms of weight using the smaller bottle. We retained an existing automatic changeover valve, which switches between bottles when one is empty, but our system has no safety cut off valve (which stops the flow of gas in the event of a major leak, perhaps caused by a traffic accident), so we turn the bottles off each time we drive.

We opted for an external refill point in a secure metal part of the motorhome skirt, rather than one in the locker, to avoid having to open the door at a fuel station. This is both for convenience (the locker door needs a fair bit of space to be fully open) and to avoid confusing fuel attendants, who might think we are illegally refilling 'normal' Calor gas bottles. Having used our system for over two years of touring, we're very pleased with it.

Our GAS IT refillable LPG system with auto-changeover valve and external filler

Instead of swapping an empty bottle for a full one, LPG bottles and tanks stay in your van (or slung under the van), and you use a specialised filler hose at fuel stations to pump gas back into them. You'll need a set of four adapters costing about £25 to ensure you're able to connect to the hoses across Europe:

- ACME Adaptor (Germany, Belgium, Netherlands)
- EURO Adaptor (Spain, Portugal)
- M10 Dish Adaptor (France, Italy)
- Bayonet Adaptor (UK)

To fill up your system:

1. Pull into the station and find the LPG pump (they're not always easy to see). Park with your filler on the same side as the pump, as the hose will often not stretch to the other side.
2. If your bottles are left 'on' for driving, isolate each of them before filling up. This isn't strictly needed but is advisable.
3. Depending on which system the LPG station is using (these can vary within a country, as well as between countries), choose the correct adapter and screw it hand-tight into your LPG system filler point.
4. Attach the filler 'gun' to your adapter, each type of adapter is slightly different, and getting the gun to attach properly can be 'fun'. We once visited several stations in Spain until we figured out how to get the gun to lock onto our EURO adapter. The gun has a trigger which locks it in place; the trigger doesn't start the flow of gas.

5. With the gun locked in place, step back and press and hold the filler button on the pump. You may need an attendant to enable the pump for you. The gas will start to flow and finally will automatically cut off. A valve in the bottles cuts in when they're 80% full. This is a standard requirement to keep the bottles safe. The flow of gas will almost stop at this point and you can release the filler button. Try not to press the emergency button on the pump, which may look a bit like the filler button, but trust us, it won't fill the bottles!

6. When you remove the gun, which you do by pulling the trigger again, a small amount of gas is released in a whoosh, which can be unnerving the first time or two you hear it. Take care removing the adapter as it will be cold, although we've never worn gloves for LPG filling. In some countries or specific filling stations, an attendant will do the filling for you.

Most countries have LPG stations, and gas refills are much cheaper than swapping bottles. Having said that, some LPG systems will cost you several hundred pounds to buy and have fitted (you can self-fit if you have the skills). The real value for us is more in convenience rather than the reduced cost of the gas, although we do you use the system heavily so will now be saving money.

Be aware that LPG stations are few and far between in some countries, so you'll have to plan ahead to ensure you don't run out. *www.mylpg.eu* is a good resource for finding stations, and *www.lpgstations.com* has a great map for seeing which countries have LPG. Don't rely too heavily on these websites as sometimes sites are closed, never existed, have run out of gas or might in rare cases refuse to fill your system.

There are no LPG stations in Finland and Morocco. In Finland it was summer for us so it wasn't difficult to make our gas last. In Morocco we easily toured for three months by staying on campsites, and using hook-up for running the fridge, cooking on a hotplate and so on.

One restriction of self-refillable LPG is the fact you have to take the van to the filling point, you can't bring the gas to the van. If you want to spend a month in the Alps skiing, you may need to decamp and drive off to find an LPG point to fill up, even if gas bottles are for sale in the resort. One way around this, if you have the space, is to have one self-refillable bottle, and a local propane bottle and pigtail. We've also met folks with a local bottle sat next to the van connected with a special high-pressure hose to the LPG refill point.

Tyres
There are endless debates about the best tyres for a motorhome. We're not experts, although having suffered a blowout from using old tyres we do now focus more on the rubber stuff than we did before. As the tyres are your only

contact with the road and we do a lot of driving, we think it makes sense to spend a bit more cash to get the right tyres.

We use a 'Mud and Snow' (M+S) motorhome-specific tyre: the Michelin Agilis Camping tyre. We're not recommending you do the same, but here are our reasons why:

- We sometimes tour over winter and in some countries tyres must have at least the M+S mark on the sidewall to be legal in winter. These 'mud and snow' tyres don't have to pass rigorous tests to achieve this designation, unlike 'full winter' tyres which have an Alpine marking (a mountain icon containing a snowflake – the Three Peak Mountain Snowflake or 3PMSF).
- If we planned to drive straight up the Alps and stay there all winter and come home again, we'd use full winters as they will offer more grip than M+S tyres. As we usually carry on touring into the summer, M+S tyres are a good compromise for us. Note that Germany has recently changed the tyre law to require full winter tyres, so it's worth researching the latest law there if you plan to visit.
- We have a set of snow chains, in case of heavy snow and ice, although we've only needed to use them once.
- We use motorhome-specific tyres as they've been specially designed for heavily loaded vehicles which sometimes stay parked up for months at a time, loading the same spot of the tyre.
- We picked the Michelin make as they meet the above two requirements and were available when we needed them, not for any other reason. So far they have performed well, although after two years use (including 18 months of long-distance touring) the front ones needed replacing.

Chemical-Free Toilet - SOG Unit

A SOG extraction unit enables you to use your toilet without chemicals. It removes the smell associated with the loo, and helps break down the waste within, simply by pulling fresh air through the cassette. A SOG is helpful for long-term touring as:

- It removes the need to find, buy, carry and use chemicals.
- It enables you to empty the cassette as often as you want, without worrying about wasting chemicals.
- It enables you to empty into sensitive systems such as the long-drop or composting toilets found in rural Scandinavia and the Baltic states.

Some long-term tourers use biological washing liquid or powder as an alternative to chemicals. We've tried these too but found the SOG unit to be more effective.

The SOG unit can be retrofitted to most motorhomes and consists of a fan fitted to the door for your chemical toilet, a microswitch which turns the fan on when the blade to the loo is open, and a pipe which feeds air through the cassette and out through the door via a charcoal filter. The unit costs about £120, plus fitting costs if you don't install it yourself.

Ours has worked very well, the only issues being an occasional smell outside the van when the fan is running in hot weather, the fact that men need to sit down to pee to stop smells coming back into the van, and we had to replace the microswitch after three years. The charcoal filter needs to be replaced at least annually to cut down on smells outside.

Solar Panel and Additional Leisure Battery
Having a 100W solar panel or two, coupled with one or two leisure batteries, is very helpful for long-term touring. Along with split relay battery charging from driving, and the odd recharge from mains hook-up, a solar system has generated all the electricity we've needed in summer touring. If you've found a fantastic aire or free camping spot, it can save you from being forced to move by running out of 12V power.

Blackout/Insulated Curtain Lining
Our van has curtains and pull-up blinds which together do an OK job of blocking bright light. We've lined the curtains with thermal blackout material, which means we can use just the curtains to keep us in the dark, and also to help keep us warm or cool in temperature extremes.

Personal Satellite GPS Trackers
While not strictly a 'van modification', we've heard of, but never used Personal Satellite GPS Trackers like those sold by SPOT LLC (*www.findmespot.eu*). You can use them to tell people where you are, or call for help, via satellite when there's no mobile phone signal. Personally, we haven't felt the need for one, as mobile phone voice networks are pretty much ubiquitous in Europe and North Africa now, and 3G and 4G internet data access is widespread. We'd perhaps only consider one if we planned serious hiking in remote areas, but if you're travelling alone, for example, you might find one offers peace of mind.

Secondary Transport – Bike/Car/Quad/Motorbike
One disadvantage of a motorhome is they're not as easy to get around in as a car or a smaller van. They tend to be on the larger side making parking trickier, and you have to securely pack everything away every time you move. Understandably, lots of people carry some form of secondary transport so they can leave the motorhome stationary and explore the local area.

Push bikes (some battery power-assisted) are the most common option, and we've also seen loads of motorhome garages, trailers and rear racks carrying mopeds. One couple we know would split up while they drove: one of them in the motorhome and the other in a car. Lots of motorhomes, especially ones which stay long term on campsites, tow a trailer with a small car, motorbike or quad bike.

We've only-ever carried push bikes with us and we haven't used them a great deal. As we tend to drive frequently, we pick up groceries from supermarkets en route, rather than needing the bikes to get them. In general, we seek out parking places within walking or public transport distance of wherever we want to visit.

If you have a motorised form of secondary transport, consider these things:

- If you have a trailer, remember the weight limits imposed by the trailer make and model, and your motorhome's tow limit. Trailers can make parking more awkward, and the spaces in most aires assume your van doesn't have a trailer. You'll also need to carry proof of your trailer's EU certification.
- If you're thinking of using an A-Frame, do your research on the countries you plan to travel through to ensure it is considered legal in each of them.
- If you store a moped on a rack or in a garage, think about its weight, and how easy it is for you to load and unload it. Some folks fit an electric winch to help pull the moped into the garage.
- Check your breakdown cover includes the second vehicle.
- You'll need insurance for the bike or car, for all the countries you plan to travel to, as well as UK road tax and MOT.
- Budget for servicing costs.
- Think about security. It's relatively easy to steal expensive electric bikes from a rack, or when they're locked up out and about.

Dogs aren't always allowed on public transport outside the UK. You can't take a dog on the bus in Spain unless it fits in a small bag and in some cases, such as Hungary and Italy, your dog will need to wear a muzzle on public transport (although the rules weren't enforced for our small dog). This might mean you need a car or quad bike, or a bike with a dog trailer or carrying basket, to enable you to take your dog with you into cities. You could consider hiring a car or using taxis, rather than taking one with you.

Places to Go

With an entire continent at your disposal, there's no shortage of places to go and visit. Where to go is entirely up to you, woo hoo! This section only aims to generate a few ideas and things to think about while planning. Guides like Lonely Planet (*www.lonelyplanet.com*) and the Rough Guide (*www.roughguides.com*) are great for finding out about the more popular places. That said, some of the very best experiences we've had were at places not listed in any guidebook, we just came across them by accident or fellow travellers pointed us towards them.

For thousands of colour photos, videos, GPS co-ordinates, ideas of costs, stories and more from across all the countries mentioned below, nip over to *ourtour.co.uk*.

By Season

If, like us, you find yourself sweltering hot in southern Spain, Hungary or Croatia in the summer months, you might wonder why on Earth you didn't head north for the summer. Same for winter, but the other way around. Having driven for what seemed like an eternity in the northern Spanish rain in December, we wished we'd headed south more quickly in the autumn. Most people have more sense than us and have a rough plan in place to be in the south in winter, and north in summer.

Some of the typical areas folks head in winter are Andalusia in Spain, Algarve in Portugal, the Peloponnese in Greece, Sicily in Italy and (outside Europe of course) the area around Agadir and the Anti-Atlas Mountains in Morocco. Of these, Spain, Portugal and Morocco are probably the busiest, although if you head inland you can still find places if you want to be alone.

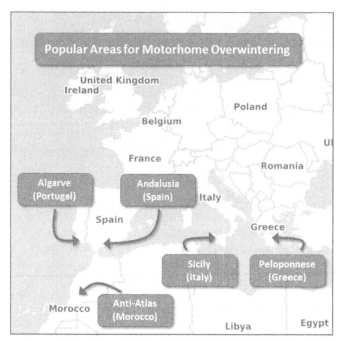

The far north of Europe opens up in summer, and you can easily drive high into the Arctic Circle in Finland, Sweden and Norway in relative warmth, plenty of daylight and without needing specialist tyres. In July and August, you might see only the smallest patches of snow, even in the far north, unless you're alongside a glacier.

The Arctic sun stays up all night, so we ended up making eye masks to help us to sleep, and a mosquito net comes in very handy in Finland! In late August we were once even lucky enough to see the Northern Lights, south of Bodø in Norway.

Christmas at Giardini Naxos in Sicily

By Country

We've provided a very short summary of our experience of touring some European countries (and Morocco) by motorhome. It's based entirely on our opinions formed during the time we spent there. On another trip, we might alter that view. For far more information on each country, have a look at *ourtour.co.uk*.

We've included this section to give some idea of what you might find, and where you might want to explore. These short notes can't hope to offer anything other than the briefest of insights into each country from a motorhoming perspective. Hopefully the information will give you a starting point from where you can do your own research, using some of the links in *Appendix B* starting on page 230, into things such as:

- **Local Driving Laws** – some countries require your dipped headlights to be switched on even in bright daylight, for example.
- **Tolls** – does the country have toll roads, tunnels or bridges? If it does, can you avoid them? If you need to pay, how do you do so?

- **Low Emission Zones** – does the country have them, where are they, do you need a sticker to access them, and can you legally access them?
- **Currency** – does the country use the Euro, or has it retained its own currency? What is the best way to obtain cash and pay for goods and services?
- **Overnight Locations** – What options are available to you: free camping, paid parking, aires, campsites, local businesses? Also get an idea what the situation is for service points: are there any free ones, are they provided at fuel stations, are they only provided at campsites and so on.
- **Maps** – do you have a good paper road map for the country? Does your satnav have the country map? Have you downloaded the *maps.me* offline maps (or equivalent for other navigation apps) for your smartphone?
- **Time Zone** – are you crossing into a new time zone?
- **Language and Alphabet** – although you may not speak it, knowing which language(s) the locals use is useful. Some countries use Cyrillic or Greek alphabets, which you don't need to know but should at least be aware of.
- **Internet and Phone** – will your internet and phones work in the country? Do any price caps apply or might you need to buy a local SIM, for example?
- **Cost of Fuel** – due to government taxation, diesel prices can change dramatically at borders so it pays to fill your tank on the right side!
- **Cost of Food and Drink** – grocery and alcohol shopping can be significantly more expensive when you cross borders (Switzerland and Norway both being expensive). Within duty-free limits, it pays to stock up before you cross.
- **Phone International Code and Emergency Numbers** – realistically as a tourist you probably won't be calling anyone locally, but if you do you'll need to know the code to dial before the number. For example, to call a German number, first dial 0049, and then the local number after removing any leading 0. Numbers for emergency services vary between countries; they generally use 112, but not all.
- **Public Transport** – if you intend to use public transport, be aware that some countries (Spain in particular) will refuse to carry most dogs on public transport. Plan accordingly if you have a pet.
- **Schengen Area** – once the Brexit transition period is complete, it will be necessary for UK citizens to know which countries are in the Schengen Area and which are not, so they can ensure they comply with the 90-in-180-day rule.

Austria

Our tours haven't yet taken us up into the mountainous Tyrol region of Austria, although we have crossed the lowland areas to the east a couple of times, including a visit to the capital Vienna, where we stayed at a stellplatz conveniently close to a city-bound railway station. As with Slovenia to the south, you'll need a vignette to use the toll roads, or a GO-Box if over 3.5

tonnes. That said, outside of Vienna and the Tyrol, Austria kindly allows 24 hour stays in legal parking places, enabling you to keep your overnight costs down.

Our impression of Austria is that it's a clean, safe, easy and pleasant country to travel by motorhome. If you plan to cross the mountains in winter you'll need to take care to ensure the passes are open, and that you have suitable tyres and chains. Otherwise there are a myriad of stellplatz, campsites and car parks where you can enjoy the clean, beautiful countryside, villages and towns.

Belgium
Just a stone's throw from the Northern French ferry ports, you can use free French motorways to be in Belgium within an hour. Once there you'll find a fairly relaxed attitude to motorhomes, with aires spread across the country, as well as campsites and free camping places where authorities and locals tolerate an overnight stay.

Belgium has a reputation for a few things: great chocolate, strong ale brewed by the monks (or whoever the monks sold the rights to), badly surfaced roads and pleasant old town centres. We'd agree with them all, although the roads aren't as bad as you might imagine, and while you will rumble along on them, the motorways are toll-free.

Bosnia and Herzegovina
Bosnia proved a fascinating country to us, although the expensive Green Card insurance sold to us at the border limited our stay to just a few days (we've since met others who haggled and got their insurance cheaper). Before visiting, our knowledge of the country was limited to memories of TV news footage showing military action and the atrocities in the 1990s. Despite being in evidence in the capital of Sarajevo, the country and international community have clearly made an enormous effort to spring the city forwards, and it felt a vibrant place to be. Although Mostar's famous bridge has been rebuilt, the rest of the city was still in need of significant investment after being all-but destroyed.

Ghosts of war aside, a chance encounter with some locals during a particularly hot spell scored us a fantastic tip: to visit the waterfalls at Kravica (GPS: N43.15849 E17.60839). For a few euros (taken in preference to local currency), we stayed overnight in the car park above the falls, enjoying hours of cool air by the waterfall in the day, as local youths proved their worth by leaping from the small cliffs.

Bosnia's still off the beaten track for motorhomes, which is reflected in the relatively small number of places to stay. That said, checking the latest *park4night.com* database there are easily enough places for a short tour of the country. One of our most memorable stays in all of Europe was the quirky Camping Paradise south of Mostar (GPS: N43.26911, E17.86447), where the

170

owner Sasha, a tee total Muslim, presented us with unlimited free cold beer and home-made grappa, while his Doberman patrolled around our van attempting to get at our dog inside. Bizarre, but unforgettable.

Bulgaria

Being in the EU, Bulgaria has no need for an insurance Green Card to travel into, so makes for an interesting and easy way to traverse the Balkans north-south or vice versa. The main roads are in fairly good condition, the motorways (such that they are) are free and there are plenty of campsites and free camping locations to stay in.

Abiding memories of Bulgaria include the enormous communist era statues extolling the virtue and power of work (these are still in place all over the country), delicious and low-cost meals out, Cyrillic road signs, dilapidated villages, the use of horse and cart as a viable mode of modern transport and welcoming people everywhere.

We generally stayed in car parks in Bulgaria: for example, at the chairlift to the beautiful Rila Lakes (GPS: N42.24274, E23.32441), outside the historic Rila Monastery (GPS: N42.13545, E23.34633), and in the centres of small towns and villages. But we also used the British-built and run campsite a few km from Veliko Tarnovo which we enjoyed (GPS: N43.075674, E25.617151). Even if you don't take the option to freely park overnight, Bulgaria is an inexpensive country to motorhome through.

Croatia

Despite being just a short drive from the Italian border, Croatia seems to remain relatively low on many British itineraries. Why this should be is a mystery, as the country is an EU member, and a delightful destination, with pure-blue Adriatic waters, beautiful stone-built coastal towns, relaxed islands, inland waterfall networks, delicious food and a great climate.

One thing Croatia isn't good for is free camping: the law against off-site overnight parking is well policed along the coast, so budget for campsites during your stay. Some sites are enormous, almost small theme parks, or you can find yourself practically in someone's back garden at a mini camp (*www.camping.hr/mini-camping*). To keep costs down, and avoid the heat and crowds, we recommend travelling in the shoulder seasons of spring and autumn and bringing your ACSI discount camping card. Also, unless you're seeking a naturist/nudist site, check to ensure your chosen site isn't partly or fully FKK (*www.camping.hr/croatian-campsites/naturist-camps*).

If you want to visit the islands, some, like Krk, have bridges which you simply drive across to reach them. For others you'll need to take a ferry, which you just turn up to, buy a ticket at the booth, and queue for the next available boat. The roads on some islands (Hvar comes to mind) are quite narrow, but easily passable in a motorhome with care. In some cases, to avoid a long back-track, you might take a bridge to get onto an island, and a ferry to get off at the other end, like we did on Pag.

Czech Republic

The Czech Republic is pretty much a mainstream destination for motorhomes, especially as it's right on the border with Germany, one of the biggest motorhome-owning countries in Europe. Although there is a relatively small number of aires, there are plenty of low-cost campsites and free (or low-cost) parking areas to enable you to tour the country at ease. If you like your lager, you can visit the home of the original Budweiser, and be sure to stock up before you leave the country. The lager's high quality and comes at a budget price.

We particularly enjoyed Prague, with its convenient Camping and Caravan Yacht Club campsite a few meters from the Vltava which slices Prague in two (GPS: N50.06167 E14.41423). A short ferry ride takes you across the river where we grabbed a tram into the city. On the way to Prague, we stayed in an official stellplatz a short walk from the lively and picturesque South Bohemian town of Český Krumlov with its UNESCO-listed castle (GPS: N48.84410 E14.36320). On the way from Prague back into Germany, we 'loved' sampling the range of egg-smelling mineral spring waters at Mariánské Lázně, where we were welcomed overnight in a nearby car park (GPS: N49.95902 E12.70183).

Denmark

We found Denmark to be a quiet, easy-going country to motorhome through. Our stopovers included a cheeky night in Copenhagen, right outside the gates to the Carlsberg Experience (handy after a few included beers), an official aire next to Kronborg ('Hamlet's Castle') at Helsingør (GPS: N56.0404, E12.6161), and a port-side aire within cycling distance of the extra-ordinary modern art at ARoS Kuntsmuseum in Aarhus (GPS: N56.13956, E10.21995).

We opted to use the bridges between Sweden and Demark, rather than a ferry, taking the Øresund Bridge from Sweden to Zealand and the Storebælt Bridge from Zealand to Funen. If you follow this route, be aware both bridges are toll, although you can pay in cash at booths. To ensure that you are charged the correct price, have your V5C to hand and use the manned lanes at the toll stations.

Estonia

Free camping was the order of the day in Estonia, where we enjoyed the countryside feel of the place, parking overnight in a variety of car parks without a care in the world. Except for the mosquitos that is, which were as ferocious as they were numerous at our free campsite in Soomaa National Park (GPS: N58.43074, E25.03012)!

With the exception of the cruise-ship-visited capital of Tallinn, Estonia didn't feel like a tourist destination to us. The towns were easy going. Modern shopping centres were available (with Western European prices), as well as plenty of smaller supermarkets to stock up at. We had no trouble finding places to stay, including within walking distance of the capital at Tallinn City Camping, a glorified car park open in the summer months, but felt calm and secure (GPS: N59.448, E24.80888).

Estonia was one of the countries where we opted to buy a local prepaid SIM card. Like in a few countries, these were conveniently available from a supermarket (in Croatia you can get them from the post office) and were already enabled and topped-up, so no need to speak the local language.

Finland
Driving across Finland feels a little like being in a computer game, where the roads are arrow-straight and all there is to see either side of the road is forest, for hours on end. Of course, if you intend to blat through the country end-to-end, that's likely all you'll see, and the fact there is no refillable LPG available will force some to do just that. There are no toll roads in Finland.

We spent about a month in Finland and came away with some of the best memories from years of touring. Like being sat in a smoke sauna surrounded by naked locals, then putting our swimming costumes on to run outside and jump into the cool of a lake (*www.rauhalahti.fi/en*). Or laughing at the antics at the World Wife Carrying Championship in Sonkajärvi, where the prize is the wife's weight in beer. Or driving, led by a small herd of reindeer as they bounced along sticking to the road, in no hurry to take to the forest. Or the great pleasure of a first night's sleep under the mosquito net we bought and fitted over the bed in the van, knowing we'd be the meal for no-one that night!

As far as overnighting goes, Finland is very easy. We freely parked in walking distance of the centre of Helsinki (GPS: N60.17213, E24.90405), and alongside lakes, by the beach, next to rivers and in the car park of a hotel. As well as a few motorhome aires, Finland provides motorhome service points in various locations like petrol stations (look out for ABC and Teboil stations), as well as obviously providing emptying facilities at campsites. Water supplies are often in heated cabinets, so can be used in winter but may need a key from the fuel station attendants to unlock.

Caravans and motorhomes are more closely aligned in Finland than the rest of Europe. Caravan drivers will wave at motorhome drivers for example, and caravans are as likely to use aires as motorhomes.

France
France has to be one of the easiest, if not *the* easiest country to take your 'camping car' (motorhome) to. French culture is highly inclusive towards

motorhomes, and there are thousands upon thousands of campsites, aires, service points and free camping locations spread across the country. LPG's available all over the place. Some supermarkets even have service points, laundrette facilities and a petrol station in the car park, so you can leave topped up on wine, LPG and diesel, wearing fresh-smelling clothes!

France is also, obviously, one of the easiest countries to get to from the UK, with various ferry options and the Channel Tunnel. If you choose to use the fast roads in France, you'll need to dip into your pocket to pay the tolls but will be rewarded with nigh-on empty roads. You can pay tolls in cash. There are also fast roads which are free in France. Check your map carefully and you'll spot them, like the A75 running up over the Massif Central from southern France, the N57 to the east of the country (useful for getting to the Alps), and the motorways in Brittany.

The country offers a huge range of landscapes, from the historic D-Day landing beaches of Normandy all the way to the high peaks of the Alps, the rolling vineyards of Champagne and the gorges and lavender fields of Provence. All accessible in your motorhome, with aires and campsites located conveniently close by. Many towns and cities are also easily accessible, with parking facilities located within walking or cycling distance, or using public transport.

Germany

If you take a copy of Camperstop Europe, and look at the edge of the unopened book, you can see at a glance how many 'stellplatz' (aires) there are in each country using the colour-coded page edges. France and Germany occupy about the same thickness of pages, and together make up about half the entire book. Germany is one of Europe's great motorhome destinations and has an incredible range of campsites and stellplatz to match that reputation. Being Germany, their quality is usually very high in terms of location and facilities.

Our own travels have taken us across much of the country. Secure motorhome parking locations outside Hamburg, Berlin and Munich enabled low-cost visits to some iconic cities. More stellplatz saw us enjoying low-stress travel along the Rhine, through the Black Forest and across the delightful old towns of Bavaria.

Germany also has the rather useful feature of free 'autobahns' (motorways). These smooth, fast roads enable you to make rapid progress around and through the country at a low cost, making it a popular transit route for motorhomes heading for Austria, Switzerland, Italy or Central and Eastern Europe.

If you're travelling in a more sedate fashion, check your map and ask at tourist information offices for the many tourist routes across the country: we enjoyed sections of the Deutsche Alpenstraße (alpine route), Deutsche Märchenstraße (fairy tale route) and the Deutsche Weinstraße (wine route).

One thing Germany is perhaps not so good for is the waistline. At least not in Bayern (Bavaria) with its schweinshaxe (baked pork knuckle) and giant one-litre Maß jugs of cold lager!

Greece

Greece has to be one of our favourite countries to travel through in our motorhome. The country offers an almost-unbeatable combination of friendly people, ancient history, delicious food, laid back attitude, wonderful scenery, relatively low costs and warm climate.

Our tour of Greece started in Patras which, along with Igoumenitsa, is one of the ports ferries sail to across the Adriatic from Italy. We 'camped on board', meaning we could stay in our motorhome on an open ferry deck, keeping our dog Charlie happy and enabling us to sleep well, cook and run the fridge on the electrical hook-up provided.

All of our previous trips to Greece have been flights to Islands, and we'd no idea what to expect of the mainland. We needn't have worried. A spring tour of the unspoiled Peloponnese, Athens, the Pelion Peninsula and Halkidiki proved a delightful experience.

We stayed on a combination of campsites, free camping and parking areas alongside tavernas which happily welcomed us in return for eating a meal. Although free camping is technically illegal, a blind eye is turned in many places. At times we were stayed in places which felt out of this world: alongside the entrance to Acrocorinth's ancient citadel (GPS: N37.88992, E22.86828), just around the corner from the jawdropping monasteries of Meteora (Hotel Arsenis, GPS: N39.70857, E21.65424), and several times right alongside the ocean where we could snorkel from the habitation door.

In terms of ancient sites, we loved all of Athens, except for the crowds (we stayed at Camping Athens, GPS: N38.00920, E23.67271). Visiting Delphi we got there early and enjoyed the heart-warming, sun-splashed mountain vistas almost to ourselves (we stayed a short drive away at GPS: N38.35183, E22.37989). We managed to pull off a similar trick at Olympia, wandering the site with just a few others, posing at the start line of the athletics track and staring in wonder at the ancient carvings in the site museum (we stayed the night before at Katakolo, GPS: N37.64765, E21.31770). The acoustics of the Epidaurus theatre amazed us. The list goes on.

Hungary

We've only stayed at a handful of locations in Hungary: at a campsite in the thermal spa town of Harkany (Termal Kemping at GPS: N45.85616, E18.23896), free camping by the country's enormous and shallow Lake Balaton (GPS: N46.71554, E17.3280), at the well-placed and friendly Camping Haller city campsite in Budapest (GPS: N47.47572, E19.08351) and free camping overlooking the Danube at Visegrad (GPS: N47.796653, E18.996542). *Park4night.com* currently lists over 400 places to stay in Hungary, so you should have no trouble making a much more extensive tour than us.

Our experience of Hungary was of a modern country, which was easy to motorhome through. We had some fun trying to stick to non-toll roads to avoid the cost of the vignette, but in the end gave up and bought the sticker from a garage, to avoid the stress of it all! Perhaps the most difficult thing about Hungary is the language, which came across as utterly incomprehensible to us. Most folks we encountered spoke at least some English though, especially in Budapest.

Italy
When we first started touring, we were often be advised there are few places to stay in Italy, that the roads are terrible, drivers are suicidal and we should generally avoid the place. Come to think of it, we've heard the same thing for several countries, and it's not yet proven to be true. Well, not entirely true. The roads aren't great, and you do come across the odd driver who thinks they are on the Ferrari test track!

We've toured Italy a number of times, including Sicily, and always end each tour with a kind of love-hate sensation. The vibrancy of the Italian people is infectious, with their outgoing nature being epitomised by the 'passeggiata' where the whole town comes out for an evening stroll and a delicious, rich gelato (ice cream). The beauty and grace of the old centres in many towns and cities is legendary, bursting with art, history and architecture, and Italian food is to die for.

But on the flip side, the urban sprawl is depressing, with graffiti everywhere. The beaches in the north are largely ruined with uncontrolled development, deserted out of season and pay-per-seat in high season. Rule breaking seems to be a national sport, which translates to the roads and car parks too, adding stress to driving and parking across the country.

With all that said, would we recommend a motorhome trip to Italy? Oh yes. Our tours have taken us from the beautiful grey rock, jagged Dolomites, past the northern lakes, through the Borolo vineyards, the hilltop towns of Tuscany down to the empire city of Rome. Into the south, we spent a few memorable days around Naples, sleeping high on Vesuvius, peering around Pompeii and being flung about by the crazed Amalfi Coast bus drivers (motorhomes are banned from the route in the daytime). Naples itself stands stark as a reminder of Italy's age-old north-south divide, surrounded by poverty, and yet inspirationally frenetic too.

Further south the larger towns and 'sostas' (aires) thin out, and free camping became the norm for us out of season. Our most memorable stays were on the lava-clad slopes of Mount Etna, at the Trulli stone houses in Alberobello, and the end-of-Europe port town of Palermo. We spent Christmas with fellow motorhomers over-wintering in Giardini Naxos on Sicily.

The country has a great network of sostas and campsites, although the quality isn't generally as high as you'll find in France and Germany. You're normally allowed to free camp without interference from the police, opening up thousands of overnight spots. LPG is widely available and although the diesel isn't cheap, the opportunity for low cost overnight stays easily makes up for it. When filling with fuel take note: you'll pay more for attendant service, that's why two prices are shown for each fuel. If you go to the self-service pumps, and fill up yourself, you effectively get a discount.

Italian motorways are toll, not as flat as we'd like, occasionally rammed with roadworks and have daft-short slip roads in places. But sometimes they're definitely worth paying for. The toll road around Naples comes highly recommended, as does any section of road when Italy's tight mountains routes simply become too much for the frazzled driver.

The very centre of old towns are usually off-limits to visiting motorhomes and cars. These areas, called ZTLs, are heavily sign-posted and automatically policed with cameras. In most cases you'll need to be a little unhinged to drive a motorhome into a ZTL anyway, as the roads are Fiat 500 territory, far too tight for a lumbering wagon (see page 120).

Latvia

Our introduction to Latvia was an overnight location just a few meters from the pristine beaches and surprisingly warm June waters of the Baltic Sea. We were bemused to find a motorhome camping area, complete with fire pits, electric hook up and disposal point, after we'd parked at the other end of the area thinking it was just a car park. At €14 for 24 hours, over weekends and in the summer, it wasn't a cheap stopover, but the access to such a beautiful beach was worth it (GPS: N57.03836, E23.40254).

Latvia's capital city of Riga proved an interesting place to visit. We found paid parking within walking distance of the city (GPS: N56.95399, E24.08127), and enjoyed the covered markets, packed with locals, inside old Zeppelin hangers.

After the excitement of two Baltic capitals and a lot of driving, we really took to the bucolic, friendly Kempings Apalkalns at Raiskums (GPS: N57.31756, E25.14966), with an open lakeside feel, top-notch facilities, and fire pits with unlimited firewood.

Lithuania

Although our visit to Lithuania only lasted a few days, Vilnius, the capital of Lithuania, was one of our favourite capitals to visit. Staying in the car park of a lively backpacker's hostel (Downtown Forest Hostel and Camping, GPS: N54.67793, E25.30221), we could easily walk into and around this compact, laid-back city.

Outside the capital, the enormous communist-era statues and museum pieces at Grūtas Park left their mark on us. Motorhomes could stay overnight in return for a few Euros (GPS: N54.02469, E24.07854).

A monument in defiance of the previous anti-religious communist authorities, was the incredible Hill of Crosses in the north of the country, where again we were allowed to use the car park overnight for a small fee (GPS: N56.0145, E23.40861).

Luxembourg

From a motorhome traveller's perspective, Luxembourg is famous for one thing: low taxation! The price of diesel and LPG is fixed across the country, and at a relatively low cost compared with its neighbours. With no tolls on the motorways, the detour could be worth your while just to stock up on fuel.

The country, small as it is, is also a pleasant place to visit in its own right. We stayed on a paid car park right in the centre of the capital, which was a little noisy but a great spot for a quick foray around the city (GPS: N49.61661, E6.12367). Further out, the Mosel flows along the southern border, with the opportunity to sleep alongside it surrounded by vivid green, vine-clad slopes.

Morocco

We've spent several months in Morocco over two winters. We loved it so much that after our first trip we wrote a guidebook giving practical advice for anyone wanting to independently tour this fascinating (and admittedly a little challenging) country. We fully revised the book in 2017 after our latest visit, and again in 2020, and were really pleased to see an increase in the number of British vans over there. The book is available as a paperback or eBook, just search *amazon.co.uk* for 'Motorhome Morocco'.

Netherlands

The Dutch are both a nation of campers, and a nation of linguists. There are campsites and aires across the country, and everyone speaks English. Although the Dutch are a welcoming bunch, their country is as heavily populated as the British Isles, so you'll be more likely to pay to park overnight than in France or Germany. On the flip side, the roads are toll-free, the towns accessible and the whole country is generally well kept and a pleasure to travel through. One favourite for us was the Den Helder Maritime Museum, which has a submarine to investigate and an aire in the car park (GPS: N52.472747, E4.639247).

Norway

Whenever people ask us our favourite countries to motorhome through in Europe, Norway always features in the answer. Why? Because of a combination of things: incredible landscapes, an edge-of-civilisation feel, the right to roam which enables motorhomes to stay overnight in some simply stunning locations and access to free 'Bobil – tømmestasjoner' (motorhome service points).

Norway isn't small, so if you plan to head from the south up to Nordkapp (the North Cape), allow plenty of time. Even if you don't detour off to the great fjords, with their twisting roads and ferries, the distances are long, speeds slow and speeding fines high. Given these facts, and the wonderful nature of the country, we'd recommend allowing as much time as you can; we were lucky enough to be there for 11 weeks.

You'll need to time your visit too. During summer you can find yourself in a sleepless daze as it's still broad daylight at 2am in the Arctic Circle, but the flip-side is very long nights in winter. Our visit was timed to be in July and August, which gave us pleasant weather even in the far north and no need for snow tyres or chains. Outside the summer months it would make sense to research likely snow conditions and temperatures and understand what equipment you might need to ensure your stay is safe, comfortable and legal.

Although Norway isn't in the EU, most insurance policies will cover it, just check the wording or ask your insurer to be sure. There are manned borders with controls on what you can import and export. Food is very expensive in Norway, especially anything with sugar in it, so stock up with as much as you can before you arrive. Tax on alcohol renders it exorbitantly expensive for many outsiders, but if you try and import more than the allowed amount there are stiff penalties if you're caught.

Poland

Although 'camping' in Poland generally still means the use of a tent, motorhomes are increasingly well catered for. You won't come across many dedicated service points, but you'll find plenty of friendly campsites where you can stay for not much money.

Poland is another country where we've been able to stay overnight within an easy walk of the capital city centre. We used a guarded parking just a few minutes from the old centre of Warsaw which, despite being near a busy road, gave us a great night's sleep (GPS: N52.25070, E21.01568).

Although you will come across some pretty poor road surfaces in rural areas, the majority of the roads we came across were in good condition. Driving etiquette left a little to be desired, especially on the road into Warsaw where a two-lane A road became three lanes, with the middle lane taken by whoever was the craziest.

One of our favourite underground escapades was in Poland, at the Wieliczka Salt Mine outside Kraków. The guided tour into the mines felt like stepping through the screen into one of the Lord of the Rings movies, with wooden structures towering up into the darkness above us. The car parking attendant at the mines happily allowed us to stay a few nights in return for a few Zloty, so we could visit Kraków by bus (GPS: N49.98494 E20.05279).

Poland's turbulent and disturbing 20th Century history is evident in a number of places across the country. We paid our respects at the Auschwitz-Birkenau concentration camp, walked the destroyed bunkers of Hitler's Wolf's Lair and got a sense of the audacity needed to pull off The Great Escape at Stalag Luft III, outside the town of Żagań. All easily accessible by motorhome, if not easily digested.

Portugal

Many UK tourists will know the southern Algarve region of Portugal, for its great winter climate, low cost eating out, friendly locals and sandy beaches. A good number of motorhomes head to the campsites and aires in Algarve for over-winter stays as a result.

Portugal has lots more to offer if you want to tour. The inland 'barragens' (dams) often provide free camping places where you can spend a night or two alongside the dam and its adjacent lake. Free camping alongside the ocean's generally tolerated out of season, and there are plenty of beaches away from Algarve which you can enjoy alone.

We've enjoyed visiting some of Portugal's heritage too. The old university town of Coimbra, once the capital city, welcomed us with a free river-side motorhome aire a short walk from the centre (GPS: N40.19928 W8.42897). Out for a meal one evening with fellow motorhomers from the aire, we were serenaded first by joyful end-of-year students in their black gowns supping jugs of Sagres beer, followed by a somewhat more morose 'Fado' band at a bar.

Remember that Portugal is on the same time zone as the UK not its neighbour Spain, which caught us out for quite a while on our first visit there.

Romania

The reputation for appalling road surfaces had us nervous about driving in Romania, but our experience was of new tarmac and smooth rolling. If anything our progress was impeded more by roadworks improving the roads, than by the roads themselves.

Romania is in the EU and has no border formalities or need for an Insurance Green Card to cross. While it doesn't have an enormous network of campsites and aires, overnight parking is generally tolerated in car parks, such as those at the country's painted monasteries.

We were drawn into the Dracula-inspired tourist traps in Transylvania (along with everyone else), but we preferred the majestic, sweeping curves of the Transfăgărăşan Pass. For a few euros we stayed overnight at the top of the pass, taking in the views and watching locals summer snowboarding (GPS: N45.60252, E24.6138).

Although clearly a relatively poor country compared to the Western European nations, Romania's towns and cities were a surprise to us. A friendly family who allowed us to free camp outside their house during the Red Bull Romaniacs Enduro (motorbike) event persuaded us to visit nearby Sibiu. While part of the taxi route was a mud road, the town itself stood proud, with a beautiful square surrounded by well-maintained buildings very similar to those found in Germany. We enjoyed a delicious, surprisingly low-cost meal in a vaulted ceiling cellar restaurant.

Slovakia

As we'd visited the capital Bratislava on a previous (non-motorhome) trip, we opted to travel through the country's smaller towns and cities. For us, Slovakia retained a relative backwater feel to it, with decades of missed investment showing through in crumbling town centres and suburbs. The flip side to this is the relative acceptance of free camping across the country (outside the capital).

The highlight of our short tour was a few nights spent in the car park at the Lomnicky Peak cable car up into the High Tatras Mountains (GPS: N49.16773, E20.2714). We enjoyed a delicious meal in the alpine style village, as well as walks in the woods and the cable car itself (although the weather closed in so views at the top were limited).

Slovenia

Tourism has long generated a good income for Slovenia, and the country happily welcomes motorhomes, although you'll be expected to use campsites and aires (*www.avtokampi.si*). To use the motorways, you'll need to buy a vignette at the border, or obtain a DarsGo Device if you're over 3.5 tonnes (*www.darsgo.si*). For these reasons, Slovenia isn't as cheap a country as you might expect.

Some of the big tourist draws are the picturesque Lake Bled, the diminutive capital of Ljubljana, the Julian Alps and Postojna Caves. These are all easily accessible by motorhome but be aware of snow conditions if you plan to travel in winter.

Spain

The climate of Spain draws large numbers of British, French, Dutch and German motorhomes for the winter months, almost exclusively along the southern coast. Although you're not guaranteed a shorts-n-T-shirt time in January, you're much more likely to see the sun than back home in Blighty.

Spain's a great country to travel by motorhome and has a reputation for its low cost of living. Campsites, especially in the north, close out of season, and there are fewer aires than you'll find over the Pyrenees in France. That said, free camping is fairly well accepted outside the heavily-visited coastal areas to the south, and there are an increasing number of aires being created in the popular areas. LPG is also widely available in Spain. Less than 20% of Spanish motorways attract tolls, and several routes have been made toll-free in recent years. On the whole, Spanish roads are in very good condition and, away from the big cities and the Med at least, empty of traffic.

Spanish cities are simply superb places to visit for their vibrancy, architecture, food and wine. The country is formed from several 'autonomous communities', each of which has its own distinctive feel, history and often language. San Sebastian, 'Donastia' in the local Basque tongue, is one of our favourites, just over the border from France with its 'pintxos' bars, and its own 'aparcamiento autocaravanas' (motorhome parking) just a mile or so from the curved bay (GPS: N43.30796, W2.01485). To the south, we loved the architecture of Seville, staying a bus ride away at a marina (GPS: N37.34032, W6.02336).

If you're crossing from France into Spain, you can avoid the Pyrenees by hugging the coast. If you opt to climb over the mountains in winter (this is general advice for any mountain range), check your route beforehand to ensure your chosen pass is open. Sometimes you're forced to use a tunnel in winter for some passes, so don't get the 'topping out' experience at the very highest point of the pass.

Sweden

Visiting Sweden after experiencing the natural high of Norway, the clean and safe streets, free aires, woods and lakes felt gentle but if we're honest, also a little boring. We've heard the same from people driving through Finland after Norway. If you plan to visit Sweden, you might want to go before you visit Norway to get the biggest impact from it.

The highlight of our stay in Sweden was a few days in the capital of Stockholm. Although a capital, the city retained a charming, easy-going nature, and we recommend a trip to see the *Vasa*, a 17th century ship lifted from its untimely resting place on the sea bed a short distance from where it was launched. Another museum we loved was the IKEA museum in Älmhult, housed in the building which was the world's first IKEA, where they kindly allowed us to overnight in the car park.

Switzerland

While parked among a few motorhomes in a large parking area at the top of a mountain pass in Switzerland, we had a knock on the door. Opening it, a friendly face asked, in accented English, "what are you doing here?" Thinking we were about to be evicted from our paradise spot, we hesitated to answer. "I mean, we never see a British motorhome up here"! It turned out to be a friendly Swiss couple and over a delicious bottle of Swiss wine, they explained how they've toured their country for years, and never used a campsite. Parked where we were, with views across the majestic Alps, we could understand why.

We followed our new friend's lead, and freely parked on several mountain roads, but we also used some great aires and campsites. Our first campsite, supermarket and fast food purchases were each an expensive shock to the system! You can save a fortune with an ACSI discount card if visiting out of season. As well as paying for an annual vignette for the toll roads, the high cost of commodities makes it well worth stocking up before you arrive, and otherwise steeling yourself for the prices. Our view was we were paying for the scenery, and it was well worth it.

Switzerland has its own version of the three-pin plug, so you may need an adapter at some sites if you want to hook-up and rubbish must be disposed of in a specific type of taxed bin bag (which cost around £3.50 each).

Clearly, like any mountainous country you need to be aware of conditions in winter and ensure you've the right equipment. In warmer months, knowing how to engine brake is essential to safely manage your brakes on the epic descents. Other than that, welcome to paradise.

Ukraine

Our few days in Ukraine were a pretty intense experience! Having travelled north through Bulgaria and Romania were we feeling brave and decided to give the country a try. Having muddled through the heavily-manned border, clutching an indecipherable Green Card insurance document we'd just bought, we soon discovered that the much-maligned road surfaces in Britain are a dream to most Ukrainians.

Ukraine isn't, by and large, a motorhome destination of choice. There are nigh-on zero campsites, practically no motorhome aires and no service points. In places main roads were so deeply potholed across their width, they were almost unpassable in a two-wheel drive motorhome.

As is often the case, the people of Ukraine came to our rescue. Our first stopover was outside a hotel we picked at random in an act of desperation. Once we'd managed to explain we didn't want a room but would sleep in the van, the staff bent over backwards to help us, moving cars and finding someone who spoke Spanish to communicate with us (sadly we don't speak Spanish).

Our second stop was at a guesthouse, where the owner confirmed by email our van would fit on his driveway, and then refused payment for two nights of parking. On a bus into L'viv, we were astonished when people on the packed bus paid the driver by passing their money forwards from person to person, with the change returned in the same way.

Unfortunately, we can't recommend a tour of Ukraine unless you have a relatively rugged motorhome. If you plan to visit, research the road conditions on your planned route before you arrive. Would we have missed our few days there though? Not for the world.

By Feature

Another way of looking at our European continent could be the diverse range of landscapes, cities and cultures it offers, all of which are accessible to motorhome travellers. We've provided a brief look at some of these features, purely as a catalyst for your own thinking as you work out your own adventure.

Mountains

Large parts of France, Spain, Norway, Switzerland, Italy and Austria are mountainous. On our first long tour, we eyed the outline of the distant Pyrenees from Biarritz with excitement, and nerves. Did we need winter tyres? What about snow chains? Were we too wide and heavy? Would our engine manage the long ascents? What about our brakes, were they up to the long descents?

Since then we've crossed the Pyrenees several times, been over and under the Alps, crossed the Carpathians in Romania, skirted the High Tatras in Slovakia, roamed along Norway's Scandes and enjoyed the High, Middle and Anti-Atlas ranges in Morocco. As well as these high ranges, we've traversed thousands of miles of lower altitude mountain terrain, particularly in Greece, Slovenia, Croatia and Bulgaria.

Mountains often offer good free camping options, particularly at the top of passes outside winter, where parking is provided for tourists. Some charge small amounts, some are completely free, but as a rule no passes have motorhome services. They can be windy and cold, so come prepared. Ski resorts often have dedicated or tolerated areas for motorhome parking, especially during the winter season when you may find yourself within easy reach of slopes and lifts, parked for free or a relatively small fee. Outside of winter, car parks for lifts are frequently quiet and make great places for a free night's sleep. Ski resorts can be pretty dead in summer, especially custom-built ones, but some double up as hiking and mountain biking venues making them lively as a result. The views from these mountainous spots can be stupendous.

Auris en Oisans French Ski Resort in summer

Some favourite mountain pass sleeping places spring to mind: the Transfăgărășan Pass in Romania (GPS: N45.60252, E24.6138), the Oberalppass in Switzerland (GPS: N46.6584, E8.67104), the Sierra Nevada in Spain (GPS: N37.09363, W3.38664) and the Rila Mountains in Bulgaria (GPS: N42.24274, E23.32441).

Volcanoes

Believe it or not, you can nip down south into Italy, drive up and sleep on an active volcano in your motorhome. Mounts Vesuvius and Etna are both relatively easy to park up on, high on the slopes, and stay the night.

We parked at a café on Vesuvius (GPS: N40.82846 E14.42685), having driven a short distance from the visitors car park which is a short walk from the crater. The view down over Naples at night was breath-taking.

On Etna we stayed at car parks on both the north (at the Piano Provenzana cable car station, GPS: N37.79708, E15.04155) and south slopes (at the Rifugio Spaienza, GPS: N37.69926, E15.00042). On our second visit the volcano was erupting every few days in a series of spectacular paroxysms, blowing ash and lava high into the Sicilian air. Yep, we'd made sure the fiery action was some miles away from where we were parked.

Lakes, Rivers, Canals and Wetlands

If you're into watersports, swimming, or are simply drawn to the serenity of a reflective body of water, you'll enjoy the huge range of lakes available across Europe. We found we could often park close to lakes and take a cooling dip in them, even the more famous and heavily visited ones like the Italian Lakes, Lake Geneva in France and Switzerland, and Lake Balaton in Hungary.

Lakes can make great, quiet and free places to spend a night. Portugal's range of barragens (dammed lakes) are one good example, as are Finland's huge array of lakes, but come armed with a mosquito net if you head here! If you plan to fish, research the local licence and permit requirements beforehand.

Europe's mighty and historically rich rivers are within easy reach when you're touring by motorhome. The Rhine, Moselle, Danube, Dordogne, Seine, Loire and many others have aires and campsites along their banks, giving the chance to tour long them, sleep beside their majestic flows, and imagine how life was alongside them in centuries past.

If you're an ornithologist, then southern France's Camargue is easily accessible from multiple car parks and aires in walking distance (we stayed at a popular aire in Saintes-Maries-De-La-Mer, GPS: N43.45399, E4.43827).

We've also enjoyed nights spent watching enormous barges plying the commercial shipping canals in Germany and the Netherlands, parked alongside their banks for the night. Many canals have switched industry over time, easing off the gas and carrying tourist traffic only, such as France's Canal du Midi which has a range of aires along its length. Greece's Corinth Canal might have been the most impressive channel we witnessed, including its amazing submersible bridge.

Fjords

Norway is the only country in Europe for fjords, despite what any over-zealous tourist offices in other countries might tell you. The epic scale of these cliff-sided inland seas makes it nigh-on impossible to imagine they were cut by mere ice.

We stayed high above Geirangerfjord at the Dalsnibba Viewpoint, one of Norway's simply incredible custom-built viewing areas (GPS: N62.04894, E7.26941). The road up to it was in great condition, although it attracted a toll. At the smaller, more intimate Naeroyfjord some fellow van-dwellers gave us a tip for a free camping place alongside the calm waters of the fjord (GPS: N60.90123, E6.8618).

The Lofoten Islands in Norway

Touring the fjords of southern Norway was a wonderful experience, and we enjoyed crossing them on the many ferries you're obliged to use unless you want to take enormous detours. If you've a motorhome longer than 6m, just be aware the cost of these ferries increases significantly with every additional metre.

Glaciers

Many high mountains carry glaciers on their backs, hulking seas of snow compacted into deep blue ice. If you're into hiking you can get some stupendous view of glaciers in the Alps and Norway. If you're not, not to worry, we've been lucky enough to park our motorhome beneath them in various places without getting out of breath:

- In Norway at the fantastic Melkevoll Bretun Camping at the foot of Briksdal Glacier (GPS: N61.66384, E6.81679).
- In France beneath the glaciers around Mont Blanc in Chamonix (roadside tolerated parking, GPS: N45.92827, E6.87674).
- In Switzerland, at the end of a toll road below the Sustenpass (GPS: N46.72937, E8.447023).

Caves and Gorges

Europe is peppered with caves, some of which are truly enormous. We've visited the famous Postojna Caves in Slovenia and the smaller but no less atmospheric Diros Caves in the Greek Peloponnese, where we stayed at the beach below Pyrgos Dirou (GPS: N36.64122 E22.38325).

If gorges are your thing, you'll find plenty of them on a European tour. We'd no idea most of the gorges we came across existed when we left home, but very much enjoyed driving and walking through them. France's Gorges du Verdon in Provence are well worth driving along, taking in the huge 800m tall cliffs. The Gorges du Tarn in Haut-Languedoc are less dramatic, but make for a fun day's canoeing (so we're told, we watched from the bank).

The Picos de Europa Mountains in the north of Spain were a welcome surprise to us, where we discovered the Cares Gorge deep within them. Driving to the start of the gorge walk at Arenas de Cabrales was a nerve-wracking experience though, and we ended up walking the last three miles to avoid the low hanging cliffs and narrow mountain road. The walk is 9km long, and although we only managed the first short section, clearly deserved its fame.

During a house-sit near Abdalajis in Andalucia we heard about the Camino Del Rey, another famous gorge walk. Until recently the walk was more of an adrenalin-fuelled climb, requiring skill and equipment to safely traverse a crumbling concrete path high on cliff faces. The walk's since been rendered safe for anyone to walk, and tickets for it are in demand so book ahead to be sure of a place.

On a much smaller, more intimate and fun scale, the Vintgar Gorge in Slovenia was a fabulous detour for us. Again a safe pathway has been built above and across the gorge, fairly low down to the flowing waters and almost an experience in meditation compared with the more intense cliff-drops mentioned above.

Beaches
We could devote an entire book to Europe's beaches, as we've enjoyed months on end up against the Mediterranean, North Sea, Atlantic, Adriatic, Baltic Sea, Irish Sea and more. The more northerly areas of Europe hold as much beauty in their beaches as those further south, if not more. The white sands of Mull in Scotland and the similarly pristine beaches of the Norwegian Arctic spring to mind.

Free camping at Toroni in Greece

The Pylos Peninsular in Greece was also a particular favourite with us, a network of small coves where we enjoyed a few days free camped alone above an idyllic beach at Lambinou (GPS: N39.36015 E23.21332), complete with its own *taverna*.

One area where the beaches were a disappointment was northern Italy. Rampant uncontrolled development's left a legacy of shanty shacks, tacky restaurants and cafes along miles on end of beach-front. Out of season these are dead, locked and an eyesore. In season the beaches are rent-a-space, packed along their length. Southern Italy's and Sicily's beaches were a far more relaxed, natural affair.

For snorkelling, we found stony Greek and Croatian waters to be the best, offering endless visibility and (sometimes with a wetsuit) enough warmth for long, comfortable forays.

Roman Ruins
One thing you can't help stumble across when touring Europe: the Romans! Unsurprisingly there are a huge array of sites across Italy, Rome being the most obvious, along with others we visited on our motorhome tours: Pompeii, Agrigento, and Sicily's Taormina and Piazza Armerina. In Tarquinia we enjoyed a visit to the tombs of the Etruscans, predecessors of the Romans, staying in a car park at Tarquinia Lido (GPS: N42.22789 E11.70270).

We've visited the magnificent amphitheatre in Nîmes, France and nearby Pont du Gard, sleeping in a free aire a mile or two away at Remoulines (GPS: N43.93817, E4.55861). We've slept in the shadow of the Pula amphitheatre in Croatia, walked the ruined town of Conímbriga (Portugal), stood above the Roman theatre in Plovdiv (Bulgaria), and wandered around a fair few other smaller sites.

Cities
Clearly Europe's peppered with magnificent, ancient cities. With a dog in tow, and mindful of security, we found it possible to visit lots of them with a little planning.

In Rome we stayed on the outskirts at the Village Flaminio campsite, using a nearby train to access the city. In Barcelona we found Spain doesn't allow dogs on their bus network, so abandoned the idea of using a campsite outside the city and instead stayed at a secure car park a couple of blocks from the Sagrada Familia (sadly no longer available). In Florence we used the Social Camper Firenze guarded sosta (GPS: N43.76236 E11.20930), a short bus trip away from the city. Prague provided the Camping and Caravan Yacht Club campsite on an island in the Vltava River (GPS: N50.06167 E14.41423), a simple but cheap site, just a boat ride away from the centre. Camping Haller in Budapest (GPS: N47.47574 E19.08428) was again a simple affair, but very friendly and helpful, and a short walk to the underground (which allowed our dog). In Athens we again used the city campsite, Camping Athens (GPS: N38.00920 E23.67271), taking a bus and underground into the centre to look around.

Vineyards
There's something enchanting about sleeping in among vines, especially when they're thick with green leaves and fat, swollen grapes. Why this is, is a mystery, perhaps the fact they're often accompanied by warmth, sunshine and calm?

France's Champagne region, and all other wine-producing regions are easy to visit by motorhome, check out the section on *France Passion* on page 90 for information about this fantastic scheme. There are free aires in among the vines, where you can see names like 'Moët et Chandon' written on plaques, claiming particular slopes for certain houses. Some of the less well-known houses even provide free aires, and in one such place we enjoyed a couple of glasses in a tasting, bought a bottle of their champagne for €15, and had a free overnight spot provided with a service point and electric hook-up, not bad value for money!

At a France Passion site in Monbazzilac, France

In Italy we got a tip-off to visit the Barolo-producing region in Piedmont, where we found ourselves in among the gentle vine-clad slopes, staying in various free sostas, entertained by the three wheeled Ape vans, and supping the odd glass of red. Further south, more free and low cost sostas provided atmospheric sleeping spots as we slowly trundled across the Chianti region in Tuscany.

Scenic Trains
The tiny, but modern Diakofto to Kalavrita mountain train in northern Peloponnese in Greece proved a fascinating trip. We stayed by a beach overlooking the Gulf of Corinth the night before (GPS: N38.20196 E22.19415), taking the train for an hour up through tunnels and gorges to the village of Kalavrita, a pretty place but sadly infamous for being the site of a WW2

massacre. After a moving walk around the village, we took the train back down, entertained by walkers coming up the track and squeezing alongside the train as it crawled past; only in Greece?

On a much grander (and somewhat more expensive) scale, the Flåm Railway in Norway is a very popular tourist attraction. The train winds its way up a valley through an impossible series of tunnels and steep climbs before returning via the same route. We stayed at Flåm Camping (GPS: N60.86303, E7.10643), a short walk from the station the train departs from and returns to, but there were plenty of motorhomes in the car park just for the day.

Finally, the Gornergrat Bahn smoothly carries you from Zermatt in Switzerland up to Gornergrat (at an altitude of 3,089m) in 33 minutes. In good weather, the train's large, clear windows offer beautiful views of the Matterhorn and surrounding mountains. From Gornergrat the vista across 4000m peaks and glaciers is jaw-dropping. We stayed at Camping Attermenzen in Randa, a few miles down the valley (GPS: N46.08571, E7.78168), and took the train up to car-free Zermatt.

Museums
On any European motorhome tour you'll soon feel like there are over a billion museums. Don't feel obliged to visit them all, or indeed any of them! We quickly learned to only take in those we had a personal interest in, or which seemed quirky and unique. The same goes for what's inside each of them: at first we felt we should be absorbed by every single object, learning over time that we might only find a few pieces of interest, which would be enough to make the visit worthwhile.

Some of the more memorable museums for us were the Maginot Line underground fortifications in eastern France, a tiny tile museum in Palermo (Sicily), Amundsen's Fram in Oslo (Norway), the enormous Deutches Museum of technology in Munich (Germany), the Museum of Egyptology in Turin (Italy) and the National Archaeological Museum in Naples (Italy). Whatever your taste in museums, there's one out there for you.

Fiestas and Festivals
While we've largely come across local events by accident, it pays to plan ahead so you don't find you missed them by a day or two. We really enjoyed the sound and light show, mechanical dragons and, of course, a few samples at the Champagne festival in December in Epernay, France. The town provided free motorhome parking and free entry for this remarkable event.

At Gythio in the Greek Peloponnese we found ourselves carrying lit candles, and being deafened by fireworks in the street, with a crowd of locals celebrating our second Easter of the year. A few days earlier we'd witnessed a more formal parade in Italy, which is Catholic, while Greece is Eastern Orthodox.

In Spain we've somehow managed to miss the vast majority of the legendary fiestas which take place there. Partly this was deliberate, as our dog Charlie was afraid of fireworks which often accompany these events. Celebrations there, like Semana Santa (Holy Week) in Seville, are huge. Plan ahead if you want to attend or avoid the hustle and bustle they naturally create.

Christmas can be an interesting time to be touring. We've found ourselves celebrating with friends we've met while on the road, eating in the sunshine and swimming in the sea. It can be a little lonely too though, as we found one New Year's Eve in Evora, Portugal when not a soul was to be seen in the streets, and all the restaurants and bars were closed.

Ideas for 12 Month Tour Routes

Europe's rather a large place, and there's a lot to see! The routes we followed were largely driven by three things: the rate at which we wanted to move through each country, the climate, and whether we could visit a country without needing special insurance or a visa. Our planning was done on the road, we didn't work out routes in much detail before we set off. We only booked into one or two campsites in advance in four years of travel.

Most folks who opt for a long-term adventure will take in several countries, but you have the freedom to do whatever you want. We've met folks doing all sorts with their time on the road including:

- David and Karen (*thegreygappers.co.uk*) who chose to spend an entire year touring Spain, tasting the country's gastronomic delights, before exploring more countries.
- Catherine and Chris who took three years to visit every country in Europe (*theworldisourlobster.com*), including Iceland.
- Adam and Sophie (*europebycamper.com*) who took a very similar route to *Example Route 3* on page 196 in 2011-2012.

The following routes are provided to give you a few ideas about route planning. There are infinite variations you can take, and there's no 'rule' you have to be on the road for 12 months. We've made all the example routes a loop coming back to the UK, because if your vehicle is old enough to need an MOT, you'll need to come back to the UK for one. All the routes set off and return to Dover. However you could the ferry from Harwich to the Hook of Holland or Newcastle to Amsterdam, or go straight to Spain on routes to Santander or Bilbao.

Example Route 1: Stay West!

This route stays largely to the West of Europe, although it includes some of the countries to the East of the old Iron Curtain. It can easily be extended to include more of the East, but it's already a fairly ambitious route for 12 months. Depending on when you set off, you may want to follow the route in reverse.

Example Tour Route 1

A few key aspects of this route:

1. Take a ferry or the Channel Tunnel to France, turn east.
2. Travel across Belgium and the Netherlands. There are tons of campsites and aires across these countries, and the motorways are free if you choose to use them.
3. Cross over into North-West Germany. Again free motorways and lots of aires. Stock up on food and booze before heading into Denmark. You'll have to pay a 'pfand' (deposit) on cans of beer, so keep them uncrushed for when you return.
4. Head north for a taste of Scandinavia in Denmark, which regularly gets one of the top spots in surveys of the World's happiest countries.
5. Travel back south into former East Germany, perhaps popping into Berlin.
6. Head into the Czech Republic for a taste of history, great food and legendary beers.
7. Cross Austria, avoiding most of the mountains for the time being by staying east.
8. Explore the rural delights of Slovenia and the beaches, towns and restaurants of Croatia.

9. Back north up through Croatia and Slovenia into Italy, popping into Venice for a look around.
10. Head down to historic Rome, and back up through Tuscany.
11. Take stunning mountain passes up and over the Swiss and French Alps and into France.
12. Enjoy Provence and the south of France before heading around or over the Pyrenees and into Spain.
13. Hug the Mediterranean coast through Spain, taking in a few *menú del dias*.
14. Amble around low-cost Algarve in Portugal before heading north.
15. Back into Spain in Galacia, across the north, with perhaps a detour into the Picos de Europe, and back into France via the Pyrenees.
16. Have a look around France before heading back home.

Example Route 2: The Arctic to Greece!

This is a full-on North-South route, topping out at Nordkapp in the Norwegian Arctic and dipping as low down as the Greek Peloponnese. It mixes up Western Europe with the old Eastern Bloc countries, and offers some magnificent terrain, cities and cultural experiences. Don't underestimate the time needed to get from Sweden to the top of Norway. This is a stunning part of the world, so you'll want to take your time, but you'll also struggle to average more than 40mph on most Norwegian roads. Again, depending on when you set off, you may choose to do this route in reverse.

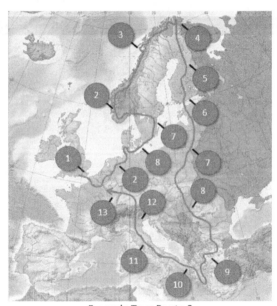

Example Tour Route 2

A few key aspects of this route:

1. Take a ferry or the Channel Tunnel to France, turn east.
2. Travel across Belgium, the Netherlands and Germany to Denmark. Stock up big style on food, beer, and anything else you might need before entering Denmark as you're not going to see 'reasonable prices' again until you get to Estonia. Be careful not to go too mad though: Norway's not in the EU and has import limits, and German cans and bottles have a deposit (a 'pfand') on them, which you won't get back until you go back to Germany with your uncrushed cans.
3. Cross the magnificent Øresund Bridge from Demark to Sweden.
4. Head up to the archipelago city of Stockholm before turning west, crossing into Norway and popping into Oslo for a few days.
5. Enjoy the fjords, glaciers and islands of Norway as you head north up into the Arctic, finally topping out at the North Cape.
6. From here it's south, through the endless trees, reindeer, lakes, mosquitoes, sausages and saunas of Finland, until you reach Helsinki and take the 'booze-cruise' ferry to Estonia.
7. The next stage takes you through the Baltic states of Estonia, Latvia and Lithuania, with small, manageable capitals and a generally easy-going atmosphere for motorhome travellers.
8. Meander south through Eastern Europe: Poland, Slovakia, Hungary, Romania, and Bulgaria all EU countries where your insurance will cover you and you'll find plenty of opportunities to overnight.
9. Arriving in Greece, where you could easily spend weeks exploring ancient sites, towns, beaches and tavernas.
10. A ferry from Patras or Igoumenitsa will whisk you across the Adriatic to Italy. Between April and October check to see if 'camping on board' is available. This allows you to sleep in your vehicle on an open deck, with your pet if you have one. The ferry staff hook you up to electricity so you can still run your fridge and, if you have an electric hob or oven, cook. You still have access to the other ferry decks too.
11. Make your way north again, up through Italy, perhaps taking in Rome, Pisa and incredible Venice as you head towards the Alps.
12. Cross the Alps into Austria, taking in the famous Großglockner Pass if you arrive in the summer months.
13. Head for home via Bavaria and the Black Forest in Germany, and finally through Alsace and up into the Champagne area of France.

Example Route 3: Europe in a Year!

What's realistic for a year's tour of Europe? If you've the energy, don't mind long driving days and want to see as much as possible, you might want to have a go at a huge route like this final example tour.

This tour heads north quickly, and would be best started in the spring, so you top out in the Arctic in the summer, head south to Greece in the autumn and spend the deep winter in southern Spain. Just keep an eye on snow conditions in the Alps if you choose to do this.

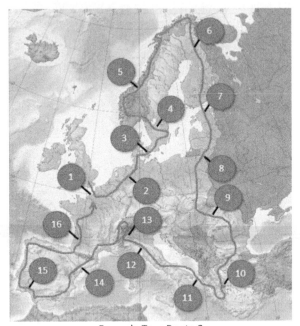

Example Tour Route 3

A few key aspects of this route:

1. Take a ferry or the Channel Tunnel to France, turn east.
2. Travel across Belgium, the Netherlands and Germany to Denmark.
3. Cross the Øresund Bridge from Demark to Sweden.
4. Drive up through Sweden, nipping over to see Stockholm before turning west and entering Norway.
5. Visit Oslo and the southern fjords before heading north into the Arctic Circle, visiting the beautiful Lofoten Islands and the North Cape.
6. Turn south, dodge the reindeer herds on your way south through Finland's forests and lakes, grabbing a few saunas on the way.
7. From Helsinki take the party ferry across the Gulf of Finland to Tallinn in Estonia. Be amazed at how cheap everything suddenly feels.

8. Nip across Latvia and Lithuania, crossing into Poland in the gap between Kaliningrad and Belarus.
9. Heading further south, across Slovakia, Hungary, Romania and Bulgaria, being immersed in Eastern Europe's history as you go.
10. Drop into Greece from Bulgaria, wander around the beaches and historical sights and swim in pure blue seas.
11. Take a ferry across the Adriatic from Patras or Igoumenitsa in Greece to Bari or Brindisi in Italy.
12. Drive up Italy and its myriad sights, sounds and tastes before heading north into the mighty Alps.
13. Swing around hairpin bends in Austria and Switzerland before turning west and crossing Le Midi, the south of France.
14. Edge around or drive up and over the Pyrenees into Spain.
15. Enjoy the towns, beaches and fiestas in southern Spain (perhaps nipping into Morocco for a while) and Portugal.
16. Drive north through Portugal, back around or over the Pyrenees into France and KA-BOOM, you're on the ferry and home, with ten thousand photos, a lot of dirty washing and a head full of memories.

Example Route 4: A 90-in-180-Day Route

This route illustrates one of the many options for UK citizens touring in the EU after the Brexit transition period when the 90-in-180-day rule kicks in. It uses Morocco and Croatia as 'waiting countries' where you can stay for a few months to avoid being longer than 90 in a rolling 180 days in the Schengen Area. Alternative routes could include Romania, Bulgaria and Serbia where UK-issued motorhome insurance is often valid, but which are outside the Schengen Area.

Alternatively, Turkey issues three-month tourist e-Visas to UK citizens for a reasonable cost, but you'll need to ensure your motorhome insurer will give you a Green Card for Turkey. There are several other 'waiting countries' outside the Schengen Area, including Albania, Bosnia and Herzegovina and Montenegro. However, it's likely you won't get a Green Card for these countries from a UK insurer, so you'd be forced to buy 3rd party insurance at the border which can prove very expensive for longer stays. Ukraine is another option, but our experience of trying to drive a non-4WD motorhome across the country wasn't a good one and we'd strongly suggest doing your research on the state of the specific roads you intend to drive if you choose that option.

Example Tour Route 4

The following assumes none of your party have spent any time in Europe in the three months prior to setting off. It also assumes you'll spend winter in Morocco, to take advantage of the weather so far south, which means setting off in the late Autumn.

1. Take a ferry or the Channel Tunnel to France, turn east. As soon as you enter France, the Schengen 90-in-180-day clock starts ticking.
2. Travel down across France, taking in the Loire Chateaux perhaps.
3. Head down past Bordeaux and the French Atlantic surf beaches, crossing into Spain at the western edge of the Pyrenees where there is no mountain pass.
4. Take in the interesting North Spain coast, visiting the beach city of San Sebastian, the Guggenheim at Bilbao and the beautiful Picos de Europa mountains.
5. The weather in Galacia in north-west Spain wasn't kind to us in our late autumn stay, and you might want to start heading south into Portugal sooner rather than later. We can recommend a trip to Porto and Coimbra, and a trip to Lisbon is easily possible before heading into the beach-rich Algarve region where you'll find lots of motorhomes overwintering.
6. Assuming it's two months since you entered France, you'll now have 30 days left on your Schengen clock. Grab a ferry ticket for Morocco and head south for the winter. You'll be issued a 90-day visa at the border. After 60 days, you'll be able to return to the Schengen zone

with a full 90 days available (30 days from original allowance plus 60 from when you were in Morocco).

7. Head back into Spain, perhaps around March so you avoid the heat which can make southern Spain uncomfortably hot in the late spring and summer. Nip into Gibraltar for the history and novelty factors before taking in in the big sights of Andalusia, Seville, Córdoba and Granada before heading east and north.

8. Find a campsite near Barcelona and take a bus into the city to visit Gaudí's architectural masterpieces, including the famous Sagrada Familia basilica which is due for completion in 2026. Be aware that you can't take dogs onto buses in Spain. Afterwards, head north into the Pyrenees, spending a few days and buying cheap diesel in Andorra before heading back down from the mountains into France.

9. Enjoy Carcassonne, the ruined Cathar Castles and the roman city of Nîmes before cruising east into the pine forests, mountains and lavender fields of Provence. Either head up and over the Alps (check your chosen passes are open – a few are snowbound until June) or travel down to the Med and take the motorway into Piedmont in Italy. From here there are too many Italian delights to list!

10. If you crossed from Morocco to Spain in March you may well be into early summer, May or June, and again your Schengen allowance will be starting to get low. To get out of the zone again, and to spend time in a beautiful country beset with Venetian ports, take a ferry across the Adriatic to Dubrovnik or Split in Croatia.

11. You could easily spend a month or two in Croatia, although bear in mind free/wild camping is illegal and actively policed so budget for campsites. Also think of the weather: it can get very hot in Croatia in summer.

12. Leaving Croatia you'll be heading back into the Schengen Area in Hungary or Slovenia. The Schengen clock starts ticking again at this point, so you need to calculate the number of days you have remaining before you have to return to the UK. Take in whichever countries you like in this region, including the Czech Republic perhaps.

13. Take advantage of Germany's free motorway network to travel across the country with ease.

14. For a taste of Scandinavia, drive up into Denmark, crossing the land border and either staying on the Jutland Peninsula, or heading east over bridges to Funen and Zealand.

15. Finally head back to the UK before your Schengen clock ticks down to nothing, driving through the Netherlands and Belgium on the way. If you spend 3 months touring the UK or Eire then your 90 days allowance will be available to you again.

The above route uses a ferry to quickly cross from Italy to Croatia. There are other options to use ferries to speed up large sections of the route, like the Barcelona (Spain) to Civitavecchia (Italy) route. This takes around 21 hours and avoids over 1200km of driving. You could also consider a ferry from Nador (Morocco) to Sète (France) which takes around 42 hours and avoids at least 1300km of driving. These ferries aren't cheap, but they do offer flexibility if your number of Schengen days available is an issue.

Some Real-Life Routes: Our Tour Maps

If you want to get an idea of more tour routes and timescales, have a look at this Google Map we created for our own travels: *tinyurl.com/ourtourmap*.

Typing the above link into a web browser will display a map, overlaid with dots. Each tour has a different colour dot, and each dot shows a location we slept in. Join the dots to see the rough route we took that trip. By clicking on a dot, you can get more information about that location, plus a link to a blog post with photos, GPS co-ordinates and videos of what we saw and did there.

Map of our European and North African night stops from *ourtour.co.uk*

Beyond Europe

Should Europe not be quite large enough, or if you fancy a little more contrast in your journey, Asia and North Africa are both relatively easy to access by motorhome. Our tours have taken us to Tunisia (via a ferry from Palermo in Sicily) and Morocco (via ferries from Algeciras in Spain). We haven't had the chance to cross into Asia yet, but the simplest route is to cross the Bosphorus River at Istanbul into Asian Turkey.

If you opt to travel outside Europe, check your motorhome insurer will issue a Green Card, providing cover for the country you intend to travel to. If they won't, your only option may be to buy 3rd party insurance at the border, which may not be palatable if you have an expensive vehicle. Also check whether a visa is needed, read the Foreign Office's travel advice, ensure your travel insurance provides cover, and check if your breakdown cover extends to the country you're planning to visit. Finally, if you plan to take a pet with you, check your destination country's animal entry requirements.

For Morocco, we've written a separate book detailing all the things we researched and learned on our tours of Morocco. It's called 'Motorhome Morocco' and is available as a paperback or eBook on Amazon.

If North Africa and Turkey aren't far enough, there are of course more options available. With the right vehicle could choose to drive further into Africa or Asia, in which case you're into 'overlanding' territory and might want to have a read of Chris Scott's Overlander's Handbook (*www.overlanders-handbook.com*). Alternatively, consider a motorhome swap with a fellow RV owner on another continent (*www.motorhomeholidayswap.com* and *www.rvworldwide.com* are two examples). We've never done this, but friends have, travelling across Canada and New Zealand for much less than the cost of shipping their own motorhome or renting one at the destination.

Getting Repairs Done in Europe

As ever, stuff will break while you're away. It's pretty much a certainty that a steady set of things will snap, die, fail to start, fail to stop, wear out, crack, fall off and generally give up the ghost. Aside from simply ignoring it and hoping it goes away, there are plenty of options for getting stuff sorted without taking the first ferry back to Dover.

Self-Repairs

Depending on your skill level, the tools you have, how confident you feel and your general level of desperation, you can fix some stuff yourself. For habitation area fixes, there are DIY shops all over the place selling Gaffa Tape, super glue, screws and fibre glass, we tend to carry stuff like this in our tool kit, along with cable ties – See Appendix A for our 'Tools and things for fixing stuff' packing list.

For minor engine repairs (we fixed a diesel leak near Gibraltar by replacing a section of hose, and fixed a radiator leak in Estonia), there are plenty of motor factors knocking about selling spares. Norauto and FeuVert in France are the equivalent of Halfords (*norauto.fr* and *feuvert.fr*). FeuVert are also in Spain (*feuvert.es*). In Estonia we used an Autoekspert (*www.autoekspert.ee*).

Finding and Using Garages

If something goes wrong with your underlying vehicle, you've these options:

- If you have breakdown cover, call them and get them to come and try to fix the issue on the roadside, or recover you to a local garage. If the cover includes a hire care or overnight stays in a hotel, this can be the best option even if you could deal with the issue yourself.
- If you don't have breakdown cover, or the issue isn't critical and you want to sort it yourself, find a local garage. You can either take to the internet and start searching for one or ask someone who lives locally, tourist information or campsite reception. Our satnav has a 'Find Help' function which lists nearby garages, which we've found hit-and-miss, but better than nothing.
- For Fiat-based motorhomes, you can search for a local garage using this site: *www.fiatcamper.com*. Don't assume a main dealer will be able to see you quickly though, we've visited two which couldn't even look at the van for 10 days!

Mechanics don't tend to speak English but do tend to be a helpful bunch. Having an app like Google Translate on your phone (with either an offline language downloaded or internet access), or using the full Google Translate website (*translate.google.co.uk*) on their computer, is a slow method of communicating but is far better than pointing and mime.

Finding and Using Motorhome Dealers

If you're in need of a motorhome dealer, perhaps to buy a spare part or to get a repair done, Google is again your friend. Search for the local word for 'motorhome' (see below), plus the nearest city, and you'll (usually) get a quick list of dealers around you – for example 'campingcar Dijon'. Alternatively, ask around fellow motorhome owners in aires and campsites.

- The French for motorhome is: *campingcar*
- The Spanish & Portuguese for motorhome is: *autocaravana*
- The Italian & Dutch for motorhome is: *camper*
- The German for motorhome is: *wohnmobile*
- The Norwegian for motorhome is: *bobil*

Long-Term Living Costs

Travelling long-term in a motorhome can be a very cost-effective way to see a continent or two (or even three!). In the following pages we aim to give you an idea of typical yearly costs, breaking them down into categories and giving you some hints and tips for keeping your costs down, to prolong your travels.

Typical Living Costs

Let's see how much it has cost some motorhome bloggers to travel for a year across Europe. These are real costs, not guesses or estimates, although we have to rely on the completeness and accuracy of the bloggers and their numbers. It's also worth noting that those of us publishing detailed figures of costs do this by tracking what we spend, this alone might tend to make us more frugal, skewing these costs towards the lower-cost end of the spectrum.

Comparing like-for-like costs can also be a little difficult. Some bloggers include all repair, insurance, consumable and side-trip costs. Some don't. Very few include van depreciation, which can double the trip cost for someone buying a brand-new van and selling it after a year. None of the costs below include the cost of buying or modifying the van, or any non-travel costs, such as house insurance, council tax and so on.

If you are planning on going full-time in a motorhome for several years, few blogger cost reports include replacing worn-out clothes and shoes, buying new gadgets, picking up new equipment for hobbies, paying for any private medical insurance and so on. This partly explains some of the big variations in yearly budgets below. Some other reasons for large cost variations include: whether any repairs were required, if the travellers have a second form of transport, whether they include fixed costs for storage or a home in the UK, how often they eat out and whether they habitually use low-cost overnight stays.

Finally, currency fluctuations and inflation can have an effect on costs. If the pound weakens, travelling in Europe gets more expensive and vice versa (although some of our biggest costs like insurance are in pounds, so aren't affected by exchange rate changes). Inflation generally pushes costs slowly upwards over time, so the older the figures are below, the more likely it is you'll be paying more.

Cost Report: OurTour Years 1 and 2

We spent two full years between 2011 and 2013 travelling almost 30,000 miles across Europe, Morocco and Tunisia. We reported costs of €32,482 (around £13,500 a year). This figure didn't include the costs incurred before we set off such as, the initial year's insurance, tax, repairs, MOT, camping cheques (which we don't recommend buying), travel insurance, breakdown cover and depreciation. Including all of these costs would bring the yearly total to around £16,000 for two adults and a dog.

ourtour.co.uk/home/how-did-we-afford-two-years-on-the-road-our-total-tour-costs

Cost Report: OurTour Year 3

We spent a further 18 months travelling between 2016 and 2017 heading as far north as Norway's North Cape, and as far south as Icht on the edge of the Moroccan Sahara. We published our costs for the 12 months of 2016 as £17,216 which included everything except insurance and depreciation.

The year's costs were inflated due to the fact we paid for two sets of MOT and servicing in one year (one of which included a cambelt change). A more realistic estimate of total costs, excluding one set of van servicing/MOT, but including depreciation would be around £18,000 a year.

ourtour.co.uk/home/how-much-does-a-year-in-a-motorhome-cost

Cost Report: Motoroaming

Karen and Myles have been travelling full-time since 2016 and have published detailed costs each year. These don't include depreciation, but do include everything else, including storage costs for their belongings back in the UK, repairs and replacing old equipment. In their first three years of travel, they spent totals of £23,776, £19,708 and £22,931, making an average yearly spend of £22,138.

motoroaming.com/money-matters

Cost Report: Home on Wheels

David and Anne spent a year touring Europe in 2018 and reported a spend of £63 per day (£22,995). This includes £3,133 spent on eating out, and £5000 on campsites. It doesn't include costs for storing furniture in the UK, motorhome or travel insurance or depreciation.

homeonwheels.co.uk/how-to-live-in-a-motorhome-fulltime

Cost Report: Tour Europe by Motorhome

Sarah and Stu spent a total of 341 days touring 21 countries between 2013 and 2014. They spent £18,909, although it's not clear if this includes insurance, consumables or van depreciation.

www.toureuropebymotorhome.com/how-much-does-it-cost

Cost Report: Our Bumble

Joanne and Craig spent 360 days covering 9500 miles across Europe in 2015, wild camping most of the way. They reported costs of £7,541, which includes van servicing, insurance, tax and warranty, but not depreciation.

ourbumble.com/touring-costs-europe-motorhome

Cost Report: Europe by Camper

Adam and Sophie travelled for 334 days from 2011 to 2012, covering 23,000 miles across 21 countries, including Morocco. They reported spending £9,570, plus another £1500 for vehicle insurance, road tax, cellular 3G internet, and a £500 trip to St Petersburg, making a total of £11,070.

www.europebycamper.com/2012/03/touring-europe-for-year-what-does-it.html

Cost Report: Aaron and Nicky

Aaron and Nicky's cost report covers 365 days between Sep 2016 and Sep 2017. They spent a total of £13,354 touring from southern Portugal to northern Norway. One-off costs are included, but not depreciation.

aaronandnickytravels.wordpress.com/2017/09/04/our-first-year-full-timing-in-a-motorhome-how-much-did-it-cost

Cost Report: Follow Our Motorhome

Andi and Paul spent 371 days touring across nine countries and covering 11,500 miles in 2017, spending a total of £20,973. The costs include one-off costs, but not depreciation.

followourmotorhome.co.uk/2018/01/01/what-does-a-years-touring-europe-cost

Cost Report: Kiri and Steve

Kiri and Steve travelled for 242 days between 2013 and 2014, covering 11,878 miles and spent £33.45 per day, which extrapolates to £12,209 for a full year. One-off costs aren't included, nor is depreciation.

www.kiriandsteve.co.uk/cost-of-motorhome-travelling-around-europe

Budget Breakdown

Let's break down some of the above figures so you can get a better idea where the money goes. This might help you plan your own budget a little better. The cost categories are broken down into one-off (yearly) costs and day-to-day living expenses, as is this is how most people track and report their expenditure.

One-Off (Yearly) Fixed Costs

Some costs are typically incurred once each year: depreciation (although this is only realised when the van is sold), motorhome insurance, travel insurance, breakdown cover and so on. These costs tend to be incurred in Sterling, so aren't affected by exchange rate fluctuations.

Vehicle Depreciation

One of your biggest costs is actually a hidden one. Most vehicles are worth less and less each year. This reduction in value is referred to as 'depreciation' and although it doesn't feel like spending money, you should factor it into your trip costs to see the full picture.

Exactly how much a van will depreciate each year will vary between vehicle make and model, wear and tear, mileage, damage, demand when you sell the vehicle, whether you sell it privately and so on. We work on an estimate of 10% depreciation a year for our second-hand motorhomes, as they get heavy use. We'd use 5% if we only used them infrequently. This equates to around £1,000 a year for the first year on our first Hymer. Our current Hymer was £1,700 for the first year, £1,530 for the second year and so on.

Brand new vehicles depreciate far more in their first year of use, maybe as much as 20%. On a £60,000 motorhome, that equates to £12,000. If you were to buy the van purely for a 12-month tour and sell it at the end, depreciation can equal the rest of your costs combined.

Motorhome Insurance

The cost of comprehensive motorhome insurance varies with a whole range of factors, as you can tell by the number of questions you're asked when you get a quote. The only way to know how much yours will cost is to get quotes from a number of companies.

When we're not full-timing, our yearly insurance is around £450. When we were full-timing it was over £1000 a year. You'll be classed as full-timing if you don't have a residence in the UK where you're on the electoral register, so if you rent your house out to travel, your insurer will class you as full-timing.

Travel Insurance

You should ensure you're covered for repatriation or emergency private medical treatment while abroad, as these costs could potentially bankrupt you. Make sure you tell your insurer about any activities you plan to enjoy, such as skiing. For long tours we buy backpacker insurance for around £100 a year per person (www.alphatravelinsurance.co.uk). Our policy allowed two returns to the UK, of 21 days each, during the two-year policy.

Pet Insurance
If you want to insure your pet while travelling, you should check whether any existing policy covers travel abroad, and if it does, how long can each trip be in duration. There are policies available which cover unlimited number of days abroad in the PETS countries (those covered by the Pet Passport). The cost will vary depending on your pet's age, breed and so on. We opted to self-insure Charlie. Money we didn't spend paying insurance premiums was ring-fenced to pay for costs as they occurred, things like vet visits, medication and inoculation boosters. As Charlie got older his costs went up a lot, but because he had a lot of money saved up which we hadn't needed to spend on him in his youth, it worked out to be a good way for us to insure him.

Vehicle Tax
Road tax, or vehicle excise duty, is payable each year for your motorhome, which can be done online when on the road. The amount you'll pay varies with a bunch of rules set by the government, depending on the age of vehicle, whether it's over 3500Kg, whether it cost more than £40,000 new, and for some vehicles the rate of emissions (*www.gov.uk/vehicle-tax-rate-tables*).

Vehicle Servicing, MOT and Repairs
Each year we fully service our motorhome before its MOT, at a local garage in the UK, which costs a few hundred pounds. Our first motorhome also cost us around £1200 during our two-year tour as it needed a new clutch fitted in France. Our current van had a new wheel bearing fitted at a cost of £280, and we've also carried out various minor repairs.

Vehicle Consumables
Tyres, batteries, exhausts and cambelts (if your engine has one), all wear out and need replacing. To give you an idea of costs, a set of four Michelin Agilis Camping tyres for our current motorhome cost us £500, and last around two years of heavy travelling. We've replaced three leisure batteries at around £100 each, one starter battery at around the same price, and a custom-made stainless-steel exhaust section at £150.

Day-to-Day Costs
These costs are incurred while you're on the road, although you may already be paying some of them to live day to day in the UK. These are the costs most likely to be affected by exchange rate fluctuations; they could easily be 20% higher (or lower) from one year to the next as the pound to the euro/Kroner etc. rates change.

Supermarket Costs
We spend more in supermarkets than we do anything else. Typically, 20% to 30% of our overall costs goes on buying food, alcohol, toiletries and so on from shops and markets. For two people we get through around £3500 a year, which equates to £4.80 per person per day. Neither of us smoke, but we do drink (cheap!) alcohol, and eat fish, seafood, meat and cheese.

Diesel
Our motorhome runs on diesel and gets about 23 miles per gallon long-term. This means we use 12.3 litres per 100km (*mpg.webix.co.uk*). A 10,000 mile journey is around 16,000km, so we would need (16000/100) x 12.3 = 1968 litres of diesel. Diesel generally costs less in Europe than the UK (*www.fuel-prices-europe.info*), but if you use UK prices you'll get a conservative idea of how much you need to budget for diesel. At the time of writing diesel is £1.34 per litre, so a 10,000 mile trip would cost roughly 1968 x £1.34 = £2637.

Overnight Costs
People spend hugely different amounts on overnight costs. Some folks never use a paid aire or campsite, so their overnight costs are nothing. In our travels we find ourselves mixing up free camping (wild camping), paid aires, free aires and campsites. Using the ACSI Camping Card reduces campsite fees out of season. On average, accounting for free nights, we spend around £4 to £5 per night.

LPG
Using a self-refillable LPG gas system reduces our gas costs significantly compared with getting Calor-type gas bottle refills in the UK. In a typical year we spend around £200 on LPG, although we tend not to spend long periods in the snow or cold climates, which would crank the cost up.

Internet Data and Phone
While the UK is within the EU (and hopefully afterwards too), you can use your UK allowance for making calls in EU countries at no extra cost. Some providers do have a limit on how many months you can do this for, so check the small print before you sign up to any contract. Also be wary of going over any monthly allowance, as out-of-plan costs can be very high (we've set up our Vodafone SIM so it stops working if we use all of our monthly allowance). We hardly use our phones for calls when abroad, preferring to use free internet solutions such as Skype, Facebook or WhatsApp calling when we have access to WiFi.

For internet access, we use free WiFi when we can find it. When there's no WiFi, or it's very slow, we use low-cost roaming internet SIM cards. We buy these in the UK before we set off. As we use around 6GB of data a month, the cost is around £200 for a year's internet access.

Eating Out
Restaurant costs vary hugely across Europe. In Spain you can get a great quality lunchtime three course meal with wine for £10 to £15 a head, plus tip. In Norway you could spend £40 each for a similar meal. If you plan to eat out regularly but are on a budget, you may want to do some research on cost comparison sites (like *www.numbeo.com/cost-of-living*) before you decide where to go.

Ferries
During our 2016 tour we spent nearly £900 on 17 ferries. This was an unusually high amount, as in addition to crossing the Channel, we cut across the Adriatic from Italy to Croatia, crossed the Gulf of Finland from Estonia, and used umpteen paid ferries in Norway. When planning your route it's worth working out if it would be cheaper to take a ferry or drive the long way around.

Replacing Items
If you plan to travel for many months or years, and want a realistic budget, you'll need to include periodic replacement of personal things such as: clothes, phones, shoes, gadgets, electric toothbrushes, and so on.

Costs at Home
If you plan to keep a house in the UK and travel, you'll need to account for any costs associated with your bricks at home. We include some costs at home in our budget such as £360 a year for a motorhome storage place at a local farm so we can come and go.

Emergency Fund
We have our finances set up so we have quick and easy access to money for emergencies, such as needing to fly home, repairs following an accident, private health treatment which we might have to pay for before reclaiming later, and so on. We aim to have around £5000 on hand to cater for these kinds of issue.

Tips for Lowering Costs
However little you spend, you'll always come across someone spending less than you. Unless you really have to travel on a shoestring, beware of the 'race to the bottom'. This involves a kind of reverse-consumerism, where motorhomers try to outdo each other spending as little as possible. We met one couple who claimed to only spend £5,000 a year on everything, which seems an incredibly low amount, even to us frugal two. Our philosophy is to spend carefully, but not to miss out on experiences which aren't likely to come around very often. At the end of the day, only you can decide what you need to spend to have an enjoyable life.

Part Three: Your First Long-Term Tour

The big costs in most people's travel budgets are going to be:

- Buying food and drink from shops and markets
- Eating out
- Buying fuel for the motorhome
- Overnight stops
- Vehicle depreciation
- Vehicle insurance
- Vehicle servicing, MOT and repairs

If you want to trim your costs, here are some options for you to consider (sadly, we doubt they will get your annual spend down to £5,000 though).

Look at Your Eating and Drinking Habits
Eating and drinking is something we need to do rather frequently! Any small amount we spend each day adds up over a year to a decent amount of money. £3 a day on a bottle of wine (a reasonable price outside the UK) will come to over £1000 a year. If you regularly eat meat, cheese and fish your costs will also be higher.

Cook for Yourself
Some of our most memorable cultural experiences came from eating out across Europe: bacalhau (salt cod) in Porto, gigandes (giant baked beans) and kokoretsi (seasoned lamb intestines) in Greece, schweinshaxn (baked pork knuckle) in Bavaria, confit de canard (salt-cured duck cooked in its own fat) in France, migas de pan (fried breadcrumbs) in Spain, and anything at all in Italy. We'd usually eat at lunchtime as evening meals are more expensive.

We can heartily recommend eating out while you travel, but it does come at a cost. On average our budget stretches to eating out once every couple of weeks. In Norway we ate out three times in eleven weeks, and two of those were, strictly-speaking, takeaway. In cheaper countries like Morocco, Portugal, Spain and Greece we ate out more frequently. The rest of the time we cooked in the van.

Choose Your Countries
The costs of diesel, food and overnight spots all vary from country to country, and these are likely to have the biggest impact on your overall spend. Unless you're on a rock-bottom budget, you'll probably find that there aren't any countries you can't afford. Countries with high diesel and eating out costs like Norway, Italy and France tend to allow free-camping, or have low-cost aires available. In places where you're obliged to use a campsite by law or other official overnight spot, such as Croatia, you'll find they tend to have lower costs.

There's no doubt that some countries are cheaper to spend long periods in. You could potter around France, Spain and Portugal in warmth and comfort for months, eating out relatively often, staying on free or low cost aires and enjoying the incredible climate for not much money.

England has high diesel costs, generally obliges motorhomes to use campsites and has relatively high food, alcohol and eating out costs. Coupled with the fact we drive on the left, this might be part of the reason so few motorhomes travel from continental Europe to the UK, compared with the other way around?

Don't Drive as Far

Each mile or kilometre you drive pushes up your fuel costs. Instead of driving all over Europe, you could opt to tour France for a year, travelling maybe 3000 miles, slashing your diesel costs compared with a North Cape to Sicily tour. Or join the thousands who travel to southern Spain or Portugal in winter, park up for the season, then drive back to a base in the UK or northern Europe in summer, again drastically cutting your diesel costs.

Free Camping/Free Parking/ Wild Camping

Free camping (often called free parking or wild camping) is an obvious way to keep your costs down. Free camping is quite possible and safe in lots of countries. Steer clear of the most popular tourist areas, and countries like Croatia which actively enforce laws against it (at least along the coast), and you won't have too much trouble finding free places to park for the night.

Aires

If free camping isn't for you, *campercontact.com* currently lists over 2700 free aires in France, and another 800+ which are less than €10. The numbers for Spain are over 650 free, and over 100 less than €10. For Germany over 1700 are free, and over 1300 are less than €10. Clearly using aires can significantly help to reduce your overnight costs!

Earning Money on the Road

Our money for travelling largely comes from income earned in the UK, saving it, or more latterly from investments in the UK. We haven't needed to work while on the road, but we have generated some income while travelling. We've also come across ways to 'work' in return for free places to stay rather than for money.

Blogging

A few years ago we made a decision to 'monetise' our blog: *ourtour.co.uk*. It carries Google Adsense advertisements (*www.google.com/adsense*) as does our YouTube channel (*www.youtube.co.uk*). It also has Amazon Associates links to products we've used and recommend (*affiliate-program.amazon.com*), as well as some paid adverts for companies we've used and again can personally recommend.

Seven years after starting our blog, and many hundreds of hours writing content, it now earns us around £2,000 a year before tax. In the early years we lost money, as the website hosting cost more than the income, possibly because we're not blogging experts and haven't made much effort to maximise the income it generates. So, while you can make money from blogging, it's hard to make any appreciable amount, and we find it best to simply love the blogging and treat any income as a bonus.

Writing
We've written a few paid articles for magazines like Motorhome Monthly Magazine (MMM). The payment for these ranged from £80 for a small article to £400 for a multi-page tour report. If you're thinking of writing for a magazine, contact them before writing anything, as they usually have a string of articles in the pipeline and may already have one on the topic you plan to write about.

With the advent of self-publishing, it's easier than ever to write and publish your own books. We've self-published this book, two books about motorhome travel to Morocco, a book about motorhome travel in France and another book which contains our first year's blog posts, all with Amazon's Kindle Direct Publishing (*kdp.amazon.com*). We uploaded our manuscripts and covers, and they took care of most of the rest: presenting the books for sale on their website, sending them to people's eBook readers, or arranging a print-on-demand service to create and post paper copies, taking payment and sending us royalties. There are no up-front costs, and so we don't need to hold a stock of books which might not sell.

While Amazon offer a fantastic service, they don't do the traditional work of a publisher. They don't arrange any editing, proofing or promotion. You need to do those yourself. If you can create and promote a good quality, popular book, you can generate a residual income stream which will drip feed money into your bank account each month. Don't underestimate the work involved though, book writing takes time and unless you manage to create a best seller, is low-income, even compared with a minimum wage job.

Digital Nomad Work
Having worked in IT and marketing for decades, we have some 'digital nomad' skills and have used these to create some income by setting up and managing websites, shooting and editing promotional videos and so on. If you also include our blogging and writing as 'digital nomad' work, and we pushed ourselves to make more money in this area, we could generate a reasonable proportion of our income on the road.

House Sitting
House sitting is a service where you give your time in return for somewhere free to live for a few days, weeks or even months. When someone wants to be

away from their house, they may want it to be inhabited for insurance purposes, peace of mind, or more likely to look after their garden and pets. If you're happy to do this, you can save yourself any overnight costs for the duration of the sit. However, you may have to pay for services (electricity, gas, wood) while you're there, so you may find it more expensive to do the sit than to stay in your motorhome.

Various websites hook up sitters with home owners, charging a fee as part of the deal; two of the biggest are *trustedhousesitters.com* and *mindahome.co.uk*. We've done two house sits through *trustedhousesitters.com*, one in the hills north of Málaga in Spain, looking after a villa and three dogs and another in Shrewsbury where we sat for three lovely pooches. We found them both positive experiences and in Spain got to see Andalusian village life close-up for a few weeks. From our experience we'd recommend you ensure you understand the home owner's requirements before you accept the sit though: out of the blue, our Spanish owner started to hint they wanted us to redecorate their villa when we were most of the way through the sit.

Workaways and WWOOFing
Workaways are another way to give your time in exchange for accommodation, and sometimes food (*www.workaway.info*). We haven't done this yet, so can't offer any direct experience, but we have chatted with fellow motorhomers who've done Workaways in Norway and Spain and enjoyed the experience.

WWOOF is an organisation which matches up volunteers with organic farms across the world (*wwoofinternational.org*). You work for free, but the host provides accommodation and food. Again, we haven't done any WWOOFing, so can't comment directly on how well the system works.

The Day Job on the Road
We've met a few folks who've negotiated with their employer for them to work part-time while travelling. Obviously, this is only possible with jobs which can be done remotely, but the widespread availability of fast and low-cost internet access and mobile phone networks makes this option logistically possible at least. You'll need an understanding boss and will need to be disciplined too: when parked alongside an idyllic Greek beach, being sat inside a slow-roasting motorhome working when your partner is out swimming takes some mental effort! We also notice that those working on the road didn't seem to relax and absorb the travel experience as much as those who cut the ties completely (if only temporarily).

Returning Home

Coming back home to the UK after a long tour can be a challenge. Many fellow travellers report 'reverse culture shock', where your own country suddenly feels like a strange place. Coming back to the UK's busy road network, expensive prices, and seeing fellow countrymen and women living what suddenly seem rushed and overly complex lives can all take getting used to.

While you might feel uplifted and refreshed from your travels, folks back home are likely to be only marginally interested in what you've been up to. You might be asked "what was it like", or "what was your favourite place", and quickly learn that a one-line answer is wanted, not a lengthy and earnest narrative.

You may also find after a few weeks at home that a listlessness sets in. Having experienced this a few times, our experience is this is best fought with a new project: a house to renovate, a book to write, a new career. Or just give in and set off again, if you can!

If your finances demand a return to work, it makes sense to start the search before you land back home (not that we did – we wanted to enjoy every last minute of our travels). We did worry that we wouldn't be able to explain a year-long gap on our CVs, but after a two-year tour we both found work within three months of returning home (one of us in only three weeks), on similar salaries to the ones we had before we left.

If you're heading back into a house you've let out, make sure the tenants know as early as possible. They need time to find somewhere to live and arrange a move. When you get back, assume some stuff will need doing on your house – minor stuff gets broken all the time, and won't necessarily be picked up even if you use a letting agent to handle the tenants.

It's worth not spending every last penny on your trip as you will need some funds to get back into life in the UK. We needed to get our car out of storage and back on the road – new tyres, battery, service and MOT etc. As our tenants wanted to stay in our house, we opted to rent somewhere smaller. We'll never forget the look on the face of the letting agent when we told them that neither of us had jobs for a credit check. Luckily, we had enough money put to one side to pay the first six months of rent upfront, avoiding the need for a guarantor.

Life Without a House - Full-Timing

Although this book is about touring in a motorhome, there are lots of folks who opt to spend long periods living in their van, eschewing the comforts (and costs and responsibilities) of a bricks-n-mortar home. Insurers tend to use the term 'full-timing' to refer to anyone travelling in a motorhome who doesn't have immediate access to a house, but it's perhaps better applied to those who sell pretty much everything and take to the road with an aim to travel for decades.

We've met a few long-term full-timers, and their motivations for living such an unusual life were varied, but often revolved around the desire to be free of the rat race, to take control over their lives. By opting to no longer own a house, they significantly reduced their expenses. This removed the need to earn more money which in turn enabled them to cut the chords which bound them to a boss or customers, the need to be at work at 9am on a Monday morning and to be restricted to two-week holidays. Instead they're on a seemingly-endless journey, stretching off into the future.

In practical terms, the main difficulty for many people in full-time travel is the necessity for a residential address for various forms of bureaucracy. Ideally, you'll be able to call on a friend or family member in the UK who is happy for you to use their address. Bear in mind you'll need to trust them to open your mail as some of it may be time-sensitive. We used this approach for two years, having first opted to receive as much communication as we could via email. Health is another important concern: even if you can easily access local state health care for free, unless you're fluent in the local language the experience can be even more stressful than it might be in the UK.

For us two, we've finally opted to mix up the life of travel with life in bricks-n-mortar. Our reason for not full-timing is simple: we found we enjoy being part of a 'fixed-location' community for at least part of the year and geared up our finances to allow for this. We understand the motivation of the full-timer though: they opt to wake in the mountains, surrounded by forest or beside the beach, spending little money and having few possessions, but feeling an enviable sense of freedom and connection with the world around them.

And Finally...

So, that's it, the end of the book. If you've read the thing from cover to cover: Well done! There's rather a lot of information in here, and as we said at the start, you really don't need to worry about all of it to get a motorhome and go enjoy it.

If you have enjoyed the book or found it useful, please take a moment to leave us a review at your favourite retailer. These really help other buyers and give us feedback too on how we can improve later editions.

We're currently in an Alpine ski resort as we write this final note, in a free aire among the pines and, if it wasn't so foggy, would have a great view of the surrounding hills and mountains. We've hot water in the shower, the TV's lined up to watch a World Cup football match, and we've a cold fridge full of tasty local food, and a chilled bottle of white. Life in a motorhome's good folks, we hope you get to enjoy it as much as we have.

Julie and Jason Buckley

About the Authors

Julie and Jason Buckley have toured Europe and North Africa several times by campervan and motorhome. Up until 2018 they travelled with their Cavalier King Charles Spaniel, Charlie. They set up the *ourtour.co.uk* blog in 2011 and have since added over 1500 articles and diary entries from over 1000 locations.

In addition to the blog, they've written and published several books, all available through Amazon:

- **A Monkey Ate My Breakfast** – a travelogue of their experiences as novice travellers driving around Morocco.
- **Funding Freedom** – a free eGuide to financial freedom, explaining how they set up their lifestyle and finances to enable long-term travel in their early 40s.
- **OurTour Downloaded** – all their first year's *ourtour.co.uk* blog posts in a single book, enabling them to be read offline at your leisure.
- **Motorhome Morocco** – a practical handbook enabling anyone to complete an independent motorhome tour of this fascinating country.
- **Motorhome France** – all the practical info you need to take your motorhome to the most visited country in the World.

When not travelling, Julie and Jason live in a small town outside Nottingham in the UK. To get in touch, or follow future travels, any of these will work:

- **Email**: julieandjason@ourtour.co.uk
- **Web**: *ourtour.co.uk*
- **Youtube**: search *youtube.com* for 'ourtour blog'
- **Instagram**: *www.instagram.com/ourtourblog*
- **Twitter**: @ourtourblog
- **Facebook**: search *facebook.com* for 'ourtour blog'

And Finally...

Things Change and We Make Mistakes...

We've tried our best to make this a useful and accurate book. We're human though and will make mistakes. Also, some of the book is very much our personal opinion, which others are 100% certain to disagree with! Things change, and some sections will date quickly, even with new editions being published.

If there's anything in here which could have a big impact on your safety, financial situation or happiness, please do your own independent research before taking action. The websites we've referenced throughout (*in italics*) have a wealth of information available, some of which will be more up-to-date than this book.

If you spot any glaring errors or obvious missed topics, please drop us a line at *julieandjason@ourtour.co.uk* and we'll be forever grateful and will of course correct future editions.

Appendix A - OurTour Packing Checklist

One rainy day, out of sheer boredom, we wrote down everything we had in our motorhome for our multi-month European motorhome tours. The list is personalised to our needs but will be a good starting point for any trip. We now use it as a checklist to ensure we haven't forgotten the potato masher again.

Legal Bits

There are things that you are legally required to carry in some countries that we don't have to carry in the UK. It's best to check the AA or RAC website for an up-to-date list of what you need for the countries you're going to.

- ☐ Spare Bulb Kit
- ☐ Emergency Warning Triangle
- ☐ High Visibility Jacket (one per passenger, must be accessible from the inside the van)
- ☐ First Aid Kit
- ☐ Headlight Converters
- ☐ GB Sticker (if you don't already have one on your number plate)
- ☐ Bike Rack Signal Board – red and white striped (if you have a bike rack on your motorhome in Spain or Italy - specifically needs to be made from aluminium)
- ☐ Spare Glasses (if needed for driving)
- ☐ Breathalyser x 2 (these were a legal requirement in France, but as no fine was ever agreed for not having them they're probably pointless)
- ☐ Car Parking Disc with Arrival Time (not strictly a legal requirement, but used in several countries for car parking where the time is limited)
- ☐ Smoke/CO Alarm (again not a legal requirement, but get one anyway)

Documentation

We know it's boring, but there are some documents you'll need to take with you and others it will be handy to have in case of a problem.

- ☐ V5C (your motorhome's 'log book' – must be the original, not an electronic scan or photocopy)
- ☐ Motorhome Insurance Certificate (ensure it covers all the countries you'll pass through for entire duration of your trip)
- ☐ Green Card Insurance (only once the UK has completed the process of leaving the EU, or if you're heading to countries like Morocco and Turkey)
- ☐ European Health Insurance Card (these are free, and enable you to access local health cover in EU countries, although they may not be valid in some countries after Brexit)
- ☐ Travel Insurance Certificate

- ☐ Driving Licences (and possibly IDPs after the Brexit transition period)
- ☐ Passports (check how old they are)
- ☐ Photocopies of all documentation (kept somewhere safe; we also scanned ours and emailed them to ourselves)
- ☐ Motorhome Instructions (always handy for trouble-shooting as stuff inevitably packs up while you're away)
- ☐ Breakdown Cover
- ☐ Mobile Phone contract details (if in contract, these are handy for bill queries and renewing)
- ☐ ACSI Discount CampingCard (gives you discounted stay at campsites out of season across Europe)
- ☐ Pet Passport, Innoculation History or other pet paperwork post-Brexit (if your four-legged friend is going abroad with you)
- ☐ Spending Book (if you're on a budget a small book to track all your spending is a big help)

Daily Servicing

Once you're on the road you'll need a few items to keep you in supplies you'd normally take for granted in a house, such as water, electricity and gas.

- ☐ Spare Keys for the van, bike locks and so on
- ☐ Hose Pipe (you can get collapsible ones, but we prefer a length of 'normal' hose pipe)
- ☐ Tap Connectors (we use Hozelock-style ones. 1/2", 3/4" and 1" screw threads, plus a male-to-male connector, cover most taps)
- ☐ Collapsible Water Carrier or Watering Can (sometimes you can't connect or get near enough to the tap to use your hose, or don't want to move your van)
- ☐ Funnel (you'll probably need one to get the water into your tank if you use a water carrier rather than a watering can. We fashioned a flat, fold-around one from the lid of an ice-cream tub)
- ☐ Power Hook-Up Cable (we don't often use mains power, so only have a single 15 metre, 2.5mm, 16A cable. If you rely on mains more than us, consider carrying a longer cable, or two cables. Remember to unwind them fully when in use to avoid over heating)
- ☐ Hook Up Cable 2 Pin Adapter (some continental campsites and aires still use the 2-pin plug as opposed to the blue European 3 pin)
- ☐ Electric Halogen Heater (save your gas and heat with electric when on hook-up, this type of heater is silent so suitable for leaving on overnight. An electric heater will not heat your water tanks. In very cold weather you'll have to use your blown-air heating/grey tank water heater to stop them freezing)
- ☐ Electric Fan Heater (we use this type of heater when we are awake and it's really cold as it's noisy but quickly heats up the van)

- ☐ LPG Connection Adapters (these four connectors cover almost all self-refill stations: ACME, DISH, bayonet and Euro-Nozzle Adapter)
- ☐ Grey/Waste Water Tank Fresh (trust us, when it gets hot the grey tank can honk. We've used this stuff, but now tend to use dissolved dishwasher tablets or a bottle of cheap cola)
- ☐ Window Vacuum for clearing the windscreen of condensation
- ☐ Fresh Water Tank Cleaner and Purifier (to keep your fresh water tank clean, either that or drink bottled water while travelling)
- ☐ Spirit Level (for ensuring your van is level and to work out where to place the levelling ramps)
- ☐ Levelling Ramps (as car parks nearly always slope when you want to sleep in them!)
- ☐ Wheel Chocks (we've used these in a couple of very steep places to give us some comfort we wouldn't roll off the mountain!)
- ☐ Anti-Slip Mats (handy if you get stuck on grass or sand)

Navigation and Finding Places to Sleep

Below are the tools we use for navigation and finding places to sleep.

- ☐ Satnav (love or hate it, without a satnav driving isn't as easy. We have a TomTom, and love the lane assist for unfamiliar motorways)
- ☐ Relevant SatNav Maps. Check which maps are on your satnav, you may have to buy others if venturing further afield (we didn't realise Greece wasn't included in the Western European maps!)
- ☐ Paper Maps (don't fully trust your satnav as they love short cuts, great for cars but not motorhomes. We always have a paper map for the country too and use it to check out the route suggested by satnav before we set off)
- ☐ Highlighter Pen (track your progress on the paper map and create a great reminder of your trip)
- ☐ Phrase Books (so you can ask for directions anywhere)
- ☐ Maps.me (free smartphone app useful for navigation if you have satnav issues, or when away from the van – download the maps on WiFi)
- ☐ Points of Interest (POI) Files (there are various files which will show you; places to stay overnight, Lidls, Service Points and campsites – we load these onto our TomTom).
- ☐ Apps for overnight stays (we mainly use *park4night* and *campercontact* we've paid for the offline versions so we can use them without internet access).
- ☐ Books for overnight stays
- ☐ Compass (handy for working out which way the sun will come up and manually orienting satellite dishes)

Outdoors, Another Room to Your Motorhome

Motorhomes aren't huge, but once parked up on a campsite the outdoors becomes an extra room, you just need to furnish it accordingly.

- ☐ Camping Chairs
- ☐ Camping Table
- ☐ Foldaway BBQ, Gas BBQ or Gas Stove (we've used all three, but currently use a gas stove as we can take it anywhere)
- ☐ BBQ Tools
- ☐ Picnic Rug
- ☐ Sunglasses / Prescription Sunglasses
- ☐ Insect Repellent
- ☐ Mosquito net (used over our dropdown bed in problem countries like Finland – fixed with bulldog clips and cable ties)
- ☐ Citronella Candles (help keep the mozzies away)
- ☐ Fly Swat (for the middle of the night mosquito cull)
- ☐ Umbrellas (we won't lie to you, it's not always sunny. We have a large golf umbrella and two fold up small ones)

Tools and Things for Fixing Stuff

We've needed to do quite a few repairs as we've travelled. Even if your van is new, it's good to have a few tools and bits to fix to stuff with.

- ☐ Ratchet Socket Set
- ☐ Multi Tool
- ☐ WD-40 Lubricant
- ☐ Assorted Cable Ties
- ☐ Gaffa Tape (also called Duct Tape)
- ☐ Super Glue (either lots of little tubes or a decent reseal-able bottle)
- ☐ Spare Fuses
- ☐ Wheel Brace (your van should have one but check before you get a flat tyre!)
- ☐ Vehicle Jack
- ☐ Precision Screwdriver Set
- ☐ Standard Screwdriver Set
- ☐ Spanner Set
- ☐ Power Pack and Compressor (we never replaced ours when it died, but when we did had it we used it for emergency power, pumping up our air suspension and in case we needed a jump start)
- ☐ Torch (LED ones last ages – we're often amazed at how dark it gets in some places we park!)
- ☐ Tow Rope (the Italian coast guard were very pleased we had one of these when we towed them off a beach!)

- ☐ Spare Engine Oil
- ☐ Disposable Gloves (to keep your pinkies clean while doing the repairs!)

Kitchen Essentials

We stock our vans with a lot of items from the kitchen of our house. But there are a few items we've bought especially for the trip.

- ☐ Melamine Plates and Bowls (they weigh less and don't break, we bought ours in the sales at the end of summer)
- ☐ Mugs (any sort, but the more stable the better)
- ☐ Wine Glasses (we used to use plastic ones, big mistake, even cheap wine tastes so much better from a glass)
- ☐ Plastic/Acrylic Glasses (for drinks other than wine, less glass means less noise and breakages on bumpy roads)
- ☐ Water/Wine Jug (a small jug to decant wine from its Lidl box into, for when we want to feel posh or have guests!)
- ☐ Plastic Food Storage Boxes (collect as many as you can – our pasta, rice, cereal etc is in upright ones, flat ones are used to house potentially leaky stuff and to stop stuff moving around)
- ☐ Double Skillet
- ☐ Large Frying Pan (if you're not taking a double skillet. Measure the width of cupboard it's going in, and the dimension of the pan across the top, not the base to ensure it will fit)
- ☐ Small Frying Pan
- ☐ Pan Protectors
- ☐ Large Saucepan
- ☐ Small Saucepan
- ☐ Remoska
- ☐ Oven Proof Dishes (we don't have an oven, but if you do you'll need some!)
- ☐ Oven Gloves (even with no oven, we still use them for hot stuff)
- ☐ Gas Hob Kettle (for when you aren't hooked up to electricity)
- ☐ Low Wattage Kettle (for when you are hooked up to electricity)
- ☐ Cafetiere or on hob Espresso Maker
- ☐ Chopping Board
- ☐ Cheese Grater
- ☐ Measuring Jug (decent size, plastic or acrylic)
- ☐ Compact Weighing Scales
- ☐ Cutlery (make sure you have plenty of teaspoons – they seem to vanish)
- ☐ Scissors (at least a couple of pairs)
- ☐ Quality Tin Opener (we forgot ours and bought a cheap one, it was faulty, it wouldn't open tins!)
- ☐ Vegetable Peeler (also handy for shaving Parmesan cheese!)
- ☐ Bottle Opener/Cork Screw (perhaps this should be at the top of the list...)
- ☐ Bread Knife (as un-sliced loaves are cheaper and last longer)

- ☐ Sharp Cutting Knife (invest in a decent one so it'll stay sharp for your trip)
- ☐ Wooden Spoons
- ☐ Spatula
- ☐ Serving Spoon
- ☐ Wooden Skewers (good for marshmallow toasting, making kebabs and poking at/fixing stuff stuff)
- ☐ Potato Masher (if you forget yours be warned they don't sell them anywhere in Italy – trust us, we looked!)
- ☐ Cigarette Lighter/Matches (for lighting the hob if the ignition fails, or a BBQ)
- ☐ Cleaning Sponges
- ☐ Cleaning Wipes (we use antibacterial wipes for cleaning the van as well as the taps and hoses at water points)
- ☐ Cleaning Scourers
- ☐ Normal Household Cleaning Products
- ☐ Washing Up Liquid
- ☐ Universal Sink Plug (as every campsite sink has a different sized plug hole)
- ☐ Dustpan and Brush (we take the carpets out in summer, so we sweep the floor)
- ☐ Mini 12V Vacuum Cleaner (if you're keeping the carpets)
- ☐ Antibacterial Hand Wash (to wash your hands with after emptying the loo!)
- ☐ Kitchen Roll
- ☐ Tin Foil
- ☐ Cling Film
- ☐ Freezer Bags
- ☐ Ice Cub Bags or Tray (for those long hot summer days!)
- ☐ Bottle Holders (free cardboard ones from the supermarket reduce clinking)

Store Cupboard Food Items

While we're in the kitchen it's worth having a few items always in your van, so you can have a cuppa at any time! We won't list loads of things, as each person has different tastes, but a few tins (soup, beans?) along with some teabags, coffee, stock cubes, gravy granules (we can't find these anywhere abroad), UHT milk, a bottle of water, a bottle or two of wine, salt and pepper, vinegar, ketchup and chocolate would never go to waste in our van!

Bathroom

- ☐ Micro-towelling Towels (we love these as they feel like normal towels but dry really fast so less damp towels hanging up around the van)
- ☐ Toothbrush
- ☐ Toothpaste
- ☐ Toiletries
- ☐ Soap

- ☐ Toilet Rolls (you can get special motorhome ones, but we use the cheaper two-ply ones and they work fine)
- ☐ Chemical Toilet Fluids (unless you have a SOG unit)
- ☐ Air Freshener (with the loo so close to the living area, it helps!)
- ☐ Medications
- ☐ Contact Lenses
- ☐ Shaving Kit
- ☐ Ear Plugs (even the best campsite can be noisy)
- ☐ Sunscreen and Aftersun
- ☐ Nailbrush
- ☐ Bags For Life (campsite showers rarely have enough hooks for all your clothes. Large supermarket bags for life – one of the thicker plastic ones with fabric handles – hang on a hook keeping all our clothes and towels dry)

Bedroom & Soft Furnishings

- ☐ Pillows
- ☐ Duvet (we have a summer tog duvet with an unzipped sleeping bag on top of it, then a blanket on top of that, so we can use whatever combination we need to keep warm/cool)
- ☐ Memory Foam Mattress Topper (beds made up from the chair cushions are comfortable with one of these, so you can imagine how lovely our pull down bed is with one on it – sleep heaven)
- ☐ Bed Sheets (a normal and brushed cotton one for cold weather)
- ☐ Spare Set of Bedding (it's not always possible to wash and dry in a day)
- ☐ Sleeping Bags (unzip and use over your duvet, or if one of you wants to sleep under the stars)
- ☐ Blankets (great for curling up under when the weather isn't so warm)
- ☐ Cushions (add a bit of comfort and colour to your van on one go)
- ☐ Sofa Throws (we use these on the seat parts of the sofas as they're easy to wash and clean)
- ☐ Hot Water Bottle

Clothing and Laundry

This was a tricky one for us as we would be travelling through most types of weather. We have one shelf each in the wardrobe, one hook each and a cupboard each – in it we have to squeeze everything from ski jackets and thermals to swim wear and wetsuit.

We've found 'technical' clothing to be really good as it's quick drying, and doesn't need ironing. Check out the camping and hiking sections in shops or online and you'll be amazed at what is out there – we even found a shirt impregnated with mosquito repellent! Here's an example lady's packing list:

- ☐ Jeans x 2
- ☐ Quick Drying Trousers
- ☐ Zip Off Trouser/Shorts
- ☐ Shorts x 3
- ☐ Skirts x 2
- ☐ T Shirts x 8
- ☐ Vest Tops x 8
- ☐ Polo Shirt
- ☐ Fleece x 2
- ☐ Mosquito Repellent Shirt
- ☐ Quick Drying Shirts x 2
- ☐ Long Sleeved Tops x 4
- ☐ Going Out Tops x 2
- ☐ Fleece/Hooded Jacket
- ☐ Swimwear (Bikini, Sarong, Beach Shoes, Wetsuit!)
- ☐ Sun Hat or Baseball Cap
- ☐ Winter wear (Thermal Leggings, Thermal Top, Ski Jacket)
- ☐ Scarf
- ☐ Gloves
- ☐ Woolly Hat
- ☐ Knickers
- ☐ Bras (1 x black, 1 x flesh, 1 x other)
- ☐ Socks (Thick Ski Socks, Trainer Socks, Walking Socks and Socks!)
- ☐ Pyjamas / Nightie
- ☐ Walking Boots
- ☐ Trainers
- ☐ Flip Flops
- ☐ Going Out Shoes
- ☐ Gilet
- ☐ Waterproof / Going Out Jacket

Don't forget all those bits and pieces you need to keep your clothes clean if you're going away for a while.

- ☐ Laundry Sack/Bag
- ☐ Washing Liquid/Powder
- ☐ Fabric Softener
- ☐ Coins for the Machines (save pound/one euro coins)
- ☐ Clothes Line
- ☐ Pegs (you can never have too many of them, you'll be amazed!)
- ☐ Drying Rack (whatever kind you can fit into your van, we use a Folding Sock Dryer which we affectionately call our 'pant chandelier' it either hangs off the bike rack or in the bathroom if the weather is bad)

Entertainment, Leisure and Tech

☐ Books
☐ Kindle/eReader (we have a Kindle as we could never carry that many physical books in our motorhome – it's great!)
☐ Board Games (we play Scrabble if you do too bring a dictionary to settle any arguments!)
☐ Playing Cards
☐ Chess Set (unused!)
☐ Snorkelling Kit
☐ Fishing Gear and Crab Line
☐ Travel Journal (notes of your adventures make a brilliant keepsake)
☐ Pens and Pencil
☐ Paper Pads (for scribbling notes or lists)
☐ Music (CDs or MP3s as the local radio stations are generally pants, unless you like the 80s)
☐ TV (ours plays from a USB memory stick, and has a built-in DVD player and FreeSat decoder)
☐ Laptop (preferably with a long battery life)
☐ Laptop Mouse (we thought we wouldn't need one so left ours at home, which was a mistake and we had to buy one)
☐ External Hard Drive (to store all your photos)
☐ Tablet PC
☐ WiFi Booster Aerial
☐ MiFi Personal 4G to WiFi Hotspot
☐ Roaming Internet and Phone SIMs
☐ Mobile Phone (we have smart phones so we can pick up the internet using free WiFi at cafes)
☐ Amazon Fire TV Stick for watching Internet TV abroad.
☐ Films/TV Series (either DVDs or electronically saved they're ideal for long nights or rainy days)
☐ Headphones (so you can watch TV without disturbing others in the van)
☐ Handheld Games System (we do puzzles and play games on our Nintendo DS)
☐ Cameras
☐ USB Memory Sticks/SD Cards (for storing and sharing photos and files)
☐ Chargers for Everything (12V if possible for lower current draw)
☐ Power Plug Adapters (our van has a couple of two pin plugs so we have one of these permanently plugged in and a spared about)
☐ Alarm Clock (we thought we wouldn't need one, but we ended up sleeping later and later each day)
☐ Binoculars
☐ Spare Batteries
☐ Bicycle (as you can't always park close to what you want to see)

- ☐ Cycle Helmet (obligatory in some countries)
- ☐ Bicycle Pump
- ☐ Bicycle Locks and Keys
- ☐ Puncture Repair Kit
- ☐ Christmas Lights and Decorations (if you're away over the festive period)
- ☐ Bunting/National Flag (for special occasions!)

Pampered Pooch

Charlie was our surrogate child so he got very pampered. He had his own space in the van, and his own cupboard for his toys, treats and medication.

- ☐ Bed
- ☐ Blankets
- ☐ Non-Spill Water Bowl
- ☐ Food Bowl
- ☐ Travel (Collapsible) Water Bowl
- ☐ Dry Food (we bought the cheapest from the supermarkets, less additives and he loved it, and swapping between foods seemed to have no effect on him)
- ☐ Tinned Food (again the cheapest – we didn't find any that he didn't love)
- ☐ Tick & Flea Treatment (check with your vet so you get the best medication for where you are travelling to – Charlie either had spot on Advantix or a Scalibor collar as both repel ticks, fleas, mosquitoes and importantly protect against leishmaniasis, which is endemic in southern Europe)
- ☐ Tick Removers (even though his treatment repelled them, he still got the odd tick so we needed these to remove them)
- ☐ Worming Tablets (again check with your vet, and make sure you stock up with enough for your trip – we struggled to get worming treatment in Italy as they only treat worms if the dog has them)
- ☐ Claw Clippers
- ☐ Fur Clippers (there wasn't always a dog groomer, so we did him ourselves)
- ☐ Comb/Brush
- ☐ Ear Cleaner
- ☐ Shampoo
- ☐ Dog Towel (microfibre for quick drying – trust us you don't want you pooch borrowing your towel after a day on the beach!)
- ☐ Lead and Spare Lead
- ☐ Collar
- ☐ Harness (an alternative to a collar but can also be used to restrain your pooch while you drive)
- ☐ Identity Disc (ensure it has the UK dialling code before your phone number if you're going abroad)
- ☐ Muzzle (in some places larger dogs will need one when in public places or on public transport, for smaller dogs the rules are usually ignored)

- ☐ Coat (pampered pooch never liked being cold)
- ☐ Toys
- ☐ Treats
- ☐ Travel Bag/Cage (we didn't have one, but if you want to restrain your dog while driving or take him on public transport in some countries you'll need one)
- ☐ Poo Bags (never underestimate how many of these you'll get through on a trip! Some of the more affluent countries do provide them for free in parks and cities so keep your eyes peeled)

Enhancements to Your Van

You can add numerous things to your motorhome to make life more comfortable on the road.

- ☐ Non-Slip Matting (for every cupboard)
- ☐ Blackout Thermal Curtain Linings
- ☐ 12V DC to 230V AC Power Inverter (for charging all your gadgets that don't have a 12V charger, running clippers and the like – do your research to ensure you get the correct specification for your needs)
- ☐ Windscreen Thermal Cover/Silver Screens (internal or external screens help keep your van warm or cool, we use external ones)
- ☐ Solar Panel and Charge Controller
- ☐ Additional Leisure Battery (an alternative or addition to adding solar panels is adding another leisure battery)
- ☐ Habitation Door Fly Screen (our current van has a built-in screen, but you can buy after-market ones too)
- ☐ LPG Tank(s) (refillable tanks or bottles which take LPG/GPL/Autogas are a big help on a multi-country trip as there is no gas bottle standardisation across Europe)
- ☐ SOG Unit
- ☐ Satellite Dish (if you want to watch live UK TV on the road)

Appendix B - Useful Sources of Information

This appendix lists some of the useful sources of information we've used to plan our motorhome tours.

Motorhome Forums

- **Motorhome Facts** – *motorhomefacts.com* – a very well-established forum. Searchable for free. Annual fee if you want to ask or answer questions.
- **Motorhome Fun** – *motorhomefun.co.uk* – again a very useful forum. Searchable for free. Annual fee if you want to ask or answer questions.
- **Out and About Live** – *www.outandaboutlive.co.uk* – run by Warners Group Publications who publish Motorhome Monthly Magazine.
- **Facebook Groups** – there are a large number of free groups on Facebook, for specific makes of motorhome for example. All offer useful information, some have negotiated discounts with insurers.

Motorhome Magazines

- **Motorhome Monthly Magazine (MMM)** – an iconic magazine in the UK motorhome world, covering a broad range of topics including tour stories.
- **Practical Motorhome** – another widely-available motorhome magazine in the UK. Focuses on the practical aspects of motorhome life.
- **Motorhome Fun Magazine** – a free smartphone and tablet-based online magazine providing no-nonsense advice and stories.

Overnight Motorhome Stopovers

- **Search For Sites** – *www.searchforsites.co.uk* – free database of campsites and other parking locations in the UK and across Europe.
- **UK Campsite** – *www.ukcampsite.co.uk* – free database of UK-based campsites.
- **Wild Camping** – *www.wildcamping.co.uk* – free forum and paid Point of Interest (POI) downloads for free camping in the UK.
- **All the Aires** – maps and details of official aires across Europe created and published by Vicarious Media (*www.vicarious-shop.com*). Focussed on France, Spain, Portugal, Belgium, Luxembourg and the Netherlands.
- **France Passion** – *www.france-passion.com* – again available through Vicarious Media. The book is refreshed each year. Buying that year's book gives you access to free camping at French vineyards, farms, restaurants etc. In practice you can usually use a book for the following year or two too.
- **Camperstop Europe** – *www.camperstop.com* – book and smartphone app listing thousands of aires across Europe.

- **Camper Contact** – *www.campercontact.com* – website and app again listing aires across Europe.
- **Park4Night** – *park4night.com* – website and app listing both official and unofficial (free and wild camping) overnight stops across Europe.
- **ACSI Camping Card** – *www.campingcard.co.uk* – the card is included with books giving off-season discounts at over 3500 campsites across Europe.

Buying Motorhomes

- **Autotrader** – *www.autotrader.co.uk* – has a section listing new and used motorhomes for sale. Can be filtered to show only private or dealer sales. Great for getting an idea of current UK prices.
- **eBay** – *ebay.co.uk* – mainly private motorhome sales. Can include a few fraudulent listings (motorhomes which don't exist) so take care, but we bought two of our motorhomes using eBay without issues.
- **Gumtree** – *www.gumtree.com* – similar to eBay – again focussed on private sales and useful for getting an idea of prices.
- **Motorhome Depot** – *www.motorhomedepot.com* – a broker for private motorhome sellers.
- **mobile.de** – *www.mobile.de* – lists motorhomes for sale in Germany. Great for seeing how much motorhomes cost there, and for looking at lots of types of vehicle, even if you don't seriously plan to go and buy on the continent.
- **MOT Status** – *www.gov.uk/check-mot-history* – shows the MOT expiry date and lists mileages, failures and advisories from previous MOTs.
- **Road Tax Status** – *vehicleenquiry.service.gov.uk* lets you check when the road tax is due, and *www.gov.uk/vehicle-tax* lets you buy tax, when you first buy a motorhome for example.
- **Outstanding Finance (HPI) Checks** – *hpicheck.com* also checks whether the vehicle has been stolen or is an insurance write-off
- **Vehicle Inspections** – The AA (*www.theaa.com/vehicle-inspection*), The RAC (*www.rac.co.uk/buying-a-car/vehicle-inspections*), AIM Vehicle Inspections (up to 3.5 tonne – *ww7.aim-vi.co.uk*), The Motorcaravan Engineer's Association (*www.mobilecaravanengineers.co.uk*)

Legal Driving Requirements Abroad

- **The AA** – *www.theaa.com* – search the site for 'Driving in Europe' for tons of advice on what you legally need to carry, rules of the road, use of lights during the day and so on.
- **The RAC** – *www.rac.co.uk* – again has a very useful section covering what you legally need to know and carry when driving in Europe, and advice on staying safe on the road.

- **The Caravan and Motorhome Club** – *www.caravanclub.co.uk* – look in the Overseas Holidays section.
- **The Camping and Caravanning Club** – *campingandcaravanningclub.co.uk* – search for 'European Travel Advice'.

Getting at Your Money Abroad

- **Halifax** – *www.halifax.co.uk* – we use their Clarity credit card abroad which has no fees for foreign ATM cash withdrawals.
- **Caxton FX** – *www.caxtonfx.com* – we use the Caxton Prepaid Currency Card for making non-cash purchases abroad.

Internet Access in the UK and Abroad

- **Motorhome WiFi** – *www.motorhomewifi.com* – these guys sell specialised motorhome equipment and SIM cards for internet access in your van.
- **Vodafone UK** – *vodafone.co.uk* – provide arguably the best value roaming SIM cards for travel across Europe (although these things change fast!), including 30-day contract options so you're not tied in for a year or more. The cards also make it appear like you're in the UK, so you can watch iPlayer and other UK-only Internet TV while you're abroad without a VPN.
- **Three UK** – *www.three.co.uk* – provide 'Internet with Legs' preloaded SIM cards which provide a set amount of data which lasts for up to 12 months. We have a couple of these as back-ups in case of issues with our Vodafone SIM. EE sell a similar card – search the internet for 'EE preloaded SIM'. Both the Three and EE preloaded cards are available on *amazon.co.uk*.
- **Prepaid SIM Data Card Wiki** – *prepaid-data-sim-card.fandom.com* – a useful resource when buying a local SIM card rather than using a UK-based SIM.

Motorhome Insurance

- **Adrian Flux** – *www.adrianflux.co.uk*
- **Safeguard** – *www.safeguarduk.co.uk*
- **Comfort** – *www.comfort-insurance.co.uk*
- **Caravan Guard** – *www.caravanguard.co.uk*
- **Saga (drivers over 50s only)** – *www.saga.co.uk*
- **Camping and Caravanning Club** (members only) – *www.campingandcaravanningclub.co.uk*
- **Caravan and Motorhome Club Insurance** (members only) – *www.caravanclub.co.uk*

Calor Gas and Self-Refillable LPG Systems

- **Calor Gas** – *www.calor.co.uk*
- **GasIT Self-Refillable LPG Tanks and Bottles** – *www.gasit.co.uk*
- **Safefill Self-Refillable LPG Bottles** – *www.safefill.co.uk*
- **Gaslow Self-Refillable LPG Bottles** – *gaslowdirect.com*
- **Alugas Self-Refillable LPG Bottles** – *www.autogasleisure.co.uk*
- **Finding LPG stations:** *www.mylpg.eu* and *www.lpgstations.com*

Low Emission Zones and Other Urban Access Zones

- **General advice on which zones exist** – *urbanaccessregulations.eu* and *www.green-zones.eu*
- **London Low Emission Zone** – *tfl.gov.uk/modes/driving/low-emission-zone*
- **Obtaining a French Crit'Air vignette** – *www.certificat-air.gouv.fr*
- **Obtaining a German Umweltzone plakette** – *www.berlin.de* (search for 'environmental zone sticker')

Motorhome Touring Blogs

This is a tiny selection of the hundreds of motorhome travel blogs available. For a longer list, take a look at *ourtour.co.uk/home/fellow-travellers*.

- **The authors' motorhome travel blog** – *ourtour.co.uk*
- **Joanne and Craig's European tours** – *ourbumble.com*
- **A multi-year full-timing couple** - *motoroaming.com*
- **A multi-year tour by a family of four** – *www.lifeinourvan.com*
- **Two Australians on multiple European tours** – *www.travelbunyip.com*
- **Every country in Europe in three years** – *theworldisourlobster.com*
- **A couple of snow-sports enthusiasts** – *winterised.com*
- **Kat offers lots of advice for motorhome travel** – *wandering-bird.com*
- **Starting with a year-long tour of Spain, now heading to Azerbaijan in a motorhome** – *thegreygappers.co.uk*

Smartphone Apps

- **Free Motorhome Magazine** – *MotorhomeFun Magazine*
- **Free Offline Maps** – *maps.me*
- **Online Maps** – *Google Maps*
- **Aires and Overnight parking** – *park4night, Campercontact, Parkopedia Parking, Campervan.Guide Free*
- **Campsites** – *searchforsites, CampingCard ACSI Campsites, ACSI Great Little Campsites, ACSI Europe*
- **Translation** – *Google Translate*
- **Satellite Dish Alignment** – *Dishpointer*

- **Voice and Video Internet Calls** – *Facebook, Skype, WhatsApp*
- **Navigation** – *CoPilot Caravan Europe*

Appendix C - Basic Troubleshooting

This section includes some very basic troubleshooting tips we've picked up while on the road. We'd strongly recommend consulting your motorhome's user guide first, then trying make-specific motorhome groups on Facebook and, if all else fails, finding a local motorhome dealer to help you out.

If you've an electrical problem, try these:

- If your 12V system isn't working, first check the van's 12V supply switch is on. Ours can be turned off at the control panel. Check your leisure batteries are registering at least 11.9V. If they're flat, they won't always recharge, and your habitation equipment won't work even if you hook-up to 230V.
- If the 230V plug sockets aren't working when hooked-up, check the site supply is working. Try another site socket or post or ask at reception if the power is off. If the site supply is live, check the RCD on your consumer unit in your van is switched to the on position – we once knocked ours off putting the shopping away.
- The underlying vehicle and your habitation area will likely have separate sets of fuses. Our current van vehicle fuses (for the van lights, fan, windscreen wipers etc.) are in the glove box. Our habitation fuses (for the living area lights, TV, heating fan etc.) are in a Schaudt-Electroblock which is installed in a cupboard by the passenger seat. Check the fuses in the relevant bank to be sure one hasn't failed. If it has, find the root cause before changing it (or at least try, we got through ten fuses once trying to source a problem in our 12V system).

If you've no water coming from your taps, try these:

- Make sure there's water in your tank, and your pump is fully submerged. Physically unscrew the top of the tank and look inside if you can, rather than relying on the water meter on the control panel.
- There could be air in the pipes, especially if the van's been drained down during storage or not used for a while. On our van we have to open both kitchen and bathroom taps on cold for a few minutes. Water starts gurgle out after a while, and we can then slowly turn our taps to hot, drawing water through the boiler.
- Check your 12V system is working for other equipment, then listen for your water pump turning on when you open a tap. If there's no humming noise, or a high-pitched whine, the pump might need replacing.

- Look under the van to see if water's being pumped onto the ground. If it is, a boiler safety valve, plug or other fitting might not be properly closed.

If your fridge won't get cold, check this stuff:

- If it's a three-way fridge, you can't run it on 12V when parked up. If you're hooked up to the mains, switch it to mains. If not switch it to gas, light it (usually by pressing in a knob and listening for the clicking noise to stop) and wait a few hours.
- Are you on a slope? If you are, get the van level using ramps or by moving somewhere flat.
- Is it over 30°C? Absorption fridges aren't great when it gets hot. Try parking so the fridge isn't in the full sun, or think about fitting an additional fridge fan.
- Fridge works on mains but not on gas? There may be a blockage in the gas burner. You can try using compressed air to blow any dust or dirt out, or visit a dealer to clean or replace the burner.

If your water won't get hot:

- If you have a combi-boiler, make sure you've switched it to hot water and not just air heating.
- Check any LEDs on the control panel, which might indicate there is no gas supply, or your leisure batteries are flat. If the gas supply has failed, try manually turning any auto switch-over valve towards the full bottle, and check the 'manifold' isolator switches (big red things normally) are turned on.
- Make sure any cold temperature safety valve is switched on (check your water heater manual – ours has to be pulled upwards).

If your van won't start, there could be a multitude of issues, but here's a quick simple list to check:

- The starter battery could be flat, especially if the van's not been used for a while, or it's very cold.
- Check you have diesel or petrol in the tank.
- Make sure your immobiliser is turned off, if you have one.
- If you've just hit a pothole, the fuel safety cut-off might have been activated. Ours is hidden inside the engine bay, and a switch has to be pressed back in before the engine will start again.

Index

Printed in Great Britain
by Amazon

44683465R00142